ALSO BY DIANE ACKERMAN

Jaguar of Sweet Laughter:
New and Selected Poems

A Natural History of the Senses

Reverse Thunder

On Extended Wings

Lady Faustus

Twilight of the Tenderfoot

Wife of Light

The Planets: A Cosmic Pastoral

THE
MOON
BY
WHALE
LIGHT

RANDOM HOUSE
NEW YORK

THE
MOON
BY
WHALE
LIGHT

And Other Adventures
Among Bats, Penguins,
Crocodilians, and Whales

DIANE
ACKERMAN

Library of Congress Cataloging-in-Publication Data

Ackerman, Diane.
The moon by whale light: and other adventures among bats, penguins,
crocodilians, and whales / Diane Ackerman.—1st ed. p. cm.
ISBN 0-394-58574-7
1. Animals. I. Title.
QL81.A24 1991
591—dc20   91-52665

Manufactured in the United States of America

Book design by JoAnne Metsch

FOR MY PARENTS,
MARCIA AND SAM

ACKNOWLEDGMENTS

Shorter versions of these essays appeared
in *The New Yorker*. Heartfelt thanks
to Robert Gottlieb, its editor in chief,
for sending me out on such nourishing
journeys.

CONTENTS

INTRODUCTION

For a month in 1989 I sailed around Antarctica, a landscape as sensuous as it is remote, whose crystal desert I had wanted to see for a long time. Some months earlier I helped raise baby penguins in quarantine at Sea World in San Diego. One fluffy brown yeti-shaped chick, which I became particularly fond of, I named Apsley, after Apsley Cherry-Garrard, who in 1911 trekked across Antarctica, and wrote a vivid and poignant book about it, *The Worst Journey in the World.* For two years, I had been writing natural-history essays for *The New Yorker,* the magazine that sent me to see and write about penguins in the wild. To be haunted by the ghostly beauty of pastel icebergs and astonished by the Antarctic's vast herds of animals is an experience few people have ever known or will ever know, and I felt privileged—and still do. Not so long ago—in the days of Sir Richard Burton, T. E. Lawrence,

D. H. Lawrence, Lady Hester Stanhope, Beryl Markham, Herman Melville, Washington Irving, and others—there was a crossroads where physical and literary adventure converged. There is also a long history of the bards called nature poets, and this brimming category includes writers as different as Lucretius and Marvell. But my prose now seems to locate me among a small tribe often referred to as nature writers. How curious that label is, suggesting as it does that nature is somehow separate from our doings, that nature does not contain us, that it's possible to step *outside* nature, not merely as one of its more promising denizens but objectively, as a sort of extraterrestrial voyeur. Still, the label is a dignified one, and implies a pastoral ethic that we share, a devotion to the keenly observed detail, and a sense of sacredness. There is a way of beholding nature that is itself a form of prayer.

In my Antarctic journal I wrote: "Tonight the moon is invisible, darkness itself has nearly vanished, and the known world, which we map with families, routines, and newspapers, floats somewhere beyond the horizon. Traveling to a strange new landscape is a kind of romance. You become intensely aware of the world where you are, but also oblivious to the rest of the world at the same time. Like love, travel makes you innocent again. The only news I've heard for days has been the news of nature. Tomorrow, when we drift through the iceberg gardens of Gerlache Strait, I will be working—that is, writing prose. My mind will become a cyclone of intense alertness, in which details present themselves slowly, thoroughly, one at a time. I don't know how to describe what happens to me when I'm out in 'nature' and 'working'—it's a kind of rapture—but it's happened often enough that I know to expect it."

I had been wondering then about the little penguin Apsley. Soon he would have fledged, replacing his thick brown down with black and white feathers, and would look very different. My plan was to gather pebbles from the rookery at Salisbury Plain, on South Georgia (where the egg he hatched from was collected), and take them back to him as a souvenir. Apsley was not the sort of penguin that builds nests from stones, but he might recognize the rich amalgam of smells.

Because I write at length about little-known animals in curious landscapes, people often ask, for example, Do you prefer whales to bats? I prefer life. Each of the animals I write about I find beguiling in and of itself; but in all honesty there is no animal that isn't fascinating if viewed up close and in detail. I chose to write about bats, crocodilians, whales, penguins, and such because each would teach me something special about nature and about the human condition: about our terror of things that live by night, or the advantages of cold-bloodedness; about intelligence and music, or our need to withstand most any ordeal to behold a nearly extinct life-form before it vanishes. Before beginning each expedition, I knew some of my motives, but I always returned nourished by unexpected experiences. What is necessarily missing from the essays is all the fun, turmoil, stress, and welcome obsessiveness that went into setting them up. The emotional marginalia sometimes included acts of great generosity of spirit, and at other times revealed less becoming sides of human nature.

Much of a nature writer's life is spent living by seasonal time, not mere chronicity, as you wait for nature to go about its normal ways. There are long pastures of quiet, broken suddenly by the indelible thrill of seeing a whale or an alligator, and then the long hours afterward, as the excitement mellows. Of course, we also live by the clock. Shifting one's allegiance between those two perceptions of time is one of the most curious and uncanny things that naturalists do. On the way out into the field, and on the return, there comes a point when the two notions of time meet, as if they were nothing more than high mountain roads converging in the wilderness, and you must leap from one to the other and quickly get your footing. I found this especially true when writing "The Moon by Whale Light," which required trips to both Hawaii and Argentina. Half the time I fretted about airplane schedules, boat rentals, getting permits and permissions, or fixing my tape recorder in the middle of lengthy interviews. But the other half I spent on the desolate, fossil-strewn beaches of Patagonia, watching the hypnotic movements of mother and baby whales. Falling asleep to their snoring and snuffling sounds, attuned only to their lives, I lived on whale time.

Entering an alternate reality that has its own social customs, time zones, routines, hierarchies, and values is not easy. You leave all the guideposts, the friends and relatives you rely on, and become part of a social group whose laws are rarely explained but include you, rule you. You have no bank account of esteem. You are judged by everyone. You are admired for your affiliations rather than your character or qualities. You meet people who wish in one way or another to exploit you. You can become distracted from yourself and enter a cone of ambiguity where you move as if you were an interloper or an outlaw. It is like waking up in a sci-fi story where people travel along a different time-line and you slide among them. In one sense, that freedom feels exhilarating, but in another it fills you with unsurpassable loneliness. It is difficult to explain the exact appeal of this paradox. Most field naturalists I know relish being new, anonymous, at their own disposal, untrackable, freed from their past, able (even required) to reinvent themselves; and yet they also tend to phone and write home often when they're in port, many times a day blazing a link to their loved ones.

Some people think I court danger. After all, I straddle alligators and swim up to a whale's mouth and climb down cliffs and stand in the midst of millions of bats and risk frostbite at the ends of the earth. Although there have been many times when I was truly frightened and a sentence such as *Why the hell do you get into situations like this?* would run through my mind, such moments passed quickly. I don't take unreasonable chances. I'm always accompanied by experts who have spent many years working with the animal we are studying and who have been close to that animal countless times, often enough to know what may be dangerous.

"How could you walk across a lagoon when there were alligators under the water and not know where the alligators were?" one woman asked, clearly horrified. Simple: I followed the invisible footsteps of Kent Vliet, who was a yard in front of me. Kent and his colleagues had been working with alligators in St. Augustine for some time, and he knew where it was probably safe to walk and also what to do if attacked. But frightened? My heart was pounding.

"How could you let a big bat tangle in your hair?" That was a different situation—bats aren't dangerous, just misunderstood. So I felt no fear at all, or, rather, was fearful for the bat, which I didn't wish to hurt in any way.

I often find things renewing about *ordeal.* When I went out into the Texas desert with Merlin Tuttle and his friends, to net wild bats and photograph them, we didn't get even two hours of sleep. By day we looked for likely batting spots and set up our nets. By night we patroled the nets or photographed bats. One night I spent hours aiming photographic lights for Merlin in an abandoned barn while startled bats peed on me nonstop. On the wall in my study I have one of the photographs of pallid bats that Merlin took that night, and it makes me smile, remembering just what the event looked, smelled, and felt like.

There were times handling alligators that I got banged up pretty hard. I didn't jump back fast enough when climbing off an alligator, and it swung its head around and clobbered me on the shin. Alligators have exceedingly powerful heads, and this was like being slammed with a baseball bat made of pure bone. My shin bruised savagely, but the bone didn't break. And that was a trivial price to pay for the privilege of being able to study an alligator intimately, to touch its mouth and eyes and the folds of its neck and the claws on its back feet and really get to know the look and feel of it up close.

At a later time, on an expedition to Japan to see certain rare albatrosses, I managed to break three ribs. Once I was sure that I would live through the injury, it became strictly a matter of pain. The pain was torrential. The top half of my body was paralyzed by pain. Every movement sent lightning forks through my chest and back. Standing absolutely still hurt badly, sitting hurt badly, lying down hurt badly, and trying to keep my balance on a small, rolling ship was agony. Once lying down, I could not get up. My muscles were too inflamed to work. On shipboard, leaving the island, the crew settled me into one of the tiny capsule bunks, which are small open cubicles recessed into the wall. I will never forget waking in pain some hours later and discovering that I was trapped in my low-ceilinged, coffinlike bunk. For two hours, I tried everything I could think of to get out. I have never known such helplessness. Because I couldn't expand my chest, I was unable to call for help, hard as I tried. Finally, a Japanese passenger across the room woke up and crawled sleepily from his bunk. I pantomimed that I needed help, that my ribs were broken, and would he drag me carefully out of my narrow bunk. Sliding his arms under my shoulders, he pulled me out like a war casualty, as pain twisted its ragged knives. Then, holding on to the ceiling, I crawled up to the middle deck and sat against a wall. But this was just pain. I know now that I can withstand great pain. I was much more concerned by how *inconvenient* the injury was for everyone. I also learned about the generosity and concern of strangers—my journey out of Japan was a trail strewn with kindness. The animal adventures recounted in this book cost me no pain as violent as broken ribs (now my benchmark for a tough trip), just the occasional allergy, bruise, parasite, or heartache.

Outside the train station in Washington, D.C., these words are inscribed: "He that would bring home the wealth of the Indies must carry the wealth of the Indies with him. So it is with travelling. A man must carry knowledge with him if he would bring home knowledge." That maxim is particularly true for a nature writer. I never mind abandoning habits, preferences, tastes, plans. I prefer to become part of the new landscape, fully available to the moment, able to revise or ad lib a perspective without warning, open to the revelations of nature. But you also need to know what you're looking at. So I read everything I can—science, folklore, novels, whatever— and then plague my scientist companions with questions. This all adds to the creative feeding frenzy that each essay sets in motion.

In writing about rock-climber Mo Anthoine, A. Alvarez cites a phrase from an unlikely source—Jeremy Bentham. The father of utilitarianism dismisses as "deep play" any activity in which "the stakes are so high," as Alvarez puts it, "that it is irrational for anyone to engage in it at all, since the marginal utility of what you stand to win is grossly outweighed by the disutility of what you stand to lose." Alvarez is wise to see that Bentham despises deep play for some of the very same reasons Mo Anthoine cherishes it. Anthoine confesses that a couple of times a year he has to "feed his rat," by which he means that wonderful mad rodent inside him that demands a challenge or a trip that will combine adventure, fun, wonder, risk, and ordeal. Although I'm not a rock-climber, I know how the rat gnaws, and I must admit there is nothing like deep play. In *On Extended Wings,* a memoir about learning to fly, I wrote:

> It isn't that I find danger ennobling, or that I require cheap excitation to cure the dullness of routine; but I do like the moment central to danger and to some sports, when you become so thoroughly concerned with acting deftly, in order to be safe, that only reaction is possible, not analysis. You shed the centuries and feel creatural. Of course, you do have to scan, assess, and make constant minute decisions. But there is nothing like *thinking* in the usual, methodical way. What takes its place is more akin to an informed instinct. For a pensive person, to be fully alert but free of thought is a form of ecstasy.
>
> Being ecstatic means being flung out of your usual self. When you're enraptured, your senses are upright and saluting. But there is also a state when perception doesn't work, consciousness vanishes like the gorgeous fever it is, and you feel free of all mind-body constraints, suddenly so free of them you don't perceive yourself as being free, but vigilant, a seeing eye without judgment, history, or emotion. It's that shudder out of time, the central moment in so many sports, that one often feels, and perhaps becomes addicted to, while doing something dangerous.

Although I never take unnecessary chances, a tidy amount of risk, discomfort, pain, or physical challenge does not deter me. At some point in the research for each of these essays, my rat found sustenance, and there were above all wonderful moments of deep play.

Why this form of play should include wild animals is no mystery. In many ways we're totemic creatures who wear the hides of animals on our bodies and, in affectionate cuteness, at times even address one another by animal names—"pussycat," "honey-bunny," "my little minx," and so forth. Animals share our world, accompany us through life, and frequently figure as symbols of one sort or another. Everyone has a bat story fluttering around in the half-lit mansion of memory. In my case, bats are inextricably linked to the first hint that I might be an artist.

In the small Chicago suburb of Waukegan, Illinois, which for some reason has driven over eighty of its onetime residents to become writers of some kind, my family lived in a bay-windowed house on the outskirts of town, where paved streets gave way to vast flat housing tracts and the tallest objects for miles were the orange bulldozers standing like mastodons in the dirt. Right across the street from us there was a small field and beyond it a plum orchard through which I sometimes walked on the way to Greenwood Elementary School. This was not the route preferred by my parents. The woods were overgrown and, as Frost wrote, dark and deep, and I was just a six-year-old with a Roy Rogers writing tablet and a mop of unruly hair my mother had temporarily tamed in a ponytail.

The route I was supposed to take went around the block, on sidewalks all the way, past the vacant lot on the corner, past the little blue frame house of Mrs. Griffith, who once phoned my mother to report: "Your daughter is talking to herself again! Lord knows what she talks about. I just thought I'd better tell you, Marcia." Then on past the bookmobile stop across from the drugstore where I sometimes bought plastic horses and riders. I loved playing with the horses, whether they were ridden by cavalrymen or cowboys, and most of all I liked it when they came with small red rubber saddles and reins that fit into the groove in the horse's mouth and even stirrups you could slide onto the foot of the rider. But the figures themselves were always frozen in a state of alarm or rest: the horses were always galloping, trotting, or standing stock-still at some invisible hitching post, the riders were always waving their arms or hunkering low in the saddle or sitting up stiffly on parade march. Though I tried to make them move, by bending or heating or twisting, I soon learned, as I would later about real soldiers and cowboys, that they could break beyond repair and disappear from my life. I never really thought of them as frozen; I thought of them as always frightened, always angry, always sad, always silently yelling.

Around the corner from the drugstore stood Victor's house. I called my cousin Tic-Toc, and he was my best friend until his mother came between us. Once she shrieked to find me talking her son into tying a towel around his shoulders and leaping from the back roof onto the brick barbecue to see if people really could fly. On another occasion we concocted a gruesome brew of unmentionable fluids to give to Normy Wolf, a nerd who lived across the street. I wanted to see if it would kill him, and we would have found out if Victor's mother hadn't caught us crossing the street with the disgusting, full mayonnaise jar. On another day I drafted Victor into a bolder experiment. Was it possible to navigate an entire house without touching the ground? His mother walked in from shopping just as I was jumping from a bannister onto a doorknob, swinging into the living room, and then leaping from couch to chair to chair as if they were ice floes. I was not a hyperkinetic child, just curious. I wanted to see if it was possible—and would have, if she hadn't banished me at once. Victor was told to play with boys from then on. It was clear girls were too dangerous.

But I didn't know I was different, truly, irrevocably different, different in what I saw when looking out of the window each day, until one morning when I was going through the orchard with three first-grade schoolmates. We were late, and there were silhouette drawings, which none of us wanted to miss, so we cut through the orchard. I can still remember the sheen of the green-and-red plaid dress that Susan Green wore. She had a matching ribbon in her hair and a petticoat that made her skirt rustle as she moved. Above us, the trees were thick with dark plums huddled like bats. Susan dragged at my arm and pulled me along because I was dawdling, staring up at the fruit—or bats—and when she demanded to know what I was looking at, I told her. She let go of my arm and all three girls recoiled. The possibility of bats didn't frighten them. *I* frightened them: the elaborate fantasies I wove when we played store, telephone operator, or house; my perverse insistence on drawing trees in colors other than green; my doing *boy* things like raising turtles and wearing six-shooters to tap-dance lessons; my thinking that the toy cowboys we played with had emotions. And now this: plums that looked like bats. All these years later, the memory of the look on their faces is indelible. But most of all I remember flushing with wonder at the sight of my first metaphor—the living plums: the bats.

THE
MOON
BY
WHALE
LIGHT

Chapter 1

IN
PRAISE
OF
BATS

One winter evening, I took a seat in a natural amphitheater of limestone boulders, at the bottom of which was the wide, dark mouth of Bracken Cave. Nothing stirred yet in its depths. But I had been promised one of the wonders of our age. Deep inside the cavern, Mexican free-tailed bats were hanging up by their toes, twenty million of them. They were the largest concentration of warm-blooded animals in the world. At dusk, all twenty million would fly out to feed, in a living volcano scientists call an emergence. They would flow into the sky with their leathery wings and ultrasonic cries, and people fifty miles away, in cities like San Antonio and Austin, would, without realizing it, rarely be more than seventy feet from a feeding bat.

"I've sat here for three hours and still seen them pouring out," the man next to me said, radiant with anticipation. If anyone should have known their habits, it was this man,

Merlin D. Tuttle, the world's authority on bats, founder and science director of Bat Conservation International, and an explorer whose cliff-hanging exploits put Indiana Jones to shame. On the ground beside us lay some of the tools of his trade: an infrared nightscope of the kind much used in Vietnam; a miners' headlamp powered by a large heavy battery that he carried in a khaki ammunition belt around his waist; a mini bat-detector, which picked up the ultrasonic echolocating calls of many species of bats. Noticeably absent were gloves, sticks, or other protective gear.

"Bats are among the gentlest of animals," he said. "They're really shy and winsome creatures who have just had bad press." *Winsome* is not a term often used by scientists. On a list of "winning" creatures, bats would not rank very high.

A blond man in his mid-forties, with gray sideburns, a mustache, and gold-wire-rimmed glasses, he had a thin, muscular build, an emphatic mouth, and wisps of hair falling across a large forehead. Before I could say anything, his eyes darted to the cave mouth, a smile drifted over his face along with the fading rays of sunlight, and I followed his gaze. Hundreds of small bats had appeared suddenly, darting and climbing, swirling and looping. Then they spiraled up and scrolled off to the east. It was an odd, small spectacle.

"Just wait," Tuttle said, reading my mind. An acrid tinge of ammonia mixed with the other night scents. "What you're smelling is the ammonia from guano—bat dung—in the cave. Two hundred and forty tons of bats roost in there and they heat the air with their body temperature. If it's a cold night, the body heat in there creates a chimney effect."

Down by the cave mouth, something slithered in the dusk, but I couldn't be sure if it was a shadow or a snake. Coachwhip snakes prowled there sometimes, hoping to eat fallen bats. The floor of the cave itself was alive with insects, small invertebrates, and other predators eager to devour any bat that lost its toehold. Because this was a nursery cave—full of mother and baby bats—the boiling cushion of hungry jaws on the cave floor was rarely disappointed. Tuttle told me that a local university had once brought out a small whale carcass on a flatbed and left it in the cave briefly for the dermestid bugs to strip clean. It took about two days. Normally, outside the cave, the bugs would be feeding on carrion. Though they were beetles as adults, their half-inch larvae were fuzzy eating machines. The cave itself sprawled 1,000 feet long, 130 feet deep, and an average of 60 feet in diameter, so there were countless crevices for bats with plenty of floor room for bugs.

Researchers who ventured into the cave wore respirators and tightly fitting clothes. Not only could they be showered with droppings from the bats overhead (1,800 adults per square yard in some places, and in the crèche, where the bald pink babies are, a squealing hungry mass of 5,000 pups per square yard), there would be the thick layers of powdery guano, the crawling beetle larvae, the infernal heat, and the intense vapor of ammonia. To the bats, it's bliss: a toasty incubator. For them, hell would be trying to live where we do, in refrigerated boxes without fresh air or sunlight, which we litter with obstacles and perfume with such irritating essences as peppermint, lemon, and chlorine bleach. Perhaps they would find it strange, as I do, that we feed on dismembered animals no longer resembling what they are; and yet, paradoxically, we insist on cooking them to the warmth of fresh prey.

Small clouds began to swell, spinning like an open funnel, as the bats orbited until they were high enough to depart. Like airplanes in a mountain valley, they must circle to climb, so they whisk around one another, wing to wing, in tight echelons. As they revolve, they pick up speed. Over open country, free-tailed bats can cruise at thirty-five miles an hour.

"They're spiraling counterclockwise. Do they always turn in the same direction?"

"No," Tuttle said. "In the mornings, when they return, they tend to go straight in. They come in real high, peel off, and then dive in fast with their wings half folded."

Shadows marched through the trees as the whirlpooling bats set off on a night's cross-country journey, to forage for food. A natural pesticide, they eat 150 tons of insects every night. Born in June, then weaned when they were about five weeks old, the new babies were strong enough to fly with their mothers, who had taught them some of the arcane arts of bathood: how to leave a cave waltzing and veer off into twilight; how to be guided by the land and feed in midair; how to swoop down to a pond with their small pink tongues out and drink on the wing; how to find the warmth they crave among the huddled masses; how to rely on the mob-law of the colony. Did they fly nonstop all night long, or did they pause somewhere to put their feet up for a spell? Did the mothers demonstrate for their own offspring, the way bird mothers do, or did the babies learn from studying the habits of the whole colony? "Probably, they break off into recognizable groups that understand where they're headed," he said. "But we just don't know. So little is known about bats."

A hawk appeared, swooped, grabbed a bat straight out of the sky, and disappeared with it. In a moment, the hawk returned, but hearing his wings coming, the bats all shifted sideways to confuse him, and he missed. As wave upon wave of bats poured out of the cave, their collective wings began to sound like drizzle on autumn leaves. Gushing out and swirling fast in this living Mixmaster, newly risen bats started in close and then veered out almost to the rim of the bowl, climbing until they were high enough to clear the ridge. Already, a long black column of bats looked like a tornado spinning out far across the Texas sky. A second column formed, undulating and dancing through the air like a Chinese dragon, stretching for miles, headed for some unknown feeding ground. The night was silent except for the serene beating of their wings. But when Tuttle switched on his mini–bat-detector, we heard a frenzy of clicks. Beyond human hearing, the air was loud with shouts as the teeming bats fluttered wing to wing, echolocating furiously so as not to collide. Like a Geiger counter gone berserk, the bat-detector poured static, and Tuttle laughed. There was no way to hear individual voices in the ultrasonic mayhem of the emergence. Such a gush of bats flowed upward that two new columns formed, each thick and beating, making long pulsing ribbons, climbing two miles high to ride rapid air currents toward distant feeding sites. Some groups twisted into a bow shape, others into a tuning fork, then a claw, a wrench, a waving hand. Buffeted by uneven currents, they made the air visible, as it rarely is. In the rosy dusk, their wings beat so fast that a strobe light seemed to be playing over them.

"Some bats live to be more than thirty years old, you know," Tuttle explained. "If someone goes on a rampage and kills a bat, they may be killing an animal that's lived on this planet for thirty years. It's not like killing a roach. For their size, they're the longest-lived mammal on earth. But unfortunately, they're also the slowest-reproducing mammal for their size. Mother bats usually only rear one pup a year. If you took a pair of meadow mice and gave them everything they needed for survival, theoretically they and their progeny could leave a million meadow mice by the year's end. If you provided an average pair of bats with the same opportunity, in one year there would be a total of three bats—mother, father, and baby. And bats cluster in large colonies in the most vulnerable places. Here we have the world's largest concentration of warm-blooded animals, and it could be destroyed in five minutes. I personally know of caves where people have wiped out millions of bats in one day."

The four largest summer bat colonies in eastern North America would not exist if Tuttle hadn't recognized the peril they were in and waged a campaign to protect them. Born in Honolulu, Hawaii, Tuttle, the son of a biology teacher who traveled often, finally settling his family in Tennessee, grew up not far from a bat cave. By the time Tuttle was nine years old, he was studying bats. He made his first serious scientific contributions when he was in high school and went on to write a doctoral dissertation on population ecology and the behavior of gray bats at the University of Kansas. A mammologist by disposition, he found the decline and plight of bats especially poignant. One day, a few years after graduate school, he returned with friends to show them the extraordinary emergence of two hundred fifty thousand gray bats from Hambrick Cave, in Alabama.

"At almost the same time every evening," he said, "you could see this big, dark column of bats, sixty feet wide and thirty feet high, going all the way to the horizon. The sound was like a white-water river. As you can see here at Bracken, a bat emergence can be one of the most spectacular sights in nature. We were all excited, with cameras ready, but the bats never came out. It was quite a shock when it dawned on us that the bats were gone. I had had a lot of emotional attachment to them. These bats had played a major role in my doctoral research and I had gotten to know them. We went into the cave and found sticks, stones, rifle cartridges, and fireworks wrappers beneath the former bat roost. I knew they had been killed. Many were banded, but they no longer showed up at their traditional hibernating caves. There were so many ways they could have died. Even a single blast from a cherry bomb could have severely damaged their sensitive hearing, making it impossible for them to use their sonar. Hambrick Cave was five miles from the nearest human habitation, not a threat to anyone, and you could get there only by boat. It was one of the last places in the world where I expected bats to be destroyed." Tuttle shook his head.

"Follow that albino one!" he said suddenly, pointing to the cave entrance, where a white ball had just appeared among what looked like a swarm of black peppercorns. Once, twice, three circuits of the bowl. It drifted far out to the rim toward us, its mouth open, then floated over the ridge and joined one of the columns. Gesturing with one hand, as if to press down a stack of invisible myths, Tuttle said, "Their mouths are open when they fly because they need them that way to echolocate. They're not snarling or mean; they're just trying not to bump into anything. We associate that look—open mouth and bared teeth—with menace, but they're not being aggressive. That's how their sonar works. Look, I'll show you." With that, he led me down into the center of the bowl, toward the cave, right into the thick of the swarming, fluttering bats, which flew around our shoulders, over our heads, beside my chin. Too amazed to flinch, I felt them graze my head with their flutters, but they did not touch me with their wings. The breeze they made blew my long hair back.

We were standing in the middle of twenty million wild bats. Tuttle swung both arms above his head, then did it again. On the third time, he grabbed a bat right out of the air.

After we filed back up to our original spot, I sat down on a boulder beside him, to see what he had captured. Its wings held closed by Tuttle's grip, its small furry brown head sticking out, a little bat looked up at us, frightened and fragile. It used its chin as a pry bar, trying to escape, but made no attempt to bite.

"See how ferocious he is?" Tuttle said.

The face was gnomic, the wet eyes black as Sen-Sen, and the body covered with a thick, fluffy brown fur. What must it have made of us—large, powerful animals, with big eyes and big teeth? It opened its mouth to echolocate, but did not snap or nip, and in any case its teeth were very small. Tuttle loosened his grip a little. Still holding the wings closed with one hand, he stroked its back with the other, following the grain of the fur, and the little bat quieted down. I knew better than to pick up a bat I might see lying on the ground—or any wild animal acting abnormally, for that matter. But a veteran bat-handler snatching a healthy bat out of the air was different.

"Want to touch?" he asked.

I ran a finger over the tiny back, felt the slender bones and the fur soft as chinchilla. Then we opened out the wings and I stroked their thin rubbery membrane, traced the elongated fingers that held up the wings, and looked at the tail from which the free-tailed bat got its name. The scientific name for all bats is *Chiroptera*, "hand wing," and even on a small version like this one the hand wings were clear.

"Isn't he a winsome little fellow?" Tuttle asked. "Here, you can let him go." When he placed the bat on my open palm, I felt a swift scuttle as it crept, wing over wing, to my fingertips, then launched itself into the air to rejoin its colony, which now had filled the sky with black magic.

Camped out on a makeshift bed on Tuttle's living room floor, I had trouble falling asleep. When I closed my eyes, I saw a negative of the night's emergence: clouds of bats floated across the inside of the lids. Anyway, his house was too alive with adventure to ignore. Though sparsely furnished in buff and brown furniture, its every decoration belonged in a museum of anthropology. On one table was a bamboo sheath full of darts still fresh with curare. On the dining-room wall, a charging elephant leapt right out of a large photograph, which Tuttle took seconds before its tusks could plunge. A witch doctor's necklace of peccary teeth sat on top of the television set, as if casually left there by the witch doctor in question. Additional artifacts came from cannibals, Masai warriors, pygmies, and such other acquaintances as he had made on his many field trips in pursuit of rare bats. A large basket, fashioned from a single palm frond, held wickerwork and shells and a stuffed cockerel with luminous yellow feathers. Porcupine quills from Thailand made a sunburst pattern on an end table. A flute carved from deer bone seemed to belong in a show of Cro-Magnon art. A knobbed Masai club looked rather like a shillelagh. Two Peruvian drums sat against the fireplace wall. There were bows and arrows, a fire-making kit once owned by canni-bals, an arrow tipped with poison and three notches that break at three points to ensure a kill. One especially curious item, a hide cap, was used for hunting by a tribe that wrapped robes of palm fiber around their bodies and crouched low like storks so the deer wouldn't recognize them and flee. A quiver of arrow tips closed with a lid made of ocelot fur. Two dope-grinding plates from South America had their own pestle attached. On one wall hung a Yanomano headdress of bright bird feathers, matching feathered pierced ear-rings across the room. A book tucked inside the end table's vault of memorabilia was titled *How to Be a Survivor.*

In contrast, the decorative tree in the skylighted foyer seemed tame. On the kitchen counter sat an open container full of meal-worms, to be used as bat food. Big bags of equipment sprawled on the floor, still unpacked, from Tuttle's recent trip to French Guiana. Before that, he had been home for a few days, newly in from Costa Rica, where he tracked and photographed the largest carnivorous bat in the world.

Vampyrum spectrum, a New World bat with big jaws and a wingspan of nearly a yard, stalks the jungles by night, using sonar to snatch birds and rats from their slumber in the foliage. It drags them back to its home in the hollow of a tree, which may be encircled with detritus from previous meals: parrot remains, rodent bits, feathers of one sort or another. Ultimately, the tree feeds on all of it, down to the corpse of the bat when it dies: the nutrients of decay are the tree's lifeblood. Indeed, to some, there may be a question about which is the true carnivore, the bat or the tree.

This large "false vampire," which Tuttle described as both "intelligent and delightful," has an enlightened home life. The male and female take turns with child-rearing and hunting duties. One stays and baby-sits while the other brings back food for the mate and the pup. Then they swap. "Those bats may very well mate for life," Tuttle had explained earlier. "We don't know, but they're certainly sharing in the duties of child rearing, and they're apparently monogamous. You've got to remember that when we talk about bats, we're talking about nearly a quarter of all of the world's mammals, and that means there's every kind of diversity you can imagine, including diversity in courtship. Among some bats, the males and females avoid each other except in the fall, when the females come into a cave to hibernate, and the males wait at strategic locations and just grab female after female and mate with them as fast as they can. Over about a two-week period, they actually burn up as much fat supply as they would need to hibernate for the whole winter. A male sack-winged bat, on the other hand, finds an especially good feeding area and guards it, letting only those females that return to the roost to mate with him feed there. So in this case, the female, instead of checking out which male has the best voice, does the best dance, or is the most handsome, picks the male that is the best provider in terms of guarding a good feeding area.

"There are bats that I call the disco bats, like the hammerheads in Africa, because the males come from miles around to a specific area, which isn't used for either roosting or feeding but is kind of like the analogy of people in bars. They go there to find mates. The males pick out territories, call, and do a little wing dance; and the females fly through and inspect the males until they find one whose dance especially appeals to them. Then they mate and the females go off to be unwed mothers. You know, it's not that different from bar scenes.

"Then there are other bats that guard a good home—a hole in a tree, a cavity in a cave ceiling, whatever, and again, the female does the choosing, based not on his personal attractiveness but on his ability to provide a good home. None of these strategies is all that foreign from what we see going on in people."

After a female gray bat mates, she goes straight into hibernation, while the male pursues other females who strike his fancy. During the summer, female free-tailed bats live together in a sorority of future mothers, a nursery colony like Bracken Cave. Some bats turn right-side-up when they give birth, but others prefer to stay head over heels. The babies are born alive and some actually help pull themselves out. A mother bat often catches its newborn in a cradle made of her wing. Clinging like a little octopus, the new bat pup stays attached by its umbilical cord for as long as an hour, while it learns the voice and scent of its mother. Its powerful clinging instinct keeps it close to her breast, where it nurses, safe from all the toothy hucksters far below on the cave floor.

Overhead, a ceiling fan turned gently but didn't cool the house, which Tuttle kept at tropical temperature. Standing open, his closet contained neatly laundered button-down dress shirts on hangers, all light blue or cream. There hadn't been time lately to shop for clothes, or even to deposit the stack of paychecks sitting in a corner. The refrigerator contained food brought in by visitors—a team from *National Geographic* had left Hershey bars (Tuttle doesn't care for sweets); someone left two boxes of Lean Cuisine (Tuttle is slender and doesn't get enough chance to eat properly). There was powdered milk; he hadn't had time to get to a store.

A set of blueprints for a birdhouse, sitting on a shelf, looked wrong. One of the first home truths one discovers about a bat is that it is nothing like a bird. Not even their wings are similar. Bats have five distinct fingers, which have bones like human fingers, and the flying membrane, as the leathery wing is called, extends along the second finger. The thumb, which has a fingernail, moves freely and can be small and straightish or long and curved in a come-hither gesture. Although bats use their thumbs to preen themselves and for other purposes, they mainly use them to grip branches, leaves, fruit, and such, or to hold on to their relatives or climb arm over arm like a primate.

Bats are extremely tidy, comb themselves thoroughly, and do not gather a mess of nesting materials for their homes as birds do. Their guano smells like stale Wheat Thins, and sometimes insects invade the guano so that it appears to be bubbling, but bats themselves live high above in penthouse roosts, where they keep their bodies well groomed. Since they don't build nests, they find shelter in whatever roof eave, cave, open brickwork, hollow tree, or other reasonably clean, secluded place presents itself. Seldom a belfry, despite the myth. Belfries are more often occupied by birds. Perhaps it was the bats darting around the church belfries at twilight, in their normal pursuit of insects, that made people think bats roosted there. Or perhaps it was the image of the devil, traditionally drawn with bat wings, and sermons that warned of his being always in the vicinity. For an orthodoxy to prevail, you need to believe in a heresy waiting at your front door, and the macabre fluttering of bats on devil's wings at sunset in the local churchyard made a persuasive reminder that evil and irrationality are not something you need to keep a day free for. People also think that bats have a special penchant for bedrooms and, if they leave their bedroom windows open when they sleep, as most people do, a wayward bat might indeed be tempted to stray in, but bats much prefer the gables of a house or a chimney or even a place under a porch. Bats roost near wherever there is a good supply of insects to feed on, and that most often is in forests, gardens, parks, along rivers, in churchyards (again, the bats-in-the-belfry idea), or around city streetlamps. Drawn to the free lunch at searchlights, they often frequent airports, along with starlings, finches, and many other winged things; since they don't hear too well in the low registers, they might not be bothered much by the engine noise.

Bats eat so much food each evening that they have weighed in at as much as 50 percent heavier after one night's dining. So insect-eating bats are a good investment for a homeowner. Bat Conservation International sells "official bat houses" for homeowners to hang up in their insect-infested yards and emphasizes what good citizens bats really are. Bats are gluttons and gorge themselves on offensive night-prowling insects. Little brown bats, the most common of the North American species, can catch up to six hundred or more mosquitoes in an hour. And as many as thirty bats may live in a single bat house. Of course, bats do change their roosts, depending on the time of year. When the females are giving birth and raising their young, they prefer warm places like Bracken Cave; when hibernating in winter, a cold place will do better.

Bat houses look nothing like birdhouses. For one thing, they don't have cutesy roofs à la Swiss chalets. I don't know why, or when, people decided that birds preferred to live in humanesque houses shaped like Victorian mansions, red barns, Kon-Tiki huts, alpine ski lodges, or kelly-green shacks in the Black Forest. Just because desperate birds do live in them doesn't mean they like them or don't feel as silly as some houses look. I much prefer the eighteenth-century bird bottle, still used in Williamsburg, Virginia—a swollen cylinder, glazed brown, that looks like a vase lying on its side. An official bat house is squarish, made of red cedar, and reminiscent of an old-fashioned mailbox hanging on someone's door. On the front is an abstract drawing of the Chinese *wu fu,* a decorative emblem worn as a medallion or as a coin or as a panel on a robe. The *wu fu* shows the Tree of Life encircled by five bats whose wingtips touch or sometimes interlock. These collegial bats symbolize the five elements of good fortune: health, happiness, long life, contentment, and prosperity. Indeed, the Chinese word for happiness, *fu,* though written differently, is pronounced the same as the word for bat. So bats occur often in Chinese conversation, especially during marriage ceremonies and other celebrations. The Chinese pictogram for bat includes the root word for "insect," so there must originally have been some confusion about what a bat was. This isn't really surprising. Many people for a time thought bats were a sort of mouse, and the word for bat in various languages reflects this misconception. In Mexico, bats are often called *ratones voladores,* "flying rats"; in Germany, a bat is the operatic *Fledermaus;* in France, *chauve-souris,* "bald mouse."

Inside the bat house there are crevices so the bats can put their feet up, and also dividers of varying widths, "to allow for different bat preferences" and bat privacy. There is a solid roof and sides, but no floor, so that squirrels and birds won't be tempted to nest, but bats can get in and out easily. If you are able to contemplate for an extended period of time exactly what "different bat preferences" might mean, then you are probably already a bat fancier and have decided whether you would prefer to attract "mother" bats or "bachelor" bats, according to the guidelines in the instructions. At $34.95, with the proceeds going to worldwide bat research and conservation, the bat houses have sold briskly—possibly, in part, as conversation pieces at garden parties.*

Of course, the simple difference between birds and bats is that a bird is a bird and, as Béla Lugosi indignantly points out to the police inspector in the 1940 film *Killer Bats,* a bat is a mammal. Except for the wings, they really look quite different. Birds have beaks, for example, but bats have teeth. Baby bats are born with milk teeth, which are sharp and hooked, to help them hold on to Mother; they grow their permanent teeth a few weeks later. But such obvious differences didn't stop people from confusing birds and bats for an extraordinarily long time. In both Leviticus and Deuteronomy, where the injunctions about eating clean and unclean meats occur, bats are identified as unclean birds: ". . . among the fowls . . . they

*Orders go to Bat Conservation International, P.O. Box 162603, Austin, Texas 78716. If you're only interested in the blueprints, BCI will send them in exchange for a contribution of any amount.

shall not be eaten, they are an abomination: the eagle, and the ossifrage, and the osprey . . . and the stork, the heron . . . and the bat." (Leviticus 11:13–19). Aesop has a fable in which a weasel snares a bat, pausing before it devours the bat to explain that it preys exclusively on birds. No fool, the bat quickly informs the weasel that it's a bat, and is let go. Later in the story, the bat meets another weasel, one that feeds only on mice, and the bat swears to the second weasel that it's a bird, and escapes again. Some Greek, Roman, and Chinese stories try to explain why the bat flies at night, and they all have to do with the bat's confused self-image. Uncertain whether it's a bird or a mouse or something else, it acts, as a result, with coward- ice or treachery or indecision, and gets banished to the nighttime world. In *Macbeth,* the three witches season their pot with "wool of bat," and in *A Midsummer Night's Dream,* the fairies dress up in bat-wing capes. "Witches' birds" bats were called in the Middle Ages. They were always associated with witches, devils, fairies, and no-goods, and it was far from lucky to have them roosting in your house, whether they were birds or not. Some people knew all along that bats weren't really birds but some sort of mousy mammal that flies, even if, as John Swan noted in his rather prosaic poem about it in 1635, "And this creature thus mungrell-like, cannot/look very lovely." In the East, where bats tend to be large and better-known, not small and secretive animals, they figure positively in myths and legends. And in this country, a Hopi story tells of a bat created out of dust and spirit that saves a maiden from rape.

In some ways, bats *are* a little like birds: they have light or nonexistent tailbones and they are exceedingly light for their wing area. But this has more to do with simple aerodynamics than with any evolutionary relationship between birds and bats. If a flying animal has short stubby wings, its stall speed will be increased, which means that it will stall even when flying quite fast. So that it didn't drop out of the sky whenever it slowed, it would need to flap its wings quickly, the way a hummingbird does. But that wouldn't be much help to an animal pursuing unpredictable insect prey. Nature evolved a better design: bigger wings. The bigger the wings, the lower the stall speed, and therefore the slower and more casual the flapping could be. Many bats have wings that are very long compared to their bodies, and it helps to make them keenly maneuverable.

Birds have small windows in their wings that open and close as air rushes through. The windows close when the bird pushes its wings down, to cup the air better, then open to let the wings lift easily for another flap. Birds molt, replacing their wing feathers annually, but bats have a thin, solid, stretchy wing. Air doesn't pass through it, and they can twist and shape it to make tight turns and even hover and do . . . well, aerobatics. Unlike bird feathers, bat wings are living tissue: if a sharp twig, say, pierces the wing membrane, it will heal over. But if it's a large hole, only the edges will mend, and the bat's aerodynamics will be altered, just as a foot injury makes a human limp. If the hole is too large, the bat won't be able to fly at all, because it could get lift with only one wing and, as pilots know, that makes it possible to do spectacular pirouettes but not much serious flying. The best animal-wing design, I think, belongs to the butterfly or moth: four panels that can be shuffled like playing cards. Compared with bats, birds have fixed wings; there isn't much flexibility in them. Still, bats can scoop things up with their wings, wrap a wing around themselves like a shawl, cradle their new babies in the bottom of a wing, sling food into their mouths with their wing. Most birds tip their heads back to drink, but bats often drink on the run, winging at water level over a pond or lake, sticking out their tongues, and delicately licking water up as they fly.

Bats fall into two main groups, microbats and megabats, and they are as unalike as otters and tigers. The megabats are the large fruit-eating bats, like flying foxes, and recent studies suggest that they are distant relations of ours—are, in fact, primates. They use their big eyes to see, instead of echolocating, and many of their brain pathways, which have the distinctive signature of primates, are organized in a way not found in any of the other twenty mammalian orders. To most people, the smaller microbats (nearly eight hundred species of mostly insect-eating bats that echolocate) look like the megabats, but Australian neuroanatomist Dr. John D. Pettigrew insists this is simply nature evolving the same pattern for similar purposes. Consider the eye. Octopuses have eyes, just as rhinoceroses do. The eye was a successful and ingenious piece of evolution that popped up in many far-flung species, each of which "invented" the eye independently. Though still a controversial topic among researchers, Pettigrew's exciting work with brain-wave study suggests that some bats are much less like mice or birds than they are like people.

Unlike birds, bats don't lay eggs. Life might be easier for them if they did. Like all mammals, they bear their young alive. Difficult though it sounds, a pregnant bat must sometimes fly with her hefty fetus inside, and then, once the baby bat is born, maneuver with it clinging to her breast. Adult bats don't weigh much. They're mainly fur and appetite. So traveling with an attached, quickly growing baby would mean becoming a beast of burden. Therefore, most bats leave their babies home as soon as possible, to crawl around the cave walls and play with other babies, while the adults go out to dine. When the mother returns, she flies through the nursery, shouting to her baby, which shouts back. So individual are their voices and smells that even in the nursery's pandemonium of thousands of calling bats, mothers and babies find one another with ease. (In a place like Bracken Cave, that means being able to smell well enough to pick out one scent among 240 tons of individuals.) A mother will flutter to her baby, scoop it up with a wing, press it against her chest, and carry it to their usual perch, where the baby will nurse at her nipple. Bats can hang upside-down with their tummies pressed against the cave wall, because their feet turn sideways, a nifty trick. And where they hang isn't random.

"Inside the cave," I had asked Tuttle, "do they all have a set place where they're supposed to be?"

"Absolutely. There are millions of bats, but every one has its own position."

"Suppose you rearranged them?" The world is storied with odd experiments, and I had visions of researchers moving bats around like peas in a shell game.

"The mother bat might not find her baby. She might lose it in the crowd."

"What if you startled the bats and they flew to other parts of the cave? Would they be so obsessive as to reassemble themselves in the right order?"

"Right. They would try to. But people disturb bats in caves, and it's a major cause of bat decline in the United States. When a bat colony is rearing young, it often roosts near a cave entrance or a particularly warm pocket of the ceiling. The cave walls in most of the United States are relatively cool compared to the body temperature of a bat. At midlatitudes, you have a cave-wall temperature of, say, 57 degrees Fahrenheit, whereas the baby needs to maintain a body temperature of up to 102 degrees Fahrenheit. This baby bat is born hairless and hangs on the wall—that's the equivalent of your being down in the basement lying naked on the cement floor. You'd get cold quickly. So for the young to grow and metabolize efficiently, they need to be in clusters with large numbers of other bats. They'll often roost in a domed ceiling or a place where the cave is extra warm. But when you disturb them, they have to move back deeper into the cave, often into colder places or where the ceiling isn't as rough, so it's harder for the babies to cling. Then they're more likely to fall off and get killed. Sometimes the mothers are so panicked by the disturbance that they drop their babies and they drown. Or the colony splits up into smaller groups at a colder roost. I've seen colonies, just after a single disturbance, move to places where it was so cold that the young couldn't metabolize rapidly enough and sixty or seventy percent of the year's young would die. Most bats only produce one young a year, so it's very important whether that one baby survives or not.

"It's also bad if you disturb a cave where bats are hibernating. Whenever a person passes by a hibernating bat, it causes the bat to raise its body temperature in preparation for a possible escape, and that generally costs the bat anywhere from ten to thirty days of stored-fat reserve. You can see that it wouldn't take too many disturbances in the course of a winter to make a bat run out of food. Then it would have to go out and feed. Not so easy to do in the winter. The bat usually dies. That's why part of BCI's work is to educate amateur spelunkers and others about not disturbing bats in caves. When most people find a bat roost, they don't understand what's happening in the life cycle of those bats or how fragile each step of that life cycle is."

Early the next day, Tuttle and I began our journey in a light plane, four hundred miles southwest, into the Big Bend National Park area, where we hoped to net and photograph several species of bats. In addition to his preeminence as a bat specialist, Tuttle was also one of the world's finest nature photographers. His photographs of bats on the wing, feeding, tending their young, and being "winsome," have appeared in journals around the world. A few years before, Tuttle had discovered and photographed how *Trachops cirrhosus*, a Central American bat, stalks its prey by sound. To enjoy the taste of the frog *Physalaemus*, the bat listens for the male frog's mating call. The louder the song, the plumper and juicier the frog. This puts the frog in an awkward position, of course. It needs to sing for a mate to perpetuate its kind, and in the tropical night it is full of sexual longing, but singing also reveals its whereabouts to any hungry *Trachops cirrhosus*. If it sings halfheartedly, the female frogs won't be impressed, even though the bat may think it's just the call of a lovesick runt. If it sings about its prowess with large, croaking, swollen pride, then a bat devours it.

Tuttle made a BBC film about the frog-catching bat and it won several international awards. Because the BBC photographers felt queasy about crawling inside a large hollow tree full of roosting bats, where venomous reptiles and insects might be lurking, Tuttle did the major exploring and setting up of scenes himself. But most astonishing, perhaps, was his skill at training the bats for the film.

He had photographs of all of it—the bats, the frogs, and his training of bats. Indeed, his archives included fifty thousand slides of bats going about their daily and nightly lives, some of them never seen before, even by most bat specialists. It was a priceless collection, samples of which traveled in museum shows. Tuttle had photographs of vampire bats leaping around on the ground like tiny hobgoblins. One was caught in a song-and-dance man's take-it-away gesture, and you could see how agile on the ground vampire bats are, unlike other bats. In fact, on one field trip, Tuttle had been holding a vampire bat when it squirmed free and ran up a colleague's pant leg. As much as anything, his amazing photographs, taken with ingenuity in risky terrain, have helped conservationists come to the rescue of bats. For openers, they have shown bats to be normal and unthreatening, tending to their young, looking cuddly, and going about their daily lives with the endearing habits most animals have. His photographs have offered incontrovertible proof that bats play an essential role in the balance of nature. They have shown with poignancy and distress how bats have been persecuted and, in some places, driven to extinction. But perhaps most of all, they have stunned people with their dazzling extravaganza of bat types.

When most people think of a bat, they picture the simple little brown bat. But a carnival of bats inhabits the world! There is the tube-nosed fruit bat, whose elongated nostrils look like party favors; the epauletted fruit bat, which has handsome tufts of fur on its shoulders and wraps its wings around itself like a blanket when it rests; the African hammerheaded fruit bat, with a long, mitered-off face, like a horse that has been punched in the nose; the spectacled flying fox that has a sharp, foxlike face, black eyes ringed with white fur, and equally sharp vision; the Javanese slit-faced bat, with huge ears and flattened nose; the funnel-eared bat that looks like a golden Pekingese; the sword-nosed bat, whose ears and nose leaf are almost as long as its body; the yellow-winged bat, with big eyes, long silky fur, and brilliant yellow wings; the greater horseshoe bat, whose horseshoe-shaped flaps surrounding the nostrils look like parts of a nebula; the Egyptian fruit bat, of the small squirrel-like face, which wraps one wing protectively around its sweetheart when ready to mate and whose young are born with human-looking, scrunched-up faces; the Chapins free-tailed bat, which puffs up its headcrest during courtship until its entire face is hidden; the brown long-eared bat, whose pleated ears can fold up and tuck under its wings; the common vampire, with a cleft chin and a pitted nose full of heat-sensing devices; the Mexican free-tailed bat, face as wrinkled as a wise old extraterrestrial's might be. A complete gallery of bats would take ages to compile, and Tuttle was doing just that—patiently photographing a lifetime of bat study.

Don Grantges was to pilot the plane the next day. His twelve-year-old son, Bert, would be along, since Bert was a junior naturalist and bat enthusiast himself, a boy who kept six bats as pets at their home in Fort Worth, Texas. Don was one of the trustees of Bat Conservation International, and he and his family had all had the appropriate vaccinations so they could be involved with Tuttle's research. Carol Grantges would be driving overland in a pickup truck packed with three hundred pounds of equipment, as well as food, since the lodge we were headed for was set, somewhat remotely, among the Chisos Mountains, on the Mexican border. Nor was there what you might call a landing strip. With a tinge of bravado, Tuttle described the runway we would be landing on as so primitive as to have terrified all the passengers on the last trip.

"When you say *primitive*," I inquired, "just what do you mean?" The answer: rock-strewn and short, with a large S-curve right in the middle of it, a mountain rearing up at one end, telephone wires at the other, and nearly always a tailwind. "Interesting," I said. It sounded tricky, but I was not overly concerned. Don, a Navy carrier pilot who flew in Vietnam, owned a Bonanza, a hot little number that can seat four if there is little luggage. As a private pilot myself, I knew to ask Tuttle, to his amusement and mystification, if the Bonanza had a straight tail or a V-shaped one. Butterfly-tail Bonanzas, as they were called, had a bad habit of losing their tails during turbulence, whereas straight-tailed Bonanzas were among the best light planes.

In the morning when we met Don and Bert at the airport, I shook hands with a grinning blond man in a black CATS Broadway musical

T-shirt and tan corduroy shorts. Blue fuel, seeping out of his plane's right tank, made a thin, tinted cascade down the wing, which puzzled more than it alarmed him. Finally, deciding it was just a loose seal around the gas cap, he pulled a bathroom scale out of the cargo hold, and we started to weigh things and load up.

Soon we were up and aloft, floating over the shiny black office building in which Tuttle's Bat Conservation International was housed, as if in its own carapace. Then the city gave way to the loopy fingerprints of the desert, the swirling patterns of sand and vegetation. In the distance was the sinewy Rio Grande, avidly patroled by narcotics agents. Tuttle napped in the rear. Bert listened to music on his Walkman. Don plotted the course, checked it against his Loran-C satellite navigation system, then bid adios to the air traffic control center, on whose luminous green radar screen we had been a small blip, and headed for wild country. There were no navigation beacons where we were going, and the desert poured along hypnotically below, with no clear signposts or fixes. But Don had flown this route before, and intuited his way among the mountain peaks and over the peppery sands.

"My gut feeling tells me the ranch is over thataway," he said at last. On cue, Tuttle and Bert sat up and began scouting the land below, then found the narrow pass in the mountains that would lead us through to Big Bend National Park and the Rosillos Ranch, with its makeshift runway. Grinning, Don pointed to a stretch of raw desert just in front of us, an insinuation of a line with a nasty switchback curve halfway down its length.

"*That's* the runway?" I asked, incredulous.

"Ain't it a beauty?"

Swooping low over the ranch, we searched for Carol's red pickup truck. Either she hadn't arrived yet or she was off visiting Helen and Buster Babbs, the caretakers who lived down the road. Or she might have been at the small grocery store in Stillwell, eighteen rut-filled miles away. Or she might have been waylaid by weather on the drive from Dallas to Austin or decided to sightsee in the mule-deer-and-rabbit-busy desert. Later, we learned that she had driven twelve hours straight through, in a lightning storm that ripped up whole trees and tossed them across the road. But for the moment she was nowhere to be seen in the chiseled range of mountains and flat sprawling scrub.

Don and Tuttle decided to scout Big Bend for the netting sites they had visited before, on four previous trips. Hunkering down low over the mountains, Don swiveled the plane around a wingtip, dipping, rolling out, and dipping again. Their eyes crawled over the ground, eating up the terrain, searching for pools of water shallow enough to wade into, small enough to stretch the forty-two-foot, thirty-foot, and eighteen-foot nets across, close to potential roosting sites like rocky cliffs and, ideally, with enough trees around to provide food as well as drink and attract more bats. All of us were hungry, and sitting low in the plane because of his height, Bert had gone pale from the roller coaster of the tight turns, so we headed back to the ranch. The plane's shadow over the ground was a black bat flying below us. For a harsh moment, it reminded me of the pilot friend I had lost a couple of years before, whose plane stopped abruptly and sent him plunging into his own shadow.

A quick flyover to check the windsock. It would be a dangerous downwind landing again. Then, just as if we were at any busy airport, Don entered the traffic pattern, made a left downwind, turned base leg, and got ready for final. A yard past the telephone wires, he threw the plane straight to the runway, touched down with the stall warning screaming like a marmoset someone had turned loose in the cabin, yanked the nose up high, to slow down as fast as possible, and swerved around the S-curve, then rolled out close to the house. His wife, the elusive Carol, an attractive woman with shoulder-length dirty-blond hair and short shorts that showed off her tanned, athletic legs, stood waving at the open-sided hangar as we taxied in.

The womenfolk decided to bunk in the bedroom, above whose door a sign warned NO DANCING. On the paneled walls, framed photographs of the ranch, deer, and cowboys on horseback told of the sort of territory we were in. Four U.S. flags and one Bicentennial flag sat in a holder on the coffee table, next to a guest book, in which the names Tuttle and Grantges appeared more than anyone else's. A large picnic table near the kitchen served as dining room and equipment drop.

Bert wanted to go out scorpion hunting, but Don set to work getting their sleeping quarters in order. On the screened-in front porch, along with animal skulls, a "museum special" rat trap, unusual stones, a 3008 rifle shell, horseshoes, and a rocking chair, there were cot beds, and Don and Bert liked to sleep right out like that, so they could hear the coyotes yowl by moonlight, drink in the desert night, and see the sunrise. But first they had to deal with any black-widow spiders nesting in the mattresses. Bert ran to the kitchen for two Dixie cups and soon they had the mattresses upended.

"Hey, here's one, I think," Don called. He and Bert discussed it. The black legs were angled like tepees and the body was shiny black, but the spider would not stay still long enough for them to check for the red hourglass on its belly. Cautiously, they tried to cage it in a cup, but it was too agile. Then Tuttle set down the photographic gear he'd been unpacking indoors, ambled out to the porch, picked the spider up with his hand, and turned it over to check. Don looked at Bert, who looked back. Tuttle had earned Bert's wide-eyed admiration long since. Picking up black widows was nothing for Tuttle; Bert still addressed him with a combination of respect and awe, always as Dr. Tuttle.

"Yep, that's it," Tuttle said after a close inspection. Nonchalantly, he carried it to the screen door and tossed it outside. It was a scorching day. Tuttle went to the kitchen sink, over which a placard warned DON'T DRINK TAP WATER, poured himself a tall glass, and drank.

"I rarely get sick," he said. "Had paratyphoid once in Peru and malaria in Venezuela. They were both awful. Otherwise, I don't get things. I've got a cast-iron stomach."

While Don and Bert continued to oust wildlife from the mattresses, Tuttle moseyed outside, and soon let out a jubilant call. He had found bat droppings all along one side of the house, right under the eaves.

"Pallids, I'm sure," he said, excited.

"How do you know?" Only the week before I had learned in Bror Blixen's writings how to judge the distance of a fleeing elephant by the warmth of its dung. Bat guano is considerably smaller, but as it turned out, the technique is similar.

"Like this," Tuttle said, squashing a pellet with his finger. "That's bird dropping," he said, pointing out a little piece. "But this here, with the grasshopper remains inside of it, that's bat dropping, and pallid bats really like grasshoppers." Despite his fifty thousand photographs, he did not yet have good pictures of a colony of pallid bats in the wild, so this was a real find. But the pallids ought to have been up there sleeping in the daytime. Where had they gone?

After a quick lunch, we set off to find our evening's netting sites. The country was so rough that the truck leapt off the road every few yards, then slithered through puddles as mud sprayed up to window height on each side. Carol had brought two navy-blue futon chairs for the enclosed rear of the pickup, but Don and Bert sat out on the tailgate instead, with Don's arm around Bert's small back, both of them hanging on for dusty life, as Carol bounced, galloped, skidded through yet another yard of washed-out dirt road. *Wurshed*-out, as Tuttle said in his rapidly developing Texas twang. Jackrabbits darted in front of us, quail flew up, and the wild sage was in thick purple bloom. Dense stands of tumbleweed, still growing, and pungent creosote bushes made a *swish-swish-swish* sound as we drove through. How perfectly spaced the creosote was. Most animals find the plant too bitter to eat, and it even poisons its own seedlings if they start to sprout too close. Whenever we came to a gate, Don jumped down to open it and Bert seized the chance to scout fast among the brush for something interesting. At the first gate, he returned with a stunningly large locust, all green and yellow, with scarlet fans under its wings. At the second gate, he found a black-and-white lizard that arced its tail up when pursued, to attract a predator's mouth to its disposable tail, not to its head (predators of all denominations swallow the head of their prey first). At the third gate, he found a baby horned toad and deposited it on my palm.

"Rub its tummy and it'll go to sleep," he urged.

Turning it on its back, I stroked its tawny little stomach with the tip of my finger, and sure enough, it quieted down.

"See," Bert said. Bert's eyes were huge with wonder as I handed the baby toad back, and he put it down under a creosote bush, where, to his preadolescent delight, two grasshoppers were busily mating.

"Come on," Tuttle said. "I'm hoping this won't take more than a couple of hours." A perfectionist in all things, Tuttle always took charge, kept track of time, and gently herded along anyone whose attention had begun to stray.

Much later, we were still bounding in and out of rough pastures, searching for standing water, pausing to appraise a site, making mental notes, then passing on to the next one. By the time we returned home, hot, dusty, leg-sore, and hungry, five hours later, Tuttle announced that we had only thirty minutes for dinner or we would not be able to set up our nets before dusk.

Carol, Don, and Bert were all obsessed with bats. Bert, especially. He had a pen pal his age, also a bat fancier, who lived in South Dakota and was personally responsible for getting the state to pass legislation outlawing the use of Rozol, a common bat poison with severe side effects for people. Neither of the two most commonly used bat poisons, Rozol and methyl bromide, is effective against bats; but they are both extremely hazardous to people, may cause birth defects, and contribute drastically to environmental pollution.

"How do you tell your bats apart?" I asked Bert.

"Well, Alex looks a lot fatter than he is. And John looks like what he should be. And there's a vein that Merlin [named after Tuttle] has that Corinna doesn't. Suzy is my oldest and most favorite. And then there's Casey, who is a free-tail."

Don was a successful land developer in Fort Worth, but in his spare time he pursued hobbies like running the New York marathon, and the whole family kept a menagerie of pets and went on nature outings. Missing the evening's bats would have been unthinkable. So grabbing slabs of cheese and a handful of Triscuits, we packed the pickup with Tuttle's batting equipment and a cooler of cold drinks and drove back down the same boggy road to two sites we had thought looked particularly promising.

"Do you know we caught six hundred bats there one trip," Carol said, exultant, as she drove with one hand and balanced a drink in the other. People, bat equipment, papers, cameras, and ice chest all leapt to the roof when she plunged into a surge of muddy road and shimmied at speed, but her drink stayed in the glass as if painted onto it.

"Mom, you're a great mudder!" Bert called from the rear as he and Don tumbled back down onto the tailgate and were tossed inside against the poles and knapsacks.

"We caught fourteen different species," Carol continued. "There are only forty species of bats in North America. So that's pretty good going."

Just before dusk, we reached the twin sites. Don and Carol would watch the first one, a waterhole frequented by zebu cattle. Tuttle, Bert, and I were to patrol the second one: an oasis, where a small spring fed a wealth of trees and bushes, tall drooping willows, cattails, a smear of algae, and many insects. Bats should find it a delectable place both to drink and dine, we assured ourselves. As we set up our equipment, a large angry hornet began dive-bombing my head, and when swatting and jumping didn't discourage it, Tuttle sighed, put down his gear, and walked up and slapped the hornet to the ground in a single move with an open palm.

"Its stinger's on the bottom," he said evenly, in a this-is-not-really-a-problem-unless-you-make-it-one tone of voice.

Then he climbed into a pair of chest-high wading boots and began unpacking long aluminum poles from the khaki sacks in which they were sheathed like machine-gun barrels. They come in six-foot lengths, so he and Don telescoped two together to make a twelve-foot pole, repeated the process, and planted them on either side of a narrow corridor between the trees at one end of the pond. From a small brown canvas kit bag, Tuttle pulled what looked like a shrunken head. No, it was a black mist net, still damp from his trip to French Guiana. Nothing had time to dry out, not even his life. Carefully, he unfolded its eighteen-foot length. Like a long hairnet, it stretched across the pond, with moveable gussets so it could be opened to as much as six feet wide.

Capturing bats for study isn't easy, since their sonar spins an intricate invisible web across the sky and, anyway, they tend to live in communal roosts high up along cliffs or, in South America, in the canopies of the rain forest, where few people have ventured, even now. Mist nets are the solution. Invented by Japanese bird hunters long ago, the thin, delicate nets are light as cobwebs but also firm enough to trap and hold birds or bats. Echolocation doesn't work with netting as intangible as a mist net's, and there is a sense in which it seems almost magical. How do you capture the flying dragon? an ancient Japanese warrior might ask a wiseman. Only with a net made of mist.

We drove to the second site, scarcely a minute away, and Don and Tuttle set up another net. The sun had begun to drain behind the distant mountains, washing the sky, the men, and the small pond with an apricot glow. The men grappled with the nets as if they were fishermen in the South China Sea. A light breeze drove small waves across the water. Thick cumulus clouds and the black threads of the net both reflected in the water, and when Don waded in, concentric circles began to flow gently away from him. He leaned back on the pole, driving it deeper into the mud. For a moment, it looked as if he was going to vault. Meanwhile, the water rose over his sneakers and short white socks. The sun glared off Tuttle's gold-rimmed glasses as he pressed down on his pole. When they pulled the fine net taut, it became invisible. Walking its length, both men inspected it for holes, and they seemed to be holding on to empty space, knotting empty space in their hands. Tuttle's forearms were tanned to the Indian red of the desert at twilight, and I had to squint hard to distinguish between him and the land.

"No need to lower the bottom," Tuttle said. Walking into the middle of the pond, he fussed with the net a little, fine-tuning it. "Give it a little more bag," he said to Don, who adjusted his end, then knotted up a small hole, as if knitting. An Impressionist would have made much of this: the pastel colors of twilight, the men bending and stretching in the rippling pool, the insects touching the water briefly, the misty filaments of the net.

Now, as night began to blue and cool the desert, Tuttle, Bert, and I returned to our spring, where the net was rigged and ready. A few tiny pipistrelle bats flashed above the trees. With night falling fast, we laid out a blue tarpaulin with a Day-Glo orange sleeping bag spread over it, put on our miners' headlamps, and strolled around the pond with the mini-bat-detector. When Tuttle turned the machine on, I flinched, and he laughed. The whirring, buzzing, creaking sounds it spat out were all made by insects, and we could have stalked them like bats if we had wanted to. Turn it off and all was silence. How exciting to discover the night packed with sounds one was not normally aware of: from the buzz of an insect to the black body radiation of Big Bang. Every few yards, pinprick eyes glittered at our feet, and Bert cast his headlamp onto them, chasing spiders as they scrambled in the dirt. When a new cloud of pipistrelles drifted over our heads to feed, we knew it first from the chattery racket on the bat-detector.

It's not hard to understand echolocation if you picture bats calling or whistling to their prey with a steady stream of high-frequency clicks. For most of us, their vocal Braille is too high to hear. At our best and youngest, we might hear sounds of twenty thousand vibrations a second; but bats click at up to two hundred thousand. They don't click in a steady stream but at intervals, twenty or thirty times a second. A *click* is the noise a bat-detector makes. Since the bats' ultrasonics are too high for human ears, we use a Geiger counter–like machine to translate the sonics into sounds we can hear: mainly clicks and warbles. Bats listen for the sounds to return to them, and if the echoes start coming faster or louder, the bat knows the insect it is stalking has flown nearer. Judging the time between the echoes, a bat can tell how fast its prey is moving and in which direction, and some bats are sensitive enough to hear a beetle walking on sand. Many can detect the movement of a moth flexing its wings as it sits on a leaf. As the bat closes in it may click faster in order to pinpoint its prey. And there's a qualitative difference between the steady, solid echoes bouncing off a brick wall and the light, fluid echo of a swaying flower. By shouting at the world, and listening to the echoes, bats can compose a picture of their landscape and the objects in it that includes texture, motion, distance, size, and probably other features, too. They shout very loudly; we just cannot hear them. This is an eerie thought when one stands in a seemingly silent grove filled with bats. They spend their whole lives yelling at the world and each other. They yell at their loved ones, they yell at their enemies, they yell at their dinner, they yell at the big bustling world. Some yell fast, some slow, some loud, some soft. Long-eared bats don't need to yell since they can hear their echoes perfectly well if they whisper. Biologist John Tyler Bonner, in *The Scale of Nature,* records a useful way to understand echolocation on a human scale:

> I can remember going through the San Juan Islands in Puget Sound in a fog. The channel between the islands is very narrow, yet it was impossible to see either shore. The ferryboat pilot first politely told all the mothers to ask their children to stop their ears. Then he blasted his horn while he leaned out the pilothouse on one side, and repeated the operation as he leaned out the other side. By judging the time it took for the echo to return, he could gauge his distance from the shore. He seemed far more composed about the process than I.

Nature is rarely so partisan as to make life easy for the bats: prey often have ears tuned to the bats' frequency, and a moth that lives in an ambient horror of owl screech, bird flap, and lizard scuttle may also know the warning clicks of an approaching bat as we would know the roar of a lion. To protect itself, the moth needs to confuse the hunting bat, and this it does by playing doggo or going into a hard-to-track spiral or making unappetizing sounds.

When a bat has its mouth full of prey, it becomes more difficult to echolocate. Some bats have evolved ways around this problem, by using their ears or other special organs. "The face of many bats is dominated by sonar equipment," zoologist David Attenborough observes, "elaborate translucent ears, ribbed with cartilage and laced with an internal tracery of scarlet blood vessels; and on the nose, leaves, spikes, and spears to direct the sounds. The combination is often more grotesque than any painted demon in a medieval manuscript." Many bats' faces do resemble submarines covered with radar equipment. Horseshoe bats, for example, have oddly shaped noses to send out echolocation sounds with and look a little like particle accelerators.

Echolocation doesn't always work flawlessly. Bats get caught up in barbed-wire fences from time to time, and some bats get killed by cars. They don't get run over. This is a report that Tuttle doesn't credit much, but one English scientist swears that willowy car aerials, with their tiny knobs, flex like insects in the breeze, and bats echolocate them as a meal, zooming in only to become skewered on the aerial or knocked against the windshield. The driver probably thinks he's being attacked by aggressive bats, and this just adds to the misery of bat conservationists.

Pipistrelles were not what we were after on this trip. Our objective was a rare, spectacularly colored creature, the spotted bat, which has pink translucent ears almost as long as its body, angora-like fur, a white belly, and a jet-black back with three white spots. It is the appaloosa of the bat world. Not many of them had been captured, and there were no good photographs of them at all. Tuttle had been after them for years. When the pipistrelles departed, we stretched out on the tarpaulin, under a night poxed with stars, stars in a coliseum of stars, and waited for the spotted bats. A bright flashing satellite cruised across the sky, appearing out of darkness to dazzle us with its speed and clarity, before it sank again into the upside-down well of the heavens. There were more constellations on view than I had ever seen before, so many that they seemed to be nesting inside each other. The Milky Way was a long backbone of light, just as the Bushmen of the Kalahari call it. A frog croaked a deep throaty *I am,* and others sounded like creaking doors or debutantes throwing kisses. There was nothing to do but wait. It is always like this for naturalists, and for poets—the long hours of travel and preparation, and then the longer hours of waiting. All for that one electric, pulse-revving vision when the universe suddenly declares itself. A ravishing tug on the sleeve of our mortality. A view of life so astonishing as to make all of life newly astonishing: a spotted bat.

To pass the time, Bert asked Tuttle to tell us about some of his bat-catching expeditions, and Tuttle, who did not believe in false modesty, was glad to oblige:

"On my last trip to Africa, my co-worker Mike Ryan and I were surrounded by bandits at two o'clock in the morning. They had spears and bows and arrows, and twenty of them crept up on us and just plain surrounded us. They planned to rob us, if not kill us."

"How did you get out of that?" Bert whispered.

"Well, we had an African assistant who had been trained by the Israelis in guerrilla warfare—close combat, psychology, everything— and he managed to lure these guys (who by now had our truck surrounded, too) all over to one side, and then he dived in the door, ducked under the window, and shone my airport landing light in their faces, which blinded them temporarily. He yelled at Mike and me to drive like hell, and we took off. We had quarter-inch dents in the back where things they threw hit the Land Rover, but we escaped.

"Of course, when we worked the upper Orinoco River, I once spent a whole night out with a native assistant, trying to hide from cannibal Indians who were looking for us. I didn't go there to have trouble with cannibals. I can tell you, we really hoped we wouldn't run into them. But there was a neat bat habitat there, and we were looking for interesting bats. We just had the misfortune of having cannibals come by at the same time.

"There are so many stories I could tell you—about the time we ran into poachers in Thailand, who had us a bit scared, but whom we talked round ultimately. There was a time when I was in a cave in Alabama, where I fell twenty-five feet and broke my leg, which isn't a great thing to do in a cave. Once I spent an evening in a wild banana grove in Thailand, where even my assigned guards wouldn't venture because the place was supposed to be full of fifteen-foot king cobras. Then there was the time we were working in a very remote area on the frontier between Venezuela and Brazil, on a natural canal connecting the upper Orinoco and Rio Negro rivers. Well, there were bandits in the area, who had heard about us, and one day they forced us into an eyeball-to-eyeball showdown. The first thing we heard was an outboard motor, and since we almost never heard any sounds having to do with civilization, we rushed out to see what was going on. There were a dozen heavily armed men coming up the river. My Indian helpers recognized these guys. So we issued guns to everybody in camp who could shoot, and hid behind rocks and boulders up by the dock. I unpacked a box of shells for each man. They each kept a handful ready and set the rest of the boxes next to themselves on the ground. When the bandits came in to land their boat, I yelled down to them in Spanish that they weren't welcome and that we would have to shoot them if they insisted on coming in. They kept coming. When they were almost to the landing spot, I warned them that the moment their boat touched the bank, we would have to kill them. They continued coming. Then I motioned for my five guys to show themselves and take aim. Three feet from the bank, the bandits put it in reverse and left. There were more of them, but we were in a better position. We had a whole expedition full of people who could have been killed by these guys, so we were dead serious. I had my camp shot up in Peru once in the middle of the night because we were *mistaken* for bandits by truck drivers, who thought it would be fun to kill a few. I've had my camp nearly bombed when we were mistaken for guerrillas in Venezuela. In fact, I had a wild ride one night up in the mountains above Caracas when we inadvertently ran into some guerrillas and were chased. Probably the only thing that saved us was that I'd borrowed the jeep that night from one of the local communist bosses. Not that

I had anything to do with the communists, but I needed transportation and the guy'd been nice to me.

"One time in Peru, I'd just recovered from paratyphoid, and this Campa Indian told us that he knew of a super place for bats. It was a cave and had about every kind of bat ever known to man, and so my younger brother, Arden, and I decided to go with him and see the cave. As it turned out it was an incredibly rugged hike, and I probably would never have gone on it, having just recovered from such sickness, if I'd known how rugged it was going to be. It was over mountainous terrain, about ten or twelve miles. When we got there, there were these big, sheer cliffs, certainly over a hundred, maybe two hundred, feet high, and the only way down the cliffs was to climb down vines from ledge to ledge. So we climbed down the vines, and it was a gorgeous place, with three waterfalls coming off the cliff into a big basin and almost continuous rainbows at the bottom. Just beautiful, idyllic. We finally got down to the bottom, thanking our lucky stars that none of the vines had broken. But we discovered you couldn't get to the cave without swimming a pond that was full of piranha and electric eels, which had anaconda tracks around it. We probably would never have swum the pond, but we'd already hiked the hike and climbed the cliffs. Though we weren't really prepared to get wet, we just stripped off our clothes down to our undershorts and went in. It was pretty spooky trying to get through this pond without getting your feet down too far, where the electric eels might be, and hoping the piranha weren't hungry. We made it across the pond, but we practically drowned trying to hold our batteries and lights out of the water while trying to keep our feet up. I had Arden stretch a mist net in front of the cave, and I went in with a butterfly net to see what kinds of unusual bats were in there. It turned out that oil birds had lived in this cave—they're a bird similar to nighthawks—and they had left piles and piles of gooey, stinking, rotting droppings, which were seething with various arthropods, from four-inch roaches to pseudo-scorpions several inches in diameter to all sorts of mites and things. The last thing I

wanted to do was wade in through this stuff barefoot and without
any clothes on, but I didn't see any way I could go back. So pretty
soon I was in this stuff up over my knees and then the passage started
sloping up sharply and there was no way to go on without getting
in up to my elbows, too. Finally, I got to the top of the slope, beyond
all the oil-bird droppings, and congratulated myself and figured
maybe now I could get to where the bats were. Then the cave
narrowed into a tight crawlway, and first I began crawling on my
hands and knees, then I was down flat on my belly, then it got so
tight that my arms were pinned up in front of me. I couldn't even
bring them back to my sides. My big concern at that point was that
I was going to come to a dead end and wouldn't be able to turn
around and back out. Sure enough, I came around a little bend and
there was a dead end. So I was lying there with my arms pinned up
in front of me, trying not to panic, saying to myself, It may take you
half the day, but if you squirm and you wriggle just right, there's got
to be a way of getting back out of here. Up until that point I'd been
concentrating on seeing where the passage went and as a result I
hadn't really looked at the ceiling that much. Now I tried to look
back over my shoulder to see how I was going to back up, and for
the first time I noticed that in the slightly concave ceiling that I
hadn't been looking up into, which was only inches over my bare
back, there were literally hundreds of scorpions, apparently gathered
to breed. There they were, all hanging down with their little tails
right over me. If you think it was hard to keep from panicking from
claustrophobia, try it with hundreds of scorpions hanging over your
heinie. I just about wore a groove in the bottom of the rock trying
to keep away from the scorpions.

"I finally got out, and you'd think the story would end there.
Ironically, it was one of the only caves I've seen in the tropics
without a single bat in it. So we took the net down and swam back
across the pond, only to find that though we'd left all our sweaty
clothes on the bank to dry, they were just covered with some kind
of vicious yellow stinging wasp, apparently looking for salt. We spent
the better part of an hour trying to get our clothes back without

getting stung too much. That day was one hell of a wild-goose chase."

It seemed almost impossible to fill the silence after a story as robust as that one. "How did you come to take that picture of the charging elephant that's hanging in your dining room?" I asked after a moment.

"Well, we were out looking for bat caves in East Africa, and we'd been around elephants all day, but I noticed this one herd that looked unusually nervous and restless. We had the back open on the Land Rover and told our assistant to stop. I was curious. It looked like these elephants would charge, and sure enough, when we stopped, one did. It was a quarter-mile away, so I wasn't too worried. I just told the driver to get the Land Rover in gear, keep the motor running, and be ready to go like hell when I told him. Then I started taking motor-drive pictures of the charge. The only thing was, I got so carried away taking pictures that it suddenly dawned on me that the elephant was going to be on top of me in about two seconds. So I yelled at the driver to go. He popped the clutch *and stalled the engine.* The elephant charged right up to the edge of the Land Rover. My colleague hit the deck. I got pictures up to about fifteen feet, then I hit the deck, too. We just froze, and this elephant was so furious it came right up and looked in the open top at us. Probably the only thing that saved our lives is that we lay still. Apparently, it decided to roll the Land Rover over. They sometimes roll a vehicle over and stomp on it—in fact, there's a woman I know who is a paraplegic from being in a car that was rolled and stomped on by elephants. Well, he put his trunk on the hot exhaust and burned it and jumped back and screamed for a second, then the driver collected himself and got the Land Rover running again and we took off. But the elephant chased us down the road for another quarter-mile. We thought we were had. Can you imagine lying there frozen, looking at this furious elephant three feet away, who'd just charged all that distance to get you?"

Bert's large eyes were open even wider than usual, drinking in the adventures. Didn't people use to think of scientists as mild-mannered stay-at-homes whose lives were small as nooses? "Tell about the time when you were sixteen, crawling around that cave."

"Well, I was dangling over a big pit, going hand over hand, and I came to what I thought was solid floor . . ."

By eleven, the winds had begun to blow, and the net bunched up and became more visible. No bats at all, though we had waited for hours. Through the infrared nightscope, the blackness showed as a magic glade full of bright green shapes. Soon the moon would be up, and then the bats would not risk coming. Predators could find them too easily in the wash of moonlight. Tuttle could not remember an expedition to the Big Bend area when he didn't net at least thirty bats. Once they netted six hundred, just as Carol had said. Discouraged, we packed up the nets from both sites and headed back home. The night wasn't lost yet. Maybe there would be pallid bats roosting at the lodge.

Sure enough, we found a barn full of pallids clumped together like a geographical survey map: brown hills and valleys, with tiny, scrunched-up, long-eared faces peering out. Under the house eaves, more pallids were huddled snugly. Ecstatic, Tuttle prepared his photo equipment, even though it was already 3:00 A.M. Don, Bert, and I held the flashes and light meter; and off we tramped again through the night, walking a few paces behind Tuttle, trying to keep all our wires untangled. We looked like bridesmaids. In the barn, Tuttle arranged us right under the bat-encrusted rafters, made a cavalcade of noises to get the bats to perk up their ears, and shot frame after frame of pallid bats roosting in the wild. The bright flashes startled them just enough to make them urinate on our hands and shoulders, and a few frightened bats flew in search of darkness elsewhere in the barn. Some hid their faces in their arms, like shy children. But Tuttle was after a shot in which a number of bats had a good "expression," as he put it. Javelinas, wild pigs, had been using the barn for socializing, and the floor was squooshy with droppings and old wood and discarded lengths of metal. Bats circled our heads in the darkness. Those huddled on the rafters peered down at us with tiny troll-like faces, remarkably long-suffering. When he was sure he had some good frames, Tuttle called it a night, and we dragged back to the lodge, leaving the equipment arrayed like an electronic explosion on the living room floor, and fell into our beds for a heavy, dreamless sleep.

In North America, bats fall into mainly predictable categories: they're nocturnal, eat insects, and are rather small. But winging through their lush, shadow-struck world, tropical bats are more numerous and have more exotic habits. Some feed on nectar so skillfully that bat-pollinated trees have evolved to profit from their visits. Mainly tropical, bat flowers tend to be pale in color (white, buff, light green), in order to be visible at night; and they are large, open and welcoming, with lots of nectar and seductive, trumpetlike mouths. One bat flower has bushy anthers that daub pollen onto the face and chest of the bat as it rams its chops in deep to drink with its long, nectar-loving tongue. Most bat flowers open only at night, high in the canopies, where they glisten with sweet nectar; they even blossom right out on the trunks of trees or on the tips of branches or on pendulous vines, so that bats can dine on the wing. The flowers stand up taut and glistening in the moonlight, as garish and available as prostitutes leaning against a streetlamp. But by morning the flowers have wilted and the bats have gone. Carnivorous bats like nothing better than a local frog, lizard, fish, or bird, which they pluck from the foliage or a moonlit pond. The American fishing bat has clawed feet dangling free (the flying membrane stops at the knees instead of the ankles) and scoots low over lake or ocean, yanks a fish out of the water, and tosses it into its toothy mouth. Some, of course, are vampires, and dine on blood. In the movies, vampires are rather showy, vaudeville types, but vampire bats rely on stealth and small, pinprick incisions made by razory, triangular front teeth. Sleeping livestock are their usual victims, and they take care not to wake them. First, they make the classic incisions shaped like quotation marks; then, with saliva full of anticoagulants so that the victim's blood will flow nicely, they quietly lap their fill. Vampire bats possess a natural anticoagulant that isn't toxic to man, so they may one day play an important role in the treatment of heart patients—that is, if we can just get over our phobia about bats.

At his busy office in Austin, Texas, Tuttle and his staff answer an average of two thousand inquiries from around the world every month. But in a sense, he has two challenges to grapple with, the second of which is persuading people about bats. Before he can do that, he first has to neutralize their fear of bats. It is an old terror. Because, as I now know, bats are sweet-tempered, useful, and fascinating animals, it makes you wonder less about the bats than about our human capacity for terror.

Things that live by night live outside the realm of "normal" time and so suggest living outside the realm of good and evil, since we have moralistic feelings about time. Chauvinistic about our human need to wake by day and sleep by night, we come to associate night dwellers with people up to no good at a time when they have the jump on the rest of us and are defying nature, defying their circadian rhythms. Also, night is when we dream, and so we picture the bats moving through a dreamtime, in which reality is warped. After all, we don't see very well at night, don't need to. But that makes us nearly defenseless after dark. Although we are accustomed to mastering our world by day, in the night we become vulnerable as prey. Thinking of bats as masters of the night threatens the safety we daily take for granted. Though we are at the top of our food chain, if we had to exist in the rain forest, say, and protect ourselves against night-roaming predators, we would live partly in terror, as our ancestors did. Our sense of safety depends on predictability, so anything living outside the usual rules we suspect to be an outlaw, a ghoul. No matter that the hawkmoths steal through the shadows of the rain forest by night. We're not awake to see them. They are mainly rumor to most of us, and if we did see them, in the twilight or by moonlight, they would look strange, hard to focus on clearly, perhaps magical.

Finnish peasants once believed that their souls rose from their bodies while they slept and flew around the countryside as bats, then returned to them by morning. Ancient Egyptians and other Arabs prized bat parts as medicine for a variety of diseases. The whole skin of a large bat was once sold as a poultice for rheumatism in India. But perhaps the most mystical, ghoulish, and intimate relationship between man and bat occurred among the Maya about two thousand years ago. Zotzilaha Chamalcán, their bat god, had a human body but the stylized head and wings of a bat. He appeared often in their glyphs, on altars, pottery, gold ornaments, and stone pillars. One especially frightening glyph shows the bat god with outstretched wings and a question-mark-shaped nose, its tongue wagging with hunger, as it holds a human sacrificial victim in one hand and the victim's heart in the other. I suppose a people as bloodthirsty as the Maya admired the vampire bat's natural gifts and couldn't resist deifying an animal whose tastes seemed so close to their own. A number of Central American tribes raised the bat to the ultimate height: as god of death and the underworld. Although it's been years since I saw them, I still vividly remember the pre-Columbian gold artifacts in the Gilcrease Museum, in Tulsa, Oklahoma, where there was a gold bat with zigzag teeth and claws of coiled might, holding in one fist a tiny death's head. Its ears were trim and soft as any mouse's, fashioned with splendid artistry by some master smith. It was a lustrous fright, a maxim in gold. There is still a bat-god-worshiping tribe in upland Guatemala, the Zotzil, a word that comes from the Mayan for "bat," and their capital city is Zimacantlán (Place of Bats). Bats have always figured in the mythology, religion, and superstition of peoples everywhere. Touching a primal nerve, it was really Bram Stoker's riveting and diabolical *Dracula* that turned small, furry mammals into huge, bloodsucking monsters in the minds of most people. If vampires were semihuman, then they could also be conniving, sadistic, and erotic, and a spill of kinky horror books began to appear about the human passions of vampires.

The last thing I remembered before falling asleep was the pallid bats huddled under the eaves of the lodge. It is almost impossible to describe their gentleness and sweetly expressive faces. When I woke and looked outside, they were gone. One of the things I like best about animals in the wild is that they're always off on some errand. They have appointments to keep. It's only we humans who wonder what we're here for.

Bert pleaded successfully, and Carol produced eggs Benedict to fuel us for the day's journey over an old mining road, a rough-and-tumble trail, and then a hike to a remote natural water tank held in the gnarled grip of an arroyo, where we were ardently hoping to net spotted bats. On the bouncing truck journey, Tuttle and I continued our conversation. Bat research, bat photography, and bat-conservation efforts caulked all the seams in his whirlwind, high-speed schedule. He was the first to admit that he was "married to his work." Indeed, BCI was to be the sole recipient in his will. There was little time to relax, but when he found some, he liked to spend it out in the wild, pursuing bats, and I was glad to be along on a field trip. The Texas desert was a state of sandy surprise and bounty: There were so many cadences of light, a vast chandelier of stars, and life followed so many strange avenues. If he had free time, Tuttle would probably have gone hiking, fishing, or camping out in the wilderness, living close to the land. But he was a perfectionist, a man obsessed by a vision.

Bats instill such repulsion in people that international wildlife organizations have been reluctant to stage a bat-preservation campaign. Advised of the plight of the panda, droves of people are moved to contribute money to protect its endangered habitat. Perhaps they think they are protecting only the pandas, but it is the entire ecological scheme in which the pandas live that the money helps. There is no hope in advertising the plight of bats. People *want* bats to become extinct. Some species depend on a very narrow range of food and habitat, and the loss of just a few critical roosting sites could spell their doom. In turn, many other plants and animals depend on bats. A few of the things we rely on bats for without realizing it: avocados, bananas, dates, figs, guavas, breadfruit, peaches, mangoes, carob, cloves, cashews, sisal for rope, kapok for life preservers and bandages, timber for furniture, chicle latex for chewing gum, balsa, and tequila (Bacardi's trademark is a stylized bat, and the company contributes to Bat Conservation International). The disappearance of bats could gravely affect the economy in a number of countries. In West Africa, the bat-seed-dispersed iroko tree produces millions of dollars worth of timber. The durian fruits of Southeast Asia provide $120 million income every year, yet each of the flowers must be pollinated by a single species of bat. The African tree of life, the baobab, which shelters so many forms of wildlife, also depends on bats for pollination. So do organ-pipe cacti and saguaro. Bats have been useful in the development of vaccines, birth-control and artificial-insemination techniques, navigational aids for the blind, and low-temperature surgery. And then, of course, there is guano, a highly prized natural fertilizer and a source of income for whole villages in third world countries.

Already extinct are the Jamaican long-tongued bat, a single specimen of which sits in a jar at the Institute of Jamaica; the Haitian long-tongued bat, whose habitats disappeared to developers; the tree-dwelling lesser falcate-winged bat of Cuba, which has been extinct for as long as two hundred years; the Puerto Rican long-nosed bat, which had a distinctive long tail and so was long at both ends; and the Cuban yellow bat, which had willowy legs and funnel-shaped ears.

"Imagine what it's like to start up an organization whose sole purpose is conservation of one of the least popular groups of animals on earth," Tuttle said, shaking his head. "I could probably raise ten times as much money if I promised people that I'd *get rid of* all the bats in their area instead of asking them to help me save them. That's how far off we are. Nevertheless, when people are properly introduced to bats, they like them enormously and they understand their importance. When I was a graduate student doing research on gray bats, I went to places where people bragged about personally burning a quarter of a million bats at a time. In one of the places a farmer had been approached by state public health officials, who, in their ignorance, came out and told him that if he didn't get rid of his bats, his cattle would die of rabies and his family would be attacked. He went in and poured kerosene in the cave and burned it, killed all the bats. I asked him how long his family had been there. His family had been living there for three generations in peace with those bats and never had any problems with rabies; nobody'd ever been attacked. I said, 'And here you let a couple of dumb city slickers come out and convince you to kill your bats.' And when I explained to him the value of the bats and what he'd done, he actually broke down and cried.

"I never had any ambition to be anything but a good scientist. I was content to be a member of other conservation organizations and support their efforts. But for years the traditional organizations just ignored bats as too hopeless. If you couldn't raise money for an animal, it couldn't be helped. That's unfortunate. Part of our problems today come from the fact that even scientists and conservationists tend to take the easy ride and find an animal that's very popular with the public. They raise funds to help that animal, but often that's so easy and tempting that other animals that are just as valuable, and sometimes much *more* valuable, remain completely ignored.

"It's obvious from the way things are going that more species are going to become extinct and more habitats lost. We're probably not going to be able to avoid that. But we are going to have to be very careful how we spend our limited resources. We have so many problems that need to be dealt with at once, we're going to have to stop dealing with just the animals that people already easily relate to because they have big brown eyes or soft fur. Most people can be appealed to at some level if they're shown pictures of a cute and cuddly 'glamour' animal with a sledgehammer over its head. But it takes a better educated, more knowledgeable person to really get concerned about something like bats. There are many animals that may be much more valuable to our ecological or economic interests that we're now ignoring because they haven't been promoted as being cute and attractive. We don't know enough to permit us to play God and decide that some animals are good and some are bad. It's a shame that people want to view animals as either good or bad. But as Emerson pointed out, a weed is just a flower out of place.

Cute and cuddly has nothing to do with intrinsic value. Some of the ugliest animals on earth are the most valuable either ecologically or economically.

"That's partly why I gave up my job at the Milwaukee Public Museum, where I was curator of mammals for eleven years, to found BCI. I had a largely research position, and I enjoy research most of all. But back in 1978 the National Geographic Society asked me to write a chapter on bats for its book *Wild Animals in North America.* I wrote the chapter but was appalled at the vicious-looking pictures of bats that accompanied the chapter. I protested, and they said, 'Well, these are all the pictures that we could find of bats.' Apparently, up until that time, nearly everyone pulled their wings out, blew in their faces, and snapped a picture. People never took the patience to show bats as they really were. And it was no different than cornering a dog and making it think you're about to kill it, until it snarled and put on the most defiant look it could, and then you'd snap a picture. Most bats' heads are about the size of the end of your finger. Often times, they're made to look like a saber-toothed tiger. It's no wonder people don't like bats. So—in self-defense, actually—I went and learned photography and ended up being the second most used photographer in the book. Then I became excited about what could be done and how much impact it could have on people's perceptions. Before I knew it, I had really gotten involved in photography. As I took more pictures, I was able to use them to educate people about bats. It just kind of grew, and today I have a collection of pictures, covering nearly a third of the world's bat species. I've photographed them on every continent. But I've always been very careful to either photograph my bats in the wild under completely nonthreatening, natural conditions or keep them in captivity long enough to get them over their nervousness about me and relaxed about doing their natural things. When you see them as they really are, they're just as inquisitive, comical, and cute as other animals. But previously, people only saw tormented individuals responding with fierce expressions. The only other bats people tend to see are ones that are sick or dying. They find them lying on the ground someplace; naturally, the bat opens its mouth wide, bares its teeth, trying to scare them away, and that's the image they get. But we ourselves wouldn't come across too well if people saw us only when we were sick or dying.

"In the Southeast," Tuttle said, "gray bats were once the equivalent of the passenger pigeon. Old-timers used to tell me about how when they were children they saw bats, clouds of bats, flying over every night and coming out of caves where there are no bats remaining today. The gray bat went from filling the night skies to having to be officially listed as endangered a few years ago. In the Southwest, the free-tailed bat, which is still probably the most abundant bat in many areas, has declined by as much as 99.9 percent in some places. The biggest colony ever dropped from thirty million to thirty thousand in just six years. Carlsbad once had over eight million bats, and now it has only a quarter of a million. How far does a bat have to decline before it's declared endangered? An even more important question is: How many bats are *essential* to maintain the balance of nature?

"By the time this has become an issue, it may be too late. Just consider how important bats are to the rain forests. And if you like, we'll just choose one plant—bananas. Bananas are prominently hit by problems such as root rot. Horticulturists have had to go back to ancestral varieties of bananas to gain disease-resistant genetic material, and without animals such as bats you can lose those wild strains. Or consider something as commonplace as peaches. There are some two thousand varieties of peaches now, but they all started in China from a type that was dependent upon bats to disperse its seeds. The sad thing is that in the Old World, where so many of these important plants come from, flying foxes are the primary pollinators and seed dispersers, and yet vast campaigns have been waged in which flying-fox colonies have been poisoned, attacked with flame throwers, napalm-bombed from the air, or dynamited.

"In Queensland, Australia, there are advertisements for people to join in big bat shoots. They go out and ring a colony site where flying foxes are rearing their young and shoot down every bat they can kill, until they're all gone. The mothers keep coming back to their young and people keep shooting until every one is dead. It's ironic, but in the late 1920s, Australia decided to wipe out its flying foxes, and they brought in a famous British biologist named Radcliffe to extinct the bats. After two years of study, he concluded that there was one point of paramount importance: that damage done by these bats is so trivial that it was a waste of taxpayers' money to try to get rid of them. On the other hand, benefits from them are enormous. In Queensland and other places where people are still trying to kill them off, these bats are major pollinators for a host of economically important plants, from black-bean trees to brush box and many medicinal and textile plants. Yet in Australia, they've already eliminated close to 99 percent of the flying foxes. Biologists have speculated that the current slaughter of flying foxes may someday prove ecologically catastrophic, yet such slaughter still continues.

"Once the bats are gone, the repercussions for the rain forests can be really serious. Norman Myers, a well-known conservationist, has pointed out that in some cases these bats are acting as *keystone* species. They are vital to the survival of incredibly important plants. Eliminate the bats and you may eliminate the plant, and that plant may be crucial to numerous other animals and plants. It is possible to start a chain reaction of linked extinctions. In Australia, people would probably have a fit to save koalas and yet they don't understand that many of the eucalyptus-tree species eaten by koalas are pollinated by flying foxes. Knowledgeable botanists argue that by the time some of the Pacific islands' flying foxes decline to the point where somebody says, 'Oh yes, they're definitely endangered now,' and give them endangered status—by that time, there'll be so few that they won't be able to perform their biological functions. They'll be biologically irrelevant and the rain forests will already be doomed. You see, rain forests often depend on bats to pollinate trees. But this is often the case when it comes to animals—by the time you eliminate them down to the point when everyone can agree that the species is officially endangered, it's already too late. So one of my concerns at Bat Conservation International is not just to save a few random populations of endangered species but to save numbers of bats that can still be biologically relevant in the maintenance of healthy environments that we've all got to share.

"The Pacific island rain forests are so beautiful, there are no thorns in them, almost nothing strange or poisonous. They're like Eden. Using the bats as a catalyst, we're now on our way, we hope, to getting a national park in American Samoa, to protect both the rain forest and the flying foxes. Samoans seem to be behind it. The chiefs are enthusiastic, too. But the reason everybody started cooperating is that we didn't go in and kick shins."

In the heyday of emotional appeals, Tuttle was unemotional, pragmatic, strategic about conservation. "Emotional doesn't solve problems," he insisted. "Reason solves problems." His success had often depended on international diplomacy and a willingness to see the point of view of the despoiler. "Take the Pacific islands' flying-fox situation," he offered. "On the island of Guam, where they love to eat flying foxes stewed in coconut milk, they will pay up to twenty-five dollars apiece for them. They've actually extincted one species of their own flying foxes and driven the other one close to extinction. In the Pacific islands in general, flying foxes are critically important as pollinators and seed dispersers for a large proportion of rain-forest trees. They are actively involved in reforestation, and as you know, the rain forests themselves are endangered. Anyway, BCI got involved trying to save the bats. I went out to Samoa and observed what the commercial hunters were doing. It was such cruel stuff. These flying foxes have wingspans of four feet. The hunters would lie in wait at roads and passes along which the flying foxes had to travel and shoot them in the wing. When the bat fell down, they'd have little kids go out and grab the bat by its broken wing and then bash it on the pavement until it was dead. They decimated bat populations. I could have gone in emotionally and gotten the humane society and everybody to write letters, you know, in an anticruelty campaign. There were so many courses we could have taken. But I chose to meet with the hunters and government leaders. I pointed out that when hunters in the United States have a valuable game

animal, they have a season on it. They don't shoot animals when
they have babies; they protect certain places where they live; they
don't allow unregulated commercial hunting. I asked: 'Do you guys
really want to extinct *your* bats just so that somebody can buy and
eat them on Guam? Why let the Guamanians come and exploit you
for the last of your flying foxes? These are bats that figure as heroes
in your legends and traditions. And they're your game animals.
They're part of your heritage. Aren't you concerned? Do you want
it said that yours was the generation that extincted the bats? Don't
you want to leave something for your grandchildren? To the government leaders, I pointed out how important the bats were economically and ecologically. Now we have important legislation there,
congressional hearings, and a proposed national park. The park will
be wonderful—it will feature these huge diurnal bats that soar right
up to you on a ridge and look at you from twelve feet away. It's such
an exciting thing for a visitor to see."

As we bounced along, a roadrunner darted across the path in front
of us, its head thrust forward and its long streamlined tail balancing
like a tightrope walker's pole. Vaguely related to the cuckoo, it has
solar-heat collectors tucked under its back feathers: When it's cold,
it reveals a section of black skin, which absorbs more sunlight. Living
among the sixty-odd species of cactus in Big Bend are more than four
hundred species of birds, and we saw an endless display of them:
doves, mockingbirds, tanagers, peregrine falcons, buntings, gros-
beaks, cactus wrens. Carol spotted a shape in the distance that might
have been a bat, up late, headed who knows where. Bats navigate
in so many different ways that it might be more precise to talk about
how they *orient* themselves. Some species with large, attentive eyes
sight on mountain ranges as much as twenty miles away. Such bats
do not fly in fog or any time when they can't see well. Like birds,
bats have been found to have brain substances that respond to
Earth's magnetic fields. Just as we do not get around entirely by
vision but also by touch, hearing, and sometimes smell, some bats
may not depend solely on one device to navigate but combine several

in a sensory collage. Gray bats apparently head for hibernating caves, which trap and store cold air like a thermos. In the fall, when the weather is still mild, certain unusually frigid caves are cold enough for the bats to start hibernating. Some of the gray bats migrate north for the winter; others go east, west, or south, wherever their frosty caves await them. Because gray bats mate in the fall, after they get to the hibernating caves, there's no way a colony could be genetically programmed to move in a certain direction. They must learn it, and the information appears to be shared from parent to offspring. Such is the hand-me-down nature of learning, at which mammals so beautifully excel.

"It's really phenomenal," Tuttle noted, "when you consider that the gray bat can't detect obstacles or topography more than a couple of meters in front of it with its echolocation system. There it is migrating hundreds of miles, from Florida to southern Virginia, even, for winter hibernation. Even blinded bats can make these trips. I mean, how do they get across highways and changes in the topography? How do they find the cave when its entrance can be so obscure that even after my knowing about it for years, I still have to hunt around, kicking through the bushes, knowing that I am within sixty feet of the cave but unable to find it? How do *they* find it? They must have a very precise ability, one that relies heavily on memorization—memorization of details beyond our comprehension. It's just mind-boggling to think of it. Imagine being released hundreds of miles from home. You're blindfolded, and you're given an echolocation system that reaches only six feet in front of you. Now, find your way home, you're told. You'd be helpless. It's inconceivable. And yet these guys are doing it all the time. So, just in terms of navigation, there are amazing things to be discovered about bats, and some of it may be useful to us."

Navigation systems seem especially to interest the Navy, which has spent a lot of money studying bats. One of its early efforts sought to discover if fishing bats used sound to detect fish. They were puzzled by how bats sensed fish down under the water, when sound should bounce off the surface. If the bats had a unique sleuthing device, the Navy wanted to know about it. As it turned out, the bats weren't really detecting the submerged fish but tiny ripples on the surface of the water, and sometimes a tail fin sticking out.

We followed the old road for only six miles, but it was a rodeo ride in the high-bucking pickup. Our voices took on a buzz from the vibration, and it felt good to get out and stretch our legs at last, pack up our gear, and set out on foot up the rock-strewn creek bed, dry in the diabolical heat. On each side, sandstone cliffs, striped like sherbet, revealed layer after compressed layer of time. How can time be so rigid in rock and so molten as we live it? Underfoot, sheets of rock swirled red, yellow, white, blue. Life blooms in such unlikely places: tufts of grass jutting out from a rock; slabs of cactus sprouting from sheer cliffside high above us, where you'd think no dirt could have settled. What savage violence had occurred there was still visible in the ripped and twisted cliffs, the swollen claws of rock jammed on top of each other. Here and there, small ponds held thousands of tadpoles, and slick gray rocks looked like basking seals. Finally, we came to a *tinaja*, the Spanish word for "jug," a small pool cupped by the rock hands of the arroyo. Red dragonflies planed low over the deep black water, with giant hornets and other insects dogfighting in the air.

It had been a long drive and a hot hike, but Tuttle began stretching a net across the first of three small pools. Each contained water of a different color, because of depth and resident algae. This was familiar and soothing work for Bert and Don, and for Tuttle, too.

"Do dragonflies have sections they call their own?" Bert asked as he steadied a pole.

"Some of them are territorial, yes," Tuttle answered.

Don pulled the net across the narrow neck of rock and water, and Tuttle followed, lifting it above a thorn bush. Idly, he whistled a few bars of "Here Comes the Bride" (he'd attended a wedding a few days earlier), then switched to some other tuneful warble. I had heard him whistle many hints and snatches of things while he worked. Never a complete song. But I had begun to think these must be the moments when he was most at peace, in the fading light of

day, among friends, in the wild, with his hands following the habit-
ual patterns of his trade. For a short time, not having to explain or
defend or champion or solicit or reform or challenge or be anything
to anyone or do anything but perceive life at its most natural and
undisturbed.

By dusk, the three nets were up. The arroyo, so narrow that only
a wedge of cornflower-blue sky was visible, was patrolled by two
crab-shaped clouds. Carol had already hiked on up ahead, on a
nature walk of her own, and at last she called to Bert: "There's an
animal up here. It's got a long tail, it's fluffy and gray. Looks a little
like a weasel." Jubilant, Bert leaped across the rocks and up the gorge
to meet her.

At 8:10 P.M. a large, billowy storm blew south of us, with swelling
gray-blue clouds and the tinges of electric green I knew to be the
signature of hail. Sunlight cut through the clouds, twisting like knife
blades, and then made corridors of light that seem almost walkable.
When night fell, lightning continued to prowl around the south rim
of the gorge. Coyotes yowled in the distance. Shooting stars began
to streak the sky with their white tears. Time for the miners' headlamps, the detectors, and the vigil.

What questions are bat specialists still tantalized by? I wondered.
Tuttle laughed. Ninety percent of the world's bat species hadn't
even been studied. Some were almost rumor—nothing more than a
description and a name. In fact, right above us that night was one
of the most plentiful and common bats in the West, the pipistrelle,
which wings in and out of the lives of so many at dusk. Yet nobody
knows where they roost. Carol had been prowling around the cliffs
up the gorge to see if she could spot any bats flying out. Shocking
though the thought is, there are bats becoming extinct throughout
the world that we may not even have discovered and named yet. Part
of people's phobia about bats, I supposed, is that they fear catching
diseases from them.

"You know, before I came out here," I said, "I had doctors, health
officials, and well-meaning academics all warning me that I could get

rabies just by inhaling around bats. I'm not sure if bats are rabid, but I know the people I spoke with were."

This was a topic that clearly burned Tuttle: "Fear of rabies from bats has been vastly exaggerated, beginning with mistakes made by researchers some twenty years ago, when bats were thought to be asymptomatic carriers of rabies."

"You mean they're not Typhoid Marys, who can carry the disease and infect others without succumbing to it themselves?"

"Of course not. They can get rabies, the same as dogs or cats can, but when they do get it, they die quickly, just like other animals do. Anyway, less than one half of 1 percent of bats contract rabies, and unlike most mammals, even when rabid, bats rarely become aggressive. Less than a dozen people in all the U.S. and Canada are believed to have died of *any* bat-related disease in the past four decades! When people *are* endangered, it's usually because they have foolishly picked up a sick bat that bites in self-defense. Just leave bats alone, and the odds of being harmed are infinitesmally small; whereas two thousand people die of falling down stairs every year.

"Eight hundred and fifty people die each year of bicycle accidents," he added, "and yet we think of biking as a safe and healthy form of exercise. Over six thousand people die of drowning each year, and yet surely it's healthy to swim. We don't get alarmed by the fact that ten or twenty people die each year from dog attacks. It's a tiny portion of the population, and everybody knows the advantages and pleasures of having pets. We recognize that we need bees: They produce honey, they pollinate our crops. We're careful to leave bees alone, that's all. It should be like that with bats. We don't get excited about the fact that more people die of food poisoning at church picnics annually than have died *in all history* from contact with bats. Now, here we have a chance of dying so remote compared to all these other things, and we're terrified of bats. Thousands of us die annually at the hands of our own spouses! Yet I don't know anybody who is afraid of getting married for fear they'll get killed by their spouse. What I'm saying is, unless you're living in abject horror of all these other threats to your life, it really makes no sense at all to be afraid of bats."

"While we're on myths," I said, "it seems like an awful lot of people can't shake the vampire image from their minds, either."

"Well, let me point out that vampire legends come from horrible, deviant behavior by *people*, not from bats or other animals. There have been people who enjoyed bathing in blood, drinking people's blood, doing all kinds of hideous things. But these vampire legends preceded by hundreds of years the discovery of a bat that drank blood. And what's the big deal? So this bat does drink blood. There are many primitive people who drink blood. The Masai mix milk with blood. I've watched people in Mexico cut the legs off a sea turtle and suck the blood out of the living turtle. Europeans make blood sausages and things. I mean, what's the big deal? We kill the whole animal every time we want to eat. The vampire seldom does that, or harms the animal at all. One other thing about vampire bats," he said, warming once more to his subject. "There aren't many animals known to be altruistic. Vampire bats adopt orphans, and they help and feed other individuals in times of need. They seem to have long memories, and they remember who has helped them in the past, and are likely to reciprocate. They're very intelligent, neat animals. Yes, they drink blood and they're occasionally a problem to cattle growers, sometimes requiring control. But to view them as hideous, grotesque, horrible ghouls—that's ridiculous. . . . Wait! There's one!"

A flutter at eye level disappeared, and just as fast its *ping-ping, ping-ping, ping-ping* disappeared with it. Surely he didn't mean a vampire bat? My mind shimmied a moment. Vampires live in Latin America. No, he had heard the cry of a spotted bat.

We looked down at the net, hidden in the dark and shadows. Tuttle flashed his headlamp over the flimsy strings of mist, picked up his infrared nightscope, and looked more carefully. Nothing. But at the next net, one pole was bobbing. For fishermen or bat catchers, a sure sign. Don and Bert jumped to the net and began disentangling the small bat, which was caught in the overlapping beams of their headlamps. It was not a spotted but a "ghost-faced" bat, one of Bert's favorites, a little squinting face in a fluffy parka of fur. Then we caught a free-tailed bat, resembling those I saw at Bracken. This time Tuttle showed me how the tail slides in and out like a sword concealed in an English walking cane. On its wings, red veins made a Christmas tree design.

"I'll show you why bats are such model animals for research. Take your light and shine it behind its wing," he instructed Bert. And suddenly a page from a *Gray's Anatomy* of bats popped into view. You could see right through the thin, translucent membrane.

"When you put it under a microscope, you can watch individual cells move through the capillaries. What's this? I never noticed this before," Tuttle said, revealing a small wedge at the corner of each wing. "Look at that pocket. Well, now . . . these fellows make a funny whistling sound when they fly."

"And you think it might be involved with the pockets?"

Shining his light squarely on the small triangle of furry flesh, he inspected it methodically. There was nothing like revelation to bring grace to a September evening. On the small bat's chin were shapes that looked like a floppy megaphone. Tuttle gently removed two ticks from its face, one from the eye, one from below the chin.

"Can I hold him?" Bert asked, putting out a finger as if for a pet parakeet to step onto. The bat hooked his feet and hung upside down, unalarmed. None of us meant to hurt him, and he was two ticks ahead of the game. Then Bert swung him gently like a small brown hammock, and he rolled to one side and took flight at the same moment. With the bat flown, it was time to return to our stations and await the next.

We lay on our backs in a geological telescope, in the still of the Texas night, with the occasional click-warble of an elusive spotted bat overhead, the stars yodeling light, the coyotes howling, the meteorites throwing their small bouquets, silent lightning forks prowling the south rim of the gorge, and peace everlasting.

● ● ●

When we returned to Austin, I visited Tuttle at his office at Bat Conservation International, where he had a library of books and articles about bats. That day, he also had two bats hanging upside-down in a mesh cage. The smaller one was Rafiki (which means "friend" in Swahili). Next to him hung a large tawny-and-golden-furred bat with black stretchy wings, named Zuri ("beautiful" in Swahili). Tuttle had brought them back from a trip to Africa, and they had traveled the country with him ever since, in a varnished box with a hot-water bottle on the bottom, to perform on countless shows, from David Letterman's to *Newton's Apple* to the *Today* show. Tuttle's efforts to smuggle them through security on every major airline had provided many pilots, flight attendants, and airport managers with priceless, batty cocktail-party stories.

The two bats were oddly matched companions in that Rafiki belonged to a standoffish species and was very much a loner, whereas Zuri belonged to a deeply affectionate species and was constantly trying to cuddle. Their keepers, Margaret and George Perry (executive director of BCI), said that they often saw Zuri inching up to Rafiki, who inched away only to be inched up to again. Once, when Rafiki was sick with an abscessed tooth and a chill, they found Zuri with his wings wrapped completely around the little bat, holding him close to keep him warm and comforted. At the time of my visit, the air-conditioning in Tuttle's office made the little bat chilly, and he had allowed Zuri to sidle up to him and press close, so they were rump to rump, like two spouses in bed. Zuri just let his wings hang, but Rafiki wrapped his wings around him and then latched his thumbs in the back for good measure. I've seen old men stand like this in parks.

Tuttle reached into the cage and pulled Zuri out by unhooking one foot at a time, as if lifting two coat hangers out of a closet. Zuri shifted his feet to Tuttle's forefinger, and Tuttle pressed gently with his thumb, just to guard against his flying off and perhaps into a glass window. Flying foxes don't echolocate, so they are as vulnerable as birds are to window bumping. Interestingly enough, both the smallest and the largest of all bats, the "bumblebee bats" and the flying foxes, share the same Southeast Asian rain forest. Bumblebee bats, weighing a third less than a penny, are also the smallest mammals on earth. Bats often look bigger than they are because their fur is so long. But flying foxes can be huge, with wings five feet wide. Though they don't inhabit the Americas, they're commonplace in a range from West Africa to the Pacific islands. Reddish-brown, with familiar foxlike faces and large black eyes, they have tiny ears and no sonar equipment sticking up from their heads. Fruit eaters, they've been known to travel as far as sixty miles for food. Hand-raised flying foxes are lovable pets, imprint quickly, and snuggle up to owners and lick their faces. BCI has members in Australia, bat mums, as they're called, who have raised injured flying foxes, set them free, and found the bats returning to visit, sometimes to show them their new babies.

Zuri hung comfortably from Tuttle's finger, watching the human pageant.

"Why don't bats faint from hanging upside-down?" I asked.

"Why don't we faint from standing right-side-up?" he retorted. "Why doesn't all the blood rush to our feet? Actually, the bat's better off, because he's sure of a good blood supply to the brain."

"Well, do bats do everything upside-down?"

"They don't fly upside-down," Tuttle offered. "Flying foxes even turn right-side-up to go to the bathroom, so they don't soil themselves."

Hanging down with most of his weight at the bottom, Zuri looked like a half-open umbrella. He turned his head up to look at me with large soulful eyes that held my gaze. One of the pupils was dilated more than the other. He sneezed. In old wives' tales, bats were thought to tangle in women's hair and drive them insane.

"Want to tangle?" I offered, as if inviting him to perform an Argentine dance. We lifted him onto my thick curly hair, which he at first slid off. Finally, he hooked his five-toed feet up and hung down one side of my head, as if he were on a motel drapery of some sort. Traveling with Tuttle, he had learned to put his feet up in some odd places, but human hair was clearly not one of his favorites. At last, he crept around my head a little, and I heard him sneeze gently again from my cologne. Then he wrapped around my neck, his tiny claws searching my smooth skin for a foothold, and he looked up at me with liquid eyes in which a thousand truths of the rain forest were hidden.

"What's the best way to show affection to a bat?" I asked Tuttle, who carefully considered the question, then said, "I'm not even sure I know the *best* way to show affection to a person." Laughs went around the room. Margaret Perry suggested petting him in the direction the fur grew right behind the neck. Lifting Zuri onto one finger, I petted his soft neck, and then we put him back in the cage. At once he scuttled over to Rafiki, snuggled rump to rump, and when settled, he began a long, thorough cleaning of his wings, chest, and body, licking methodically like a cat, to get rid of the minute oils, salt, perfume, and human essence he found on me. It was obvious that he felt dirtied. He washed up slowly, good-naturedly eyeing us, then closed his eyes and began to doze. After all, it was sleep time for bats. Nonetheless, when anyone drew near, he opened one eye and peeked out over his arm to see who was there.

At dinnertime, Tuttle and I tried the patio of the Four Seasons Hotel downtown, on the Colorado River, a few blocks from the pink-granite capitol building and right across from the Congress Avenue Bridge. We had not come for the margaritas or the lobster enchiladas but to watch an emergence as dazzling as the one we had seen at Bracken Cave. Tucked inside the crevices under the bridge were three quarters of a million bachelor free-tailed bats. They made Austin the summer home of the largest urban bat population in the world. As the sun ladled thick pastels into the river, two crew boats pulled gently, side by side. Could they see the bats when they passed under the bridge, I wondered? Sweethearts had begun to stroll across the bridge hand in hand, waiting for the emergence. Sodium lights from the Hyatt Hotel cast a trail of copper coins across the water. Suddenly, smoke billowed from underneath the bridge. No, not smoke but a column of bats. Then two columns soared high and flew in parallel, like the long black reins of an invisible sleigh. Bats kept surging out, and soon four columns stretched miles across the sky. A few strays looped and fed near us, passing like shuttles through the weave of the trees. The night was noticeably free from insects, but that was no surprise. These bats would eat five thousand pounds of insects that one night alone.

In a medieval simile of the Venerable Bede's, life is depicted as a beautiful and strange winged creature that appears at a window, flies swiftly through the half-lit banquet hall, and is gone. That seems about right for a vision of creation as beautiful as this one was, which soon included the city lights, the sunset doing a shadow dance over the water, and four columns of bats undulating across the sky.

Chapter 2

THE
EYELIDS
OF
MORNING

Nothing looks more contented than a resting alligator. The mouth falls naturally into a crumpled smile, the eyes half close in a sleepy sort of way, the puckered back looks as harmless as the papier-mâché maps of the Rockies children make in elementary school. The thick toes hug the mud like tree roots. Because their massive jaws curve upward, alligators appear to be laughing even when in repose. They seem caught in a great big private chuckle. And they do have something to be smug about. After all, they've seen the disappearance of the dinosaur and the Neanderthal. They are a hundred times more ancient than human beings.

Crocodilians, birds, and dinosaurs had a common origin about 230 million years ago, in the Mesozoic Era, when they sprang from a group of early reptiles called the thecodonts. Today there are three groups of crocodilians: crocodiles, alligators and caimans, and gharials (lissome, skewer-nosed animals that frequent the Ganges). According to the fossil record, there once were sixty-foot-long aquatic crocodilians and some that hunted on land and wielded six-inch teeth. In the heyday of huge, miscellaneously talented dinosaurs, they not only competed with, but somehow outwitted, the forces that killed the dinosaurs. Living relics, today's crocodilians have survived with only minor changes since the days of tar pits and thunder lizards, and part of our fascination is how out of place they look. They are genuine "Mesozoic leftovers," as George Campbell, author of a natural history of crocodilians, dubs them. And children are just as wild about crocodilians as they are about dinosaurs, which they lump together into one big carnival of monsters.

I was reminded of this on a sunny February morning in 1988 at the St. Augustine Alligator Farm, where I'd come with zoologist Kent Vliet and other researchers from the University of Florida to "bleed alligators," as Kent called the taking of blood samples. He and his colleague Lou Guillette, a reproductive physiologist who worked with reptiles, were studying the effects of captivity on hormone cycles.

"When you capture an alligator, its hormones sometimes go screeching up for hours, then plunge for days," Kent explained. "There are a lot of things we'd like to understand about their hormonal cycles. The basic problem is that alligators in captivity reproduce much less successfully than alligators in the wild. It might be a result of how densely the animals live. When animals are under stress, they produce stress hormones that block up the biochemical pathways that help with the production of sex hormones. If corticosterone levels rise, reproduction drops. So we've developed a threefold project. The first part is just to look at the effect our taking blood and handling the alligators has on their hormones. The second part is to look at alligators in different densities and compare the hormone concentrations. The third part is sort of a little background check to make sure that alligators in captivity cycle hormonally like wild alligators do. Throughout the year, we take blood samples monthly, sometimes even biweekly."

This meant regular gator roundups, which meant first rounding up half a dozen or so people who were keen to grapple with alligators. Although Kent was a heavily built man in his thirties, with a beard, thinning hair, and large, powerful hands, collecting alligators every month all by himself would have been an ordeal. It took a lot of volunteers to handle alligators, and on this occasion Kent and Lou had six others: Debby, an effervescent graduate student in zoology with a mop of brown curls, known locally as the possum lady, because of her work with local opossums; Sylvia, a quiet, dark-haired Nicaraguan graduate student studying the brown caiman of Colombia and Central America; Barry and Jimmy, two outgoing blues and folk musicians and alligator enthusiasts; Kent's roommate, John, a tall, thin graduate student with a lot of field experience, who spent most of the year in Venezuela studying the spectacled caiman and the Orinoco crocodile. Since he was soon to be a zoologist, I asked him what one does, exactly, and laughing, he answered, "A zoologist is someone who stops along the roadway to pick up dead animals." Some of us had traveled together by van, along with the equipment; the rest had arrived separately. But there was no way to miss the rendezvous site, announced by billboards with paintings of giant alligators, jaws open wide enough to hold a lion tamer and his lion.

The St. Augustine Alligator Farm is the oldest existing alligator farm in the world. And that seemed only fitting, since St. Augustine is the oldest city in the United States and crocodilians are some of the oldest living reptiles. The farm was started in 1893 by George Reddington, the conductor, and Felix Fire, the fireman, of a train that ran from Jacksonville down to St. Augustine Beach. As the train wove through the swamps, people often saw basking alligators and they would ask the trainsmen to stop so they could watch. Fire and Reddington had to stop anyway, to remove alligators from the tracks, and one day they decided to round up the animals, put them in a bathhouse on the beach, and charge people a quarter for a look. The current owner's father, a haberdasher, had bought the farm and another one in Jacksonville in 1937, blending the herds to produce a collection of the largest, oldest, and fattest alligators ever, and the farm had stayed in the family since that day. Most of the gators were caught fifty years before, and when we arrived there were acres of them lying so close together they looked like a relief map of the Himalayas. In one pen alone lived 128 alligators, whose average age handlers estimated at sixty to ninety years. Some showed white calcium deposits on their tails, scar tissue from fights. Most were old and scarred and a few were missing an eye. Not only was it hard to tell where one began and another ended, they were for the most part lying as still as masonry.

"How would you know if one died?" I asked.

"You've got to look for flies around their eyes," Kent said, practically.

"When they die, do you bury them?"

"Burial's rough. A nine-hundred-pound alligator needs a big hole. We had a big old alligator die here once, and I weighed its head— just its head—at a hundred and fifty pounds!"

Though it was a cold day, which felt ten degrees cooler in the shade, large crowds meandered from one exhibit of crocodilians to the next. Each year, a quarter of a million people made this pilgrimage to ogle the last of the giant reptiles. Munching on popcorn or hot dogs, they gawked at caimans from Central and South America; a Nile crocodile from Africa; false gavials from India; American alligators; saltwater crocodiles from Sri Lanka; American crocodiles; highly endangered Chinese alligators; Morelet's crocodiles from Central America; smooth-fronted caimans from South America; broad-snouted caimans from Uruguay; Cuban crocodiles; African dwarf crocodiles; and Siamese crocodiles. Regular shows in a small amphitheater revealed the basics of "alligator wrestling." But the most popular place was a shallow, swampy lake containing hundreds of alligators, most lurking just out of sight below the chilly water— and that made them even more frightening to many people, because they seemed to dwell in their subaquatic world as mysteriously as they do in our subterranean dreams. Raised wooden walkways led out over the swimming animals. Children raced down these platforms and leapt onto the rails, in a frenzy to see the huge, potbellied alligators (which have grown obese from never having to hunt prey), while parents screamed and moved cautiously down the center of the boardwalks. One woman looked like she was walking the plank. Another, bold with curiosity, leaned over the fence and tried to look underneath the boardwalk.

The first time I saw Kent in a National Geographic film, *Realm of the Alligator,* he lay up to his neck in this pond full of them, armed only with a five-foot cypress cudgel. Floating among alligators, he was observing them on their own terms, at eye level, hoping to decipher their body language and visual cues. Scanning the water for signs of submerged gators, he occasionally nudged away animals that got too close. It didn't surprise me that a zoologist might wish to enter the alligator's world as completely as possible. Not much is known about alligators. They don't train well. And they're unwieldy and rowdy to work with in laboratories. So the best way to study them is out of doors. But it was while watching that film that I first realized how passive, otherworldly, and deeply maternal alligators could be. They make tender mothers and languorous, sensual swains.

Alligator courtship rituals are lengthy and oddly delicate. It all begins with a female's affectionate pestering. She swims up to a male and rubs him gently along the face, nuzzles his neck a little, nudges him with her solid black shoulders, and alternately caresses and gently pushes his head. Then she might bump him lightly or climb onto his back and slide right over his head with her full weight. Sometimes she actually mounts the male and rides him around the lake. All this to get his mind off unromantic things, like squabbling with other males or staking out a territory. Once he gets the message, he starts necking, too. There is much stroking of heads, because so many touch receptors group there, especially along the sides. If you think about it, this makes sense for aquatic animals. Alligators are creatures of the water's edge who have dual citizenship in the wet and dry worlds. Though not technically amphibians, they live in a similar twilight of water and sky, and they are masters of the narrow realm where the two worlds collide. They touch to orient themselves to one another, the water, the air. Sometimes they blow bubbles at each other and cough gently. After a long period of weighty caressing, the male puts his head over the female's neck or head, presses her down, lifts his front leg and hind leg on one side, and slides up over her. Mating involves maneuvering their cloacal vents (which lie underneath and at the base of the tail) together and it's difficult to get them in position. The male clutches the female with his fore-limbs, embraces her, angles his head off to one side, and swivels so that he's at a ninety-degree angle to her body, bracing himself against her back or pelvis with his hind limbs. He searches with his tail, and when he finally gets the tip of it underneath the female, all he has to do is pull his tail forward, draw the bases of their tails together, and insert his penis into her cloaca. It's a difficult position in which they look like mating Swiss Army knives.

"Have you ever seen crocodilians mating out of water?"

"I'm not really sure it's possible."

"In the National Geographic film, you were swimming in the lake. Do you still do that?"

Kent secured the rope to one of the boardwalk's stanchions. "No. I haven't done that for a long time."

"How come you stopped?"

"Because I didn't need to do it anymore. Anyway," he said wearily, "it was starting to become a circus. People went crazy when they saw me out in the water, up to my neck with the gators. I first began doing it for two reasons. I was pretty sure that alligators were communicating with subtle visual signals. Slight changes in body posture and body elevation in the water—things like that. But being on this boardwalk looking down on them, I wasn't able to see those slight changes very well. I thought that if I could get at an alligator's eye level, it would be pretty easy for me at least to see what's relevant to an alligator. So that was the first reason. The second was that at that time I was studying courtship behavior, and I thought if I could swim with the gators, if I made up a fake alligator and actually went out and could stimulate them into courtship with this fake alligator, it would be a wonderful experiment. I'd be able to intensify or eliminate acts of courtship and see what effect it had on their response."

What had he made the fake alligator out of?

"I took the skull of an alligator, filled it with foam to make it neutrally buoyant, painted it to look like a live animal, hung it on a big pole, and I swam out with it."

"Do you think they believed it was a gator?"

"I think they did initially, and then after a while they realized it was a setup. I could never get an alligator to remain interested for any length of time."

"Maybe the model alligator didn't smell right."

"No, I'm sure it didn't smell right, didn't move right, maybe it didn't hit hard enough in courtship or something. It was really very interesting for me. There was a lot I learned. It's remarkable how powerful those animals are. I usually talk about courtship being a very slow and gentle process; it looks like they're just sliding up and bumping along each other. But there's a hundred-and-fifty-pound female and a four-hundred-pound male in the water, and when they start to bump, you really feel it. Courtship involves a lot of pressing, which is extremely important behavior to both individuals. I think it's because it allows the alligators to judge the size and fitness of the partner. The alligator doing the pressing can feel how strong the lower alligator is when it's resisting and the lower alligator can feel how strongly it's being pressed. When I played around with this fake, which by the way I called *syn-gator,* I could press right up on top of an alligator and I could actually rest the bottom of the pole on the bottom of the lake and lean on that gator with all my weight, and I couldn't budge a gator an inch. And yet they dunk each other left and right. They're immensely powerful."

Some visitors to the farm found Kent's experiment hair-raising. Maneuvering a fake alligator head, floating at alligator level in the lake, Kent must have looked wholly uncivilized to them. To the people of the Sepik River, in Papua New Guinea, however, the crocodile is an ever-present danger that they both fear and worship.

In their mythology, a giant crocodile swam to the surface of the sea with the Earth on its back, and it continues to hold it there, above the sea. Life-size, meticulously carved crocodile heads decorate the prows of their canoes, which support their passengers the same way the crocodile supports the Earth. They wear crocodile-motif wristbands and other ornaments when they dance. After a head-hunting raid, they blow a wooden trumpet, shaped like a crocodile's head, to signal their return and the number of enemy heads they're carrying. A Papua New Guinean would have found the sight of Kent in the lake wearing an alligator head a small ripple in his large estuary of belief.

Kent had performed his courtship mummery in spring, courting season. In winter, crocodilians stop eating entirely and become lethargic. With mythic fright, people picture them as voracious eaters whose razory jaws feed a limitless appetite. But the truth is that crocodilians eat infrequently, perhaps as little as once a week in the spring and summer, and in the winter, they don't eat at all. In the wild, they dig dens with their feet, mouth, and tail or they lie on the bottom of a lake or flooded prairie to await the warmer weather. They don't actually hibernate; their metabolism lowers and they fast. It's their dens that make them such good citizens. Because "gator hole" ponds tend to stay wet in the winter, they support whole communities of animals. Even cattle sometimes water at gator holes. These days, civilization inadvertently makes wildlife ponds suitable for crocodilians too, on golf courses, in real estate developments, and even in back of one power-and-light company in Miami, which was amazed to discover in its labyrinthine canals a nesting community of Florida's American crocodiles (chiefly marine animals), which are almost extinct in the wild. But then many crocodilians are seriously endangered. Crocodilians come from tropical and subtropical regions—if one drew a band of their habitats around the world, it would be a line that at the top went through the United States at the northern part of North Carolina—and that means crocodilians live largely in developing countries, where they succumb to commercial hunting and mutilation. If the animal doesn't have a commercially valuable skin, then it's hunted by local people as a source of food. Or some simply lose their habitats to power plants and industry. Progress sometimes steps on nature's toes, and there's not always much one can do about it. But high-fashion crocodilian products are strictly a luxury item, and life, including crocodilian life, can go on without them. One needs a pair of shoes, one doesn't need a pair of crocodile shoes.

Just below the boardwalk, a nose and a pair of bulbous eyes appeared through the duckweed scum on the water. It seemed a fitting paradox that one of the heaviest and most lumbering animals on earth should live under a blanket of the world's smallest and most delicate flowers. Mixed with the duckweed there was *Wolffia,* an even smaller plant. Almost as little is known about *Wolffia* as about alligators; it was not long before that its flower had been photographed through a scanning electron microscope. Heavy as the alligators are, they depend on the fragile flowers for warmth. When the wind blows the duckweed down to one end of the lake, as occasionally it does, all the gators gather at that end, too. That day the winds were calm, a thin, even blanket of confetti-size leaves floated on the water, and the two dark eyes peering up at us like twin snorkels were coated in the greenish-yellow flecks. Kent ran to the rail and lowered a rope noose in front of the animal's head. Carefully, he slid the noose over the head to the thick, heavy neck muscles and pulled up sharply, closing the noose. Then he lassoed another alligator. Now that there were two to work with, our team went into action, getting the hypodermic needles ready, the logbook, tape measure, rolls of electrician's black tape, and other tools of a zoologist's trade. Kent climbed right over the fence and into the lake, took the free end of the rope as if it were nothing more than a leash on a small schnauzer, and began pulling the alligator onto a small tree-studded island.

"Could sure use some help here!" he called.

Lou and John scrambled over the fence and stepped carefully

through the water (gators might be sliding along the bottom), and I crawled over, too.

"Watch your feet! Watch the water! Watch under the board-walk!" Kent warned me as I followed right behind Lou and John, trying to place my feet where they placed theirs. Barry and Jimmy had begun picking up ropes and lassoing gators at different sections of the lake. A tug-of-war crew secured each animal to a tree, fence post, or the boardwalk stanchions. Pulling together on the rope, we tried to hoist our animal out of the water, but it thrashed about, waving its enormous head, and then suddenly hurled itself into a series of fast rolls, an alligator's typical getaway move.

"Okay. Back off a little!" Kent directed as the rope spun in our hands. "Let him wear himself out a bit." We let the rope go slack. As soon as the gator leveled out, we heaved again, this time dragging it onto the shore, where I tied the rope to a strong tree. Now the alligator opened its mouth in a toothy threat display and hissed long and loud. A real full-bodied textbook *hissss* that jangled your nerves and made your shoulders cringe. *Hissss.* It is the first time I had ever truly understood the word. What's more, I seemed to have backed up. So had the others, all except for Kent and John, who made these trips often and moved deftly, with a kind of informed nonchalance, at just the right distance from the jaws, which the alligator swung in a wide arc.

"They can jump," Kent said, making a back-it-up motion with his open palms.

What a strange, beautiful creature it was, with bulging eyes and stubby legs and powerful jaws and rows of sharp teeth and a thick white tongue and pointy scutes (the puckered armor that gives alligator hide its distinctive look). Each scute has a keel down the center of it, and in some species the scutes are arranged geometrically. Its eyes, especially, fascinated me. All crocodilians have a third transparent eyelid, or nictitating membrane, goggles of a sort, so they can see while swimming underwater. But they also have football-shaped pupils, which stay vertical to the horizon no matter what angle the head turns. Even if the gator tilts its head straight up, the pupil floats like a gyroscope, so vision won't be distorted. It's a handy adaptation. The secret to an alligator wrestler putting one to sleep—or "hypnotizing" it, as they sometimes brag—may be that when you turn an alligator upside-down you disorient it, disturb its equilibrium, and upset its eyes' ability to focus. Naturally, it lies still, as would a human with severe vertigo. But another feature of the eyes has contributed to their near extinction. Crocodilian eyes reflect light. Cruise the Okefenokee Swamp at night, hold a flashlight against your forehead, and shine it toward the shore, and you're likely to see pairs of red burning coals—alligator eyes: a perfect target for hunters. Other animals' eyes shine, too, and for the same reason: There's a thin reflective layer, the *tapetum lucidum* (Latin for "bright carpet"), which acts as a mirror just behind their retinas.

Once, in the Amazon, I went out in an inflatable Zodiac at sunset to "shine" caiman eyes along the shore. There were precious few caimans to shine, since, like the manatees that inhabited the river, they had been overhunted for food, hides, and souvenirs. The "baby alligators" tourists used to take home from Florida were really baby caimans. The souvenir-doll "alligators" wearing top hats and tuxedos, or dressed as doctors, lawyers, or professors (complete with pince-nez), tend to be baby caimans, too. But it is easy to confuse the three main types of crocodilians, which look similar in a lot of ways, especially if there isn't time to check the animal out thoroughly. Here are some rules of thumb: Alligators have round snouts, whereas crocodiles have pointed, triangular snouts. Alligators' nostrils have a space between them and look like an open V that doesn't meet at the bottom (whereas crocodiles' nostrils are closer together). Alligators have much less aggressive personalities. If you can see both upper and bottom teeth, it's probably a crocodile; but alligators have more teeth (eighty) than crocodiles do (seventy). Crocodiles look speedier, more aerodynamic, and they are renowned for their savagery. Gharials are mild-mannered, fish-eating crocodilians with long, slender, graceful snouts and, sometimes, a big knob right at the end. And caimans look like alligators but have short, blunt noses.

Within the order of crocodilians, there are about twenty-nine different forms, including such rapacious and unpredictable predators as the Nile crocodile, which kills more people in East Africa than any other wild animal except the hippopotamus (of course, this is a minor number compared to the yearly deaths from auto accidents, malaria, sleeping sickness, and AIDS), and the gigantic saltwater crocodile of Australia, New Guinea, Indonesia, and other places, which can grow to around twenty-three feet long and is responsible for some of the supposed shark attacks. These "salties" usually live in the brackish waters of coastal mangrove swamps but also make their way into freshwater rivers from time to time. Not only are they unpredictable, they're athletic, and have been reported by locals to stalk their prey. These are the crocodiles newspapers like the *National Enquirer* often feature, with such headlines as "I FOUGHT OFF A MAN-EATING MONSTER WITH MY BARE HANDS." In that sensationalized story, a man swimming near his yacht in the Solomon Islands related how he "screamed in excruciating agony as the crocodile sank its teeth into my back and chest and shook me like a floppy little rag doll." The Cuban crocodile, although not a "man-eater," is apparently not an animal to be feckless around, either. But there are also shy and retiring crocodilians like the African dwarf crocodile, the smooth-fronted caiman, our American alligator, or its cousin the Chinese alligator, which Marco Polo wrote about in the thirteenth century.

What we had now in our lasso was an American alligator, but it was impossible to tell from the outside whether it was a male or a female. It began a low snarling growl. Sneaking up behind it, Kent climbed onto its back, tucked his knees behind the gator's front legs as if he were a jockey getting into position, and at the same time pressed the gator's head against the dirt so that the mouth closed. Then he reached around and under either side of the jaws, as if gripping a big sandwich in two hands, held the jaws closed, leaned back, and lifted the head.

"Tape!" he called. Debby ran up with a roll of electrician's tape and wrapped the jaws half a dozen times, then Kent set the head

back down. It could still swing its head like a club, but it could not
open its jaws to bite. Alligators have large, steely muscles for clamp-
ing shut on prey. Though it's virtually impossible for even the stron-
gest man to open an alligator's mouth once it has closed on
something, the muscles for opening the mouth are very weak. Kent
was a strong, heavyset man, but holding a gator's jaws shut is more
a question of leverage than sheer muscle. The alligator lifted its left
rear leg, tucking it close to its body, and Kent quickly shifted his
weight, so that the gator did not roll. Then he slid a large palm right
over the animal's eyes and at last it quieted.

"Want to hold the eyes?" he asked me. Kneeling on the sand right
beside the taped jaws, I waited for Kent to lift his hand off. The
bulging eyes popped up like a scene in a storybook. When I rushed
my hands toward them, the nictitating membrane slid across from
left to right, the top and bottom eyelids closed, and when I pressed,
the eyes dropped down into the head. They felt springy under my
palm.

"Amazing," I whispered. To see how it happened, I lifted my
hand just a little, felt the eyeballs pop up, saw the eyelids open, the
nictitating membrane float from left to right, the elliptical pupils
perfectly horizontal. Then I replaced my hand and the eyes vanished
back into the head. Meanwhile, Kent inserted a hypodermic needle
into a fold just behind the head and withdrew a syringe full of blood,
which he handed to Lou, who labeled it and put it in a fishing-tackle
box.

"You want to sex it?" Kent asked invitingly as he leaned back and
held up the heavy tail, exposing a small slit, which is the cloaca, a
cavity in which the sex organs lie.

Debby took my place as blindfold as I leaned under the tail and
slid my first two fingers inside the cloaca, squooshy and cool.

"I don't feel anything special in there." My fingers withdrew
covered in a heavy, sweet, pungent musk. Both male and female
gators give off musk, and scientists think there may be both water-
borne and airborne portions of it. After a gator bellows, there is often
an oily sheen on the water all around it.

John double-checked. "Female," he confirmed. But Kent had already smelled the musk in the air and recognized it as female. Gingerly, he climbed off, and Debby and Sylvia measured the head, the body, and the tail, calling out each number—27; 40.5; 39—as if ordering up a suit. John attached a small numbered band on the webbing between the toes of a hind foot. Kent painted a broad orange stripe on the gator's nose with a grease crayon so we'd all know not to catch it again that day, and checked its general condition. Then he climbed carefully onto the next gator, which was tied to another tree nearby, and the ritual began again.

"Try sexing this one," he said, holding up an even heavier tail. When I inserted my fingers into its cloaca, I felt a slippery hard length lying off to the left side, its penis.

"*Mister* Gator. No doubt about it."

"It's not so easy," Kent cautioned. "A female alligator has a clitoris, and sometimes you can feel it way up in the cloaca, which can make sexing alligators real confusing."

"Does this mean that a female alligator can have an orgasm?"

"Well, we don't know. Don't know about sperm transport, either. But there aren't muscular ejaculations in the male. Crocodilians have relatively short bouts of copulation—twenty to thirty seconds—compared to other reptiles. To answer the orgasm question we'd have to do hormone levels during copulation, which would be very difficult. They're pretty private about mating. And they don't make good laboratory animals when they're big enough to mate. They'd tear the place apart! I knew a scientist once who worked with monitor lizards in a lab, even had them walk treadmills, but gators are too stubborn to walk a treadmill. They'd probably just lie there and be carried along by it. So I don't think we're going find out some things for quite a while."

Across the lagoon, a medium-size alligator basked on the shore. After setting our two sampled alligators free, we climbed up the railings and raced across the boardwalk. Kent just waded across, a lasso in one hand, looking around cautiously as he moved. John got there first, just in time to grab the tail as the gator dove into the water. Then Barry and I grabbed the tail too, and with all three of us hanging on, we managed to keep the gator from escaping, but we were not strong enough to drag it onto land. A rope around its hind parts might have hurt it, and its head flailed somewhere under the duckweed-coated water. Looking for the jaw, Kent inserted a hand straight into the opaque water where he thought the head should be, calmly, as if he were reaching into a vest pocket.

"Mouth is open, damnit," he said, withdrawing his hand. Then he tried again.

"Are you crazy!" Debby screamed as Kent's hand disappeared below water and the gator began to thrash so much it unsettled our footing. We looked like a scene from an ancient cautionary tale about wrestling with the Leviathan. Some researchers insist that the Leviathan mentioned in the Bible really is a crocodile. Peloubet's *Bible Dictionary* says: "In Job 41:1 and Psalms 74:14, the crocodile is without a doubt the animal intended." In Job 41, there is a long descriptive passage about the rigors of fighting the Leviathan, of which the following is a sample:

> Who can open the doors of his face? His teeth are terrible round
> about. His scales are his pride, shut up together as with a close seal.
> One is so near to another, that no air can come between them.
> . . . His eyes are like the eyelids of the morning . . .

What a lovely description of the day opening its many veils just as a crocodilian does its elaborate eyelids. Crocodilians were almost certainly the dragons of yore. In Chinese, alligators are called *tulong,* or "earth dragon," and the etymology strongly suggests that the Chinese dragon began with myths about the alligator. Knights may have fought large prehistoric crocodilians in the Near East, or they may simply have mythologized the dragons' size and ferocity. Dragons were often depicted as fire-breathing, but in certain temperatures and atmospheric conditions, crocodilians can emit vapor from their nostrils when they bellow, and in the magic-loving eyes of the Middle Ages, the vapor might have looked like smoke. "We are ignorant of the meaning of the dragon," Argentinian writer Jorge Luis Borges writes, "in the same way that we are ignorant of the meaning of the universe, but there is something in the dragon's image that fits man's imagination and this accounts for the dragon's appearance in different places in different periods."

Finally John managed to slide a noose safely over the gator's hips and we hauled it up onto the shore, hissing and growling, jaws snapping. It swung its head at us in an irritated bluff but did not charge. Quickly, Kent slipped a noose over its head, cinched it up tight, and tied the gator to a nearby tree.

"You want this one?" Kent asked me.

"Absolutely." I stepped forward.

"Wait! Get farther away from the head," he said. "Gators can strike fast and—remember?—I said they can jump. Swing around behind it. Move in fast and confidently and get the eyes covered as soon as possible, and be sure to keep your knees behind its front legs, so it can't swing its jaw around and bite your leg."

"Right." In one quick motion, I climbed onto its back, tucked my knees behind its front legs, and ran a palm down its forehead to cover the eyes and push the mouth closed against the dirt. I gave both of us a moment to quiet down, then slid my hands under its bottom jaw and quickly grabbed both jaws, holding them shut. What took strength was lifting the heavy head up without falling forward, while at the same time holding the jaws tightly closed so that Sylvia could tape them.

"Hurry! Hurry!" I told her as my grip weakened. But once that was done, I tried to relax and soothe the alligator by putting a hand over its eyes.

"What do you suppose is going through its mind?" I asked Kent, who was preparing the hypodermic.

"Not a thing. It's probably like a dial tone."

"I see you don't romanticize their intelligence."

Kent laughed. "They have a little tiny brain," he said, his eyes opening wider with each diminutive. "Even the biggest animal we work with today will have a brain of only about an inch long and half an inch wide. That's a *little* brain. But they're so capable at what they do. They're so well adapted to the kind of life they lead, they just don't need those higher brain functions. They're amazing for other reasons. They're perfect reptiles."

"What's the *essence* of being reptile?"

"Taking energy when you can get it and never expending it unless you have to. They're just an extremely efficient energy system."

"Mammals must seem messy and extravagant to you by comparison."

"Mammals *are* extravagant. Mammals are high-speed race cars. Reptiles are BMW cars, and they're really gas-efficient."

When you think about it, there are many advantages to being cold-blooded and getting your life energy from external sources—like basking in the sun—rather than from a private inferno you carry in your body. That inferno must be stoked carefully and kept at a precise heat. An alligator can't digest food if its body temperature is too low. We can eat any old time, and it probably doesn't do us much good—it just makes us fat. The alligator can't do that. Nor is there anything vulgar about relying on a heat source outside your body. Humans store information outside our brains, in writing. We help warm ourselves by burning wood, bridling waterfalls, digging up coal, plumbing natural gas. We must eat to keep our temperatures up, and most often we do that by heating our food to the steaminess of freshly killed prey. In our own warm-blooded bias, we see alligators and other cold-blooded animals as low, primitive, far less advanced than we, who lord over them as the pinnacle of physiological adaptation. But what a misconception that is. They are not less well adapted than we are because they're cold-blooded; they're just highly developed in different directions. They are merely another one of the many treats of being, another way in which matter declares itself. And if we weren't such chauvinists, we would admire how being cold-blooded allows them to seek out niches in which we are incapable of living. Some years ago, naturalist Harvey Pough worked out that it would be impossible for mammals to maintain a body size as small as a little frog's or fish's, perhaps only two and a half to three millimeters long. Our sort of metabolic system just couldn't manage it. It is impossible for us to have an elongated body, like a snake's, lizard's, or salamander's, because we'd lose too much heat. Our metabolic rate would need to be gigantic to keep that long body warm. There are many pluses to being cold-blooded that we high-handedly ignore. One is that it allows reptiles to be as efficient as alligators, which may catch only three or four good meals a year at best and the rest of the time not worry about eating. They lose little energy, because they're not hot-rodding around the landscape, busily burning up their energy stores. Even when warm-blooded animals lie still or sleep, they are at fast rev, burning up energy to maintain body heat. If we mammals don't get something to eat every day or two, our temperature drops, all our signs fall off, and we begin to starve. Living at biological red alert, it's not surprising how obsessed we are with food; I'm just amazed we don't pace and fret about it all the time.

"One big problem for scientists," Kent said, "is that it's hard for us, who are built on a very fast time clock, to perceive cause and effect in alligator behavior, because they're built on a slower clock. This is especially true in winter. I say something to you and you respond immediately. When an alligator says something to another alligator, it may be fifteen or twenty minutes before the other responds. You really have to be paying attention to see the cause and effect in their behavior, since it's on a very different time scale from the one we're used to. This poses a real problem for researchers. It's very difficult, as a warm-blooded animal, to understand the behavior of a cold-blooded one."

When they saw our troupe of gator handlers at work, children begged to join in. Why are children charmed, obsessed even, by such violent predators as crocodilians and sharks, which aren't at all cute and cuddly? Indeed, some of these species tear their victims apart with melodramatic savagery. Alligators usually do this while rolling, and two may grab the same animal and roll in opposite directions to rip it apart. Dinosaurs, at least, are so big that they defy a child's comprehension. Children play with them as little things, as toys. In

museums, they do see them full-size, but only as skeletons or mummified, not alive. So the monsters stay totally mythic and, above all,
dead, sealed forever in the safety zone of the past. But alligators and
crocodiles are massively alive, and children would climb right into
the water with them and try to play if their parents didn't prevent
it. On the other hand, adults often asked us what we were being paid
(nothing), then shuddered and yelled to us across the lake: "There
isn't enough money in the world to make me do that!" As a final
gesture, one man swatted the air with a hand, slamming an invisible
door shut on the whole idea, and said: "I'd *never* do that. *No way.*
I mean *never!*" But, leaning against the wooden rails of the boardwalk, he shielded the sun from his eyes and continued watching us
for hours. Each time I looked up, he was there, quietly shaking his
head no, as if in answer to some prolonged question.

Sitting on an alligator is an ideal way to learn about its anatomy.
Some people think that "alligators wear a built-in ugly job," as one
writer puts it. If so, they haven't looked at one very closely. Alligators
have beautiful undulating skin, which feels dense, spongy, and solid,
like the best eraser. And they're full of anatomical surprises. Their
nostrils are surrounded by strong muscles. Leaning forward, I
touched the nostrils with the tips of my fingers, and in response, they
squeezed closed and then opened again. An alligator is efficient
underwater, aerodynamic and sleek. Not only does it retract its eyes,
it can close its nostrils, tuck in the two spongy musk glands under
its neck, close its movable ear lids, and seal off its throat with a wide
drape of flesh. The throat drape is especially important, so that it
doesn't drown when it drags its prey underwater. Though it has a
four-chambered heart, it can reroute the blood and stop circulation
to the lungs while it's submerged. An alligator should have an excellent sense of smell, because it can close off the glottis and throat,
isolate the nostrils, and direct a small sniff of air straight into the
olfactory chamber, right next to the brain's olfactory lobe. That a
creature so beautiful, wild, and mysterious could be turned into a
handbag or pair of shoes gave me a slow chill.

Kent drew a wide stripe of orange grease crayon down the gator's nose.

"Can alligators smell as well as sharks can?"

"Oh no, they don't smell nearly that well," Kent said. "I mean, they aren't smelling anything *in* the water; they smell only airborne particles. Their nostrils are closed underwater."

"So if you cut yourself in the lake, they couldn't home in on the blood?"

"Not unless maybe they could taste it. You know, they don't have any lips, so stuff goes in their mouth very easily. They have pretty good sight, their hearing is pretty good. I wouldn't say that they were highly evolved in any of their senses, but they're very fine predators because they're *generalists.* All of their senses are good. I think that's the key to their survival."

"Generalists make the best predators? Have you told that to your department chairman?"

"I bet he already knows it."

Running one hand along the yellow side of the alligator's jaw, I caressed the black speckled touch receptors. Its mouth quivered a little as I lightly touched a protruding tooth. When you look down on an alligator, if you let your sense of perspective go, you'll swear you're flying over the Rockies at thirty thousand feet. Its back is covered in miniature mountain ranges: horny plates that pucker and interfold and are geometrically arranged. Only the top of the alligator is full of these spiky ridges. Alligator-hide apparel is made from the smooth, soft belly skin. By wearing their skins on our feet and over our shoulders like talismans, I suppose we domesticate them in a symbolic way. Some people even carry alligator briefcases and luggage, in which they tame parts of their lives.

Peter Brazaitis, superintendent of reptiles at the Bronx Zoo, had told me a little about the history of marketing crocodilian hides when I spoke with him earlier in New York. A slender, lightly tanned middle-aged man, wearing a khaki shirt and earth-brown trousers with a brass belt buckle in the shape of a sea turtle, he had sat down at a conference table in front of a National Geographic wall map of the world. On a nearby counter, a small, tantalizing wooden box said simply LIVE ANIMALS, and had a drawing of a flamingo and a turtle, although there was certainly no way a flamingo could fit into it. Through the open office doors, I saw the back access doors to some of the exhibits in the Reptile House. On each door ran the warning: THINK BEFORE YOU OPEN. I hadn't realized that officials of the Bronx Zoo wore large badges in the shape of law-enforcement shields. Peter's number was 503; he pinned the shield at heart level, and it gave him the look of a knight. "Up until and right through the sixties," he had explained, "there was a great commercial pressure to hunt these animals. For one thing, technology improved: Airplanes could get into very remote areas, so it became easy to bring skins out of previously inaccessible regions and sell them on an international market. By the end of the 1960s, it became clear that many species of crocodilians were on the verge of extinction. Some of the most critically endangered were the Chinese alligator, the American alligator, the Orinoco crocodile, and the Cuban crocodile; in fact, almost every species of crocodilian became threatened or deeply endangered. Any of the animals that had a beautiful, classic skin, which made the best leather, were right at the brink of extinction. You see, the industry would use a species until it was exhausted and then switch to another species and just go on down the line. At the end of the 1960s and the beginning of the 1970s, CITES [the Convention on the International Trade of Endangered Species] was formed as part of the United Nations. The signators of its treaty agreed to abide by certain rules in taking some species and realizing that others were endangered or nearly extinct, and they agreed to provide protection. In the United States we went a step further. We passed the Endangered Species Act, and what it did was ensure that we abide by the regulations of the CITES treaty. In addition, we put animals on our list that we felt were endangered even though CITES hadn't flagged them yet as endangered. Each of the countries that signed CITES became an enforcement agency, a real watchdog for the other countries. If a species was protected in Brazil, it was automatically prohibited from import into the United States or any other CITES country. And this is the way it remains to this day."

"Surely that helped the animals."

"That's what one would think, and it did save a few species. That wasn't the problem. The real problem revolved around identification. If you look at a live animal, you can tell exactly where it came from. You say, 'Yes, this is the jacara caiman.' But if you have it in a pair of shoes, you have trouble, because for a few of the species of crocodilians, there are no identifying characteristics you can see on a small piece of their leather. Being able to prosecute violators or prohibit or refuse import to a particular group of skins really depended on being able to identify that species in trade. Many hides came into the country that could not be *legally* demonstrated to be endangered species even though we knew they were."

"So endangered species are poached, and then their skins are smuggled through other countries, to throw the CITES nations off the track."

"Yes, they get laundered. By 1983, Bolivia, Paraguay, and Brazil went to the CITES secretariat and confessed that they couldn't control the illegal hunting. They don't have the money to fund forces of people in their remote regions. Also, commercial hunting is very well organized. The traffic routes for smuggling skins are basically the same as those for smuggling drugs—Singapore, Hong Kong, Brazil, Paraguay, Bolivia. Some nations decided to do a comprehensive study of the animals throughout Central and South America, to get some idea of what populations are left, and then work out regulations with some pep in them. This is a large, long-term project that began in 1985. I'm leading the team in Brazil."

"Is the United States still importing endangered-crocodilian skins?"

"More than 80 percent of all [finished] wildlife products comes through the port of New York, because most of the tanneries are in Europe—in Italy and France. And, unfortunately, there are less than a dozen inspectors for the entire port of New York.

"Are they conversant in the skins? Could they tell what's what?"

"Only up to a point. I've trained many of them, but there is a constant change of personnel, as in any agency, so there are always new people coming and going. If I were to look at a thousand skins that came out of a particular country as a finished product, I would probably be able to say with certainty which ones were endangered species only about 60 percent of the time. And if I can't do better than that, and I happen to be one of three people in the world who has that expertise, you can imagine the problem.

"We can account for every single alligator skin that comes out of the United States. But here's the tragedy: Once we created a *legal* market, we essentially said to the industry, 'Okay, there's no reason why you can't use the skin commercially.' Well, they started an ambitious campaign, pointing out that alligators were not only legal but farmed like cattle. That happened in 1979, after the first harvest of the American alligators, then again in 1982 and in 1983. When that happened, their advertising created a demand that was greater than what the legal sources could supply. American alligators' skins, when they were first exported, went for $7.50 a foot for, let's say, an average seven- to eight-foot animal. The same skin today, raw, is bringing $48 a foot to the hunter. Every time the skin changes hands, from the hunter to the dealer to the tanner to the importer to the manufacturer, it almost doubles in price. In developing countries, someone poaching a crocodilian skin can make a whole year's income from it. We just made it too profitable to break the law."

In 1967, the government declared alligators an endangered species, and hunting them, or even carrying them across state lines, was a federal crime, so Kent still had to have a license even to transport their blood samples. But by the late 1970s the Department of the Interior decided that the alligator had made an "amazing comeback" and demoted it from "endangered" to "threatened," which permitted a certain amount of supervised killing, or harvesting, as it is euphemistically called. Most alligator people will tell you that it's impossible for so many animals to be born in such a short time; so what probably happened is that the shy animals felt safer in the open once people stopped hunting them, and the swamps seemed packed with alligators all of a sudden. Nonetheless, the Florida Game and Fresh Water Fish Commission has a "Nuisance Alligator Control Program," in which it has hired the only people expert enough to hunt alligators—the ex-poachers it used to fine. As naturalist George Campbell once observed: "This is a little like hiring bank security guards from the ranks of ex–bank robbers on the grounds that they possess the necessary skills." There is a law in Florida against luring and feeding alligators, since taming them makes them dangerous and more of a nuisance.

In St. Augustine, as I sat astride a beautiful alligator, I thought of the other treasures they provided. Their red blood cells are dense and large and have been highly successful in the early diagnosis of arthritis in humans. As effective as this technique can be, it's a little elaborate; not many laboratory technicians wish to keep alligators around for the occasional extraction of blood. Thanks to Mark J. W. Ferguson's research on palatal development in alligators, scientists have also discovered that if they remove an embryo or late-term fetus from a woman, they can perform surgery on the fetus to correct harelips and other deformities, and reimplant it in the uterus. The child will be born without surgery scars, because a fetus doesn't produce visible scar tissue.

Lifting one of its stubby front feet a little, I separated the five digits—three with claws, the outside two without. When I glanced behind me, I discovered that the hind feet had only four digits, three with claws, the outside one without. The broad, powerful jaws evolved to crush hard-shelled animals, like turtles. The tail's picket-fence scales looked very dinosaurlike. Alligators use the broad surface as an undulating paddle when they swim, but they may also use it as armament when they fight. John lifted up the tail, and Sylvia checked inside the cloaca. It was a female. She was a small, beautiful alligator, with healthy legs and loam-black eyes. Her skin puckers were still sharp, which was unusual. Captive alligators frequently get worn smooth over the years, just from climbing over one another. They act as living emery boards. And the alligators tend to spread, the way a human's feet do in summer: Because captive animals spend more time than usual on the land, their sheer weight flattens them. But this little female was still relatively narrow-waisted, and as she shifted beneath me, her muscles felt dense and powerful, thickly resilient, like coiled steel or solid rubber. With the sampling and checking done, a simple truth occurred to me, one that I suspected was first commented on by an ancient Chinese sage: *The hardest part of riding a dragon is getting off.* Lifting my hand, I saw her eyes popping up slowly. Then the two lids opened, the transparent membrane pulled aside like a vaudeville curtain, and she grew suddenly alert. Jumping up while falling backward, I stumbled just enough for her to swing her head around fast and thwack me hard with her taped jaw. A large bump started to swell on my shin. Kent wagged a Didn't-I-tell-you-to-be-careful finger at me.

"Nothing bruises as bad as alligators bruise," he said, comfortingly. "When they get you, the bruise stays for four or five weeks. Figure they're hitting you with a solid club made of bone."

With a snake-handler's long pole, he loosened the rope and slid it over the alligator's head. Then John pulled the tape off her jaws. Suddenly, she pressed up onto her toes and started to trot, in what's called a high walk, back into the water. The team of wranglers moved down the shore to the next two animals, while I sat on a tree stump, rubbing my shin and scouting the water for the female we had just set free. In a moment, she surfaced a few yards away. Floating parallel to the shore, with just her nose and eyes showing, she watched me and I watched her.

We don't encounter crocodilians much in our daily lives. But they're often on our minds. When we dub someone a "creep," we're comparing him to something reptilian, vaguely snake- or alligator-like, and we may go on to call him "low-down," "thick-skinned," or "cold-blooded." The cad might even cry "crocodile tears" and make our skin "crawl." "Later, alligator," we still sometimes say by way of goodbye, even if it is part of a phrase made popular decades ago. There are all those goofy-looking alligators on tennis shirts. Why should the alligator become the mascot of country clubism? Athletes drink Gatorade for stamina. Despite our passion for totemic terms of endearment—my little chipmunk, my little pussycat, etc.—crocodilians never seem to enter into our menagerie of affection. My little alligator?—I doubt it. For W. C. Fields, maybe. My little saltwater crocodile?—Probably not. Though crocodilians are the pinnacle of the class of animals known as reptiles, we often read about our "reptilian brain," that haunt of warlike emotions and throbbing irrationality, den of our darkest motives. But probably the best-known crocodilian ever is the one in J. M. Barrie's deliciously silly and wise classic, *Peter Pan.* As you may remember, the crocodile had swallowed a clock, so "the way you got the time on the island was to find the crocodile, then stay near him till the clock struck." Of course, he had also swallowed Captain Hook's severed arm, and as Hook lamented: "Followed me ever since, from sea to sea and from land to land, licking its lips for the rest of me." This presupposes a certain endearing ideé fixe on the part of the crocodile, but in a world where small children can "sniff danger" in their sleep, revenge is the least one can expect of reptiles. Crocodilians are often seen as con men, sleight-of-jaw artists. One minute you think a log is floating beside you, the next, it's dragging you underwater. Crocodilians don't fight fair—that is, aboveground. Instead, they appear almost magically, as if conjured into being, and carry you off to an underwater realm where they have all the advantages. And once they do grab you, there's no negotiating. The jaws are sealed like a crypt. Still, crocodilians don't figure much in monster films, but that's probably because filmmakers don't realize, for example, that crocodilians can run short distances on land and have been observed climbing six-foot-high chain-link fences.

This is all just as well, because people are frightened enough of crocodilians. When the famous naturalist William Bartram explored Florida two hundred years ago, he wrote: "The alligators were in such incredible numbers, and so close together from shore to shore, that it would have been easy to walk across their heads, had the animals been harmless." Ever since, cartoonists and writers of adventure sagas have been obsessed with the idea of people running over alligator heads. This really isn't possible, as the experience of a stuntman on the James Bond film *Live and Let Die* showed. To film Bond running across the heads of alligators, handlers tied the alligators' bodies together to form a living raft. However, Roger Moore's stand-in kept slipping between the heads, where he got bitten. They did repeated takes of the scene and finally ended up having to patch together both the scene and the stand-in.

As a lassoed alligator flailed in the water, palm fronds swayed nearby. A dozen white egrets flew from a tree. The alligators had turned the lake into a sanctuary for birds that did not have to worry about prowling raccoons, cats, or other predators, including the overfed alligators, which in turn did not need to bother with hunting. They were fed processed meat with vitamins, not live chickens or nutria or other game. It is against the law to feed live animals to other animals in public. So tourists don't get to see zoo animals as what they really are. But then most people do not want to see that anyway.

"Lordy, he's big," Kent said as he straddled the back, struggling to hold the colossal jaws tight for Steve to tape. "I know this guy. He's a dominant male. I saw him the day he busted his nose in a fight." The usually rounded nose had a piece missing and looked like an *M*. His neck muscles hung large as Christmas wreaths. His mottled black skin shone with crusted mud. Right at the end of his tail, a round hole, which had once held a tag, looked as if ready for an oversize key chain. Though Kent recognized the animal, we performed all the tests anyway. Lou got a syringe ready, which was a little awkward since he had a large white bandage on one finger. Although he got the cut in his laboratory, people assumed he was bitten by an alligator, and for the fourth time that morning, he yelled to a concerned visitor that, Yes, he was okay, No, he didn't need to be rushed to a hospital. No, he hadn't been wounded by a renegade alligator. Reaching inside the cloaca, I confirmed that it was a male. John patted his pockets, looking for the tape measure. Twelve noon. A cannon fired at a nearby fort. Then the sound of distant thunder filled the air. In the delft-blue sky, one small cloud floated and the sun was tough as an anvil. A slow-motion thought occurred. I had just heard bellowing. The noon cannon had set them off. I remembered reading that when a space shuttle flew over a few years earlier, making two sonic booms, all the alligators had looked up and begun a furious reply.

"Where's that coming from?" I asked quickly.

Kent handed the syringe of blood to Lou and pointed across the lake. "Better hurry. But approach *quietly* when you get in range." Kent knew that more than anything I wanted to see the water dance, the strange subsonic upside-down rain that alligators make when they bellow. Sprinting through the trees and bushes, I climbed a cyclone fence, ran down a pathway, and slowed up when I got to a tree-studded enclosure with a sinuous stream and a wide beach for basking, where nearly 150 alligators lolled in and out of the sun. A high wooden fence corralled them. Quietly, I climbed in, crouched at a safe distance, and watched. Surely they had seen me, but they were used to wet, mud-caked handlers, and anyway, these alligators were well-fed, laissez-faire animals who did not go looking for trouble. They just slithered into slightly different positions. Sun streamed through the trees as the gators languidly floated around and on top of one another, drifted apart, climbed onto land, crawled into the shade, and slid back into the water, where scaley tails and backs slowly shuffled. It was like watching the breaking up and reassembly of ancient continents. A white tooth lying in the sand at my foot caught my eye, and I picked it up. Because alligator teeth are large and hollow, colonials used to fill them with gunpowder. Now I saw that the sand was littered with teeth. Alligators lose teeth throughout their lives, and new teeth push up from the socket to replace the old. In their lifespan, which parallels a human's, they may have as many as three thousand teeth.

A large alligator stretched high out of the water, swinging its tail as a counterweight, so it could lift its enormous head. Then it puffed up its throat, and the tail flagged like an Irish setter's. A thundering bellow filled the air like distant war games, and the water danced high all around its body in an effervescent fountain full of sparkle in the sunlight. Another alligator rose up with tail waving, gulped hugely, dropped down, tensed up, then the water frizzled all around it, as if someone were spraying atomizers full of diamonds, and at last it bellowed. Few sights and sounds are as astonishing.

We may *see* the water dance, but alligators *hear* the ultrasonic signal, made only by male alligators, for some as yet unknown purpose. They use it in courtship, but also among other males, perhaps to assert their dominance. It may, in part, be the simple outcry that all animals seem to make (and humans, too) when, driven by some deep-down cosmic loneliness, they bay at the moon or croak with swollen throats, declaring to the bright, blooming confusion of the universe the ever-astonishing fact that they are alive: *Here is what I am. Here is who I am. Here is where I am.* Females bellow, too, and slap their heads on the water with great panache as males do, but they are not water dancers. It may be that females communicate in equally graceful and mysterious—but harder-to-observe—ways. Maybe the water dance is not simply a way to produce infrasound, maybe it is a signal *in addition* to the infrasound. Scientists need to be choreographers and code-breakers as well as observers. Who can understand the subtle semaphore of a glance? In that pen full of males, the response was instantaneous: Many twitched to attention or shifted their position. However, females read infrasound signals especially well, as if such sounds were billets-doux just for them, and they would by now be dashing toward these crooners. But whether they *feel* the sound as vibrations that make their scales tingle and titivate their yen to mate or *hear* the sound isn't fully understood yet, because no one's successfully tested their hearing in such low registers. Thus far, ten species of crocodilians are known to do the water dance, and it is always performed by the males. In fact, it's the only crocodilian behavior—other than pregnancy and egg laying—mastered by only one sex. Some crocodiles use the motion all by itself, without the flamboyant bellow, effervescing the water two or three times in a row. Males never bellow without doing the water dance at some point in the general rhythm of their bellowing. But in the head-slap display, when they tilt their heads at about a thirty-

five-degree angle to the water surface and slap and splash the water
noisily, they sometimes invoke the water dance, sometimes do not.
Sometimes they water-dance before they head-slap, and at other
times they head-slap and water-dance all at once. When they get
good and truly inspired and want the water to sizzle like frying bacon
for many minutes, they can even do a whole suite of water-dances—
as many as eight or nine. This suggests that the dance is a separate
behavioral act, one they can choose to use whenever they think it
necessary in the private agenda of their lives.

After all the bellowing had stopped, I retraced my path back into
the lake and found Kent and the others busily wrestling with a male
that had begun to hurl itself into tight spins. Its belly flashed a
beautiful glossy yellow with each turn, and its neck scales looked like
large green curds. How could anything that heavy float? But doesn't
the moon float? What is an alligator compared to that? A white,
fleshy half-moon sat low in the sky, invisibly tugging on the water
in the lake, the cycles of the female alligators, and the moods of us
three women.

"Did you see the water dance?" Kent asked, puffing a little and
trying to maneuver the alligator into a position near the shore where
it would not hurt itself or any of the handlers. Before I could answer,
something alerted him, and he turned quickly and scanned the
opaque water behind him, which he seemed to be sectioning with
his eyes. It was like trying to look from one world into another, from
life into death. No amount of urgent staring will clear the water or
make the forces that lie beneath it visible. There can be only hints
and signs—a certain wavering of the current, a surface shimmer.
People who walk in the woods come to know the signs that animals
leave on the ground, but water animals leave signs, too. When I was
in the Amazon, I watched pods of pink dolphins arc across the river.
Just before one would surface for air, a narrow window seemed to
shine on the water, bright and mirrorlike, and then a dolphin would
leap right through the window, making a small soughing sound as
it inhaled and plunged back under. The dolphin windows were signs
I grew to search for. Kent read the water for small whirlpools in the

duckweed, signs of underwater motion, but it was a false alarm. While the alligator quieted, we all decided to rest on the shady bank.

The sound of cows mooing, and then of a big truck struggling to get out of a mudhole, as I knew by then, was really the distant bellowing of alligators. An early traveler through Florida once wrote that the bellowing "most resembles very heavy distant thunder, not only shaking the air and waters, but causing the earth to tremble; and when hundreds and thousands are roaring at the same time, you can scarcely be persuaded but that the whole globe is violently and dangerously agitated." Picture the swamps sizzling up around thousands of bellowing alligators, each male creating its own private water dance, all of them part of a dizzying group spectacle that must have driven the females berserk.

"The water dance was fabulous," I said. "There should be a musical accompaniment. . . . Well, I guess, in a sense, there is."

"You know," Lou said as he fussed with his now-drenched bandage, "a lot of things can set an alligator bellowing. The American Museum of Natural History once proved that they prefer B-flat."

"B-flat? On any special instrument?"

"Doesn't matter. You see, back in 1944 they had a big alligator named Oscar, who seemed to respond when they strummed steel rods at certain frequencies but not at others. So one night when an orchestra was using the museum auditorium, they asked a French horn player to help them out with an experiment. He played a little, and whenever he hit B-flat, Oscar went nuts with bellowing. Then they tried a cello and the same thing happened. The instrument didn't matter, just the right pitch."

I remembered Alan Hovhaness's "And God Created Great Whales," which includes the mournful ragas of humpback whales, those oceanic troubadours with a song in their bones. Had no composer, I wondered, written a composition in B-flat for alligator and orchestra? Three herons swooped low over the water and disappeared behind a tall stand of ficas. A chilly breeze cut through the glade. Sylvia hid her hands in her pockets, and I pulled on an extra navy-blue sweater. If we had been alligators, we would have found a patch of sunlight to bask in. When the sun comes up, they sprawl in its hypnotic warmth; when they get too hot, they slither into the shade. Maintaining the right temperature is crucial, so they must constantly ad-lib, and sometimes that makes them seem a little finicky: arranging the tail out of the water but the rest of the body in it, or just the head underwater or one leg and the tip of the nose in the sun, the rest of the body curved into the shadow. The human equivalent would be taking off one's cardigan but putting on a pair of socks and, maybe, a hat.

"This must be a far cry from your boyhood in Oklahoma," I said to Kent.

"That's a fact. There's not much to do in Oklahoma. On a Friday night, we used to go out and find a pasture full of cows. We'd sneak in among them when they were asleep and push them right over. You don't have to shove them too hard and they fall." He made a toppling motion with his hands. "You should see the look on their faces! They don't know what happened to them when they hit the ground. Cow rolling's what we called it."

At last, the alligator wore itself out a little. "Well all right, let's have a go at him," Kent suggested, and we began hauling it onto the shore, but every few feet it dug its toes into the mud and hauled back. For a tense moment, as my feet skidded forward in the mud, there was some question about which of us was hauling in whom and for what purpose. The alligator did not seem to be straining at all, just sitting in the shallow water and gently leaning back, like a skyscraper whose foundations had shifted.

"Whatever you do, *don't lean forward,*" John warned. "Make sure that if you fall, you can fall backward or to the side." As the rope cut into our hands, I was glad for the heavy cowhide gloves I had thought to bring, even though I knew Kent was right when he advised me, with characteristic understatement, that a "pair of gloves probably aren't much help against an alligator's teeth." There was something faintly scrambled about wearing a cow's hide to grip hemp (which the cow would have chewed on) to catch an alligator (which would have chewed on the cow). For the moment, it was a

Mexican standoff: the six of us sweating and straining, the alligator hunkering down in the water, none of us advancing or retreating.

You'd think the alligator would have attacked us or at least run forward, jaws open, growling and hissing, in a grandstand bluff. We were puny compared with it. We couldn't outswim it, outmuscle it, or even outrun it for short distances. But we had on our side one unlikely and powerful weapon. Alligators measure their prey by its *height.* To a crocodilian, a high animal is a big animal, even if in reality it's only a lightly built child. Alligators can adjust their height by only a few inches, and they have short, stubby legs. So, faced with an overzealous crocodilian, the best thing to do is look tall and intimidating. In shallow water, stand up and raise your hands. Of course, the best plan is not to swim where crocodilians are known to travel and not to lure them out of the water by feeding them marshmallows and other tidbits, as people in Florida and Georgia invariably do. One day, their "pet" alligator, which roams a nearby lake or canal, confuses a white sneaker for a big marshmallow or decides to bunk in the house, and there is instant turmoil. That's when the fish and wildlife commission is called in to remove the "nuisance" alligator.

At last, we dragged the alligator partway onto the shore, and it walked the rest of the way up the bank as nonchalantly as a willful dachshund.

"I've sometimes wondered about the fish and wildlife program here in Florida," Kent said. "They basically just run roughshod over the alligators in this state. When they started what they call experimental harvests here, I did go out and hang around a little bit, to see what they were doing. I hated it. The people doing it weren't just the ex-poachers, but other people they'd picked up for this harvest. I mean, it's kind of a good idea to pick up ex-poachers. They don't actually use people who've been caught poaching. If they have an alligator violation, they can't do it. Most of the guys will admit though that they *used* to poach animals—they just never were *caught.* The obvious advantage is that if they're hiring these guys to kill alligators, they aren't going to be out poaching alligators. So they've eliminated the poaching problem. The second advantage of it is that these guys do know how to catch alligators. You can't just go out and pick up Joe Blow off the street and expect him to know how to get an alligator out of the lake. What's not good about it is that people have been illegally poaching for a long time. Now you're allowed to go out and do it anyway. And some of those guys make a lot of money off it."

"Seventy percent of the hide proceeds and all the money they can make off the meat or any of the other products," Lou added.

"Anyway, I just don't think there's that big a nuisance problem. There *is* in the sense that alligators wander and end up where they shouldn't be, and you have an alligator eating dogs and stuff. But there certainly aren't two thousand five hundred nuisance alligators a year, which is the number they're killing in Florida. Then they also have special *hunts,* where they're killing another one thousand five hundred or so. And now they're establishing a new program, which they hope will increase, in just a year or two, the number of alligators that can be killed annually to eight thousand. That's an awful lot of an until-recently-endangered animal. You see, their whole philosophy is that a wild animal is being wasted if it has economic potential that isn't being used. That's a rather mercenary way to think about wild animals. But there's a sense in which I also think that the nuisance program, at least, is essential—not to protect people from alligators, but to protect alligators from people. Because people, whether it's right or wrong, really fear alligators. They fear what alligators are capable of doing, and if the general public thought there was no program that offered them protection against potentially dangerous alligators, then they'd be much more willing to set up programs that were even more harmful to the gator population. It gives them a way to vent their fears. They kill two thousand five hundred alligators a year just to have a sense of security."

Killing a token number of animals to work some sort of protection racket seems senselessly primitive and wanton.

"What do you do when you're trying to discourage an alligator?"

"Before I started swimming with them, I tried to develop a few safeguards in case I got into trouble. One is that I never swim in deep water. I always swim in water that is shallow enough so that if I stand up, at least half my height shows—because I know that will slow them down, if not stop them. And it does work. I've never had an alligator go into a full charge at me. I've had alligators that were careening toward me, *starting to* go into a charge. I stood up—and, boy, they just stopped dead in their tracks."

"What does a charging alligator look like?" I asked. "The only ones I've seen have been in movies, and those have probably been staged."

"It's a phenomenal thing. A charging alligator is incredible. It starts by swimming fast, then as it builds up power, it churns hard with its tail, its head starts rising up out of the water. And when it really goes, it lunges out of the water—I mean, its entire head, shoulders, and about half its body come right out of the water, with its arms folded back and its mouth wide open—and it just growls and keeps coming on strong. Then it closes its mouth and dives and hits what it's charging at under the water and drags it away."

"Wow," Debby said, more exhale than comment.

"Why do they seem to be so crazy about dogs?" I said.

Kent laughed. "They sure do seem to have a thing about dogs. They really love them. I used to think it was because dogs are low prey that hang around the water's edge, but I've changed my mind on that. I think they just like the taste of them, the way we like the taste of certain things."

"Will they stalk them? Will they stalk anything?"

"They're not great stalking animals, like some crocodiles are. Some crocodiles are very good ambush predators."

"It's a funny idea, thinking of them waiting behind a bush."

"Well, they don't wait behind bushes; what crocodiles do is sit way out in the middle of the lake. If they see you on shore, they'll submerge and swim all the way to you underwater, and then they'll just come charging onto the shore and take you out before you know what's happening. In fact the guys that farm crocodiles have to continually watch the crocs, because if one goes underwater, you have to move up- or downshore fast—he's going to come charging out, and if you're still there, you're in big trouble. Now, alligators can't do that. They just aren't built to do it. Occasionally, you'll see one try to do it, go underwater, but then you see it popping up in the wrong place. It gets lost, you know, and it kind of looks around and goes back down and tries it again. They just don't attack the way crocodiles do. Alligators are big crocodilians, but they're shy and retiring, very passive creatures, even the largest males. Crocodiles, on the other hand, are agile and mean and fast, superpredators that consider humans prey items. Alligators just aren't like that. They're real pussycats."

But *very large* ones, I thought as we watched the antics of the huge alligator tethered a few yards from us. Nearby, a smaller alligator floated, mainly submerged, only its eyes, nose, and back showing, like a small archipelago. A sweet, pungent muskiness drifted through the air. A heavy molecule that doesn't diffuse well, musk was nonetheless easy to detect here at the farm, because we were so mobile—we could walk across the boardwalk, wade into the water, or perch on a bank. Surprised by the musk, I took a step into and out of a cloud of the subtle, lightly cloying aroma. Though many perfumes contain animal musk, most people recognize only the strong musk of a skunk, which really hasn't the same quality as alligator musk. One of the mysteries about alligator musk is whether its airborne component, which we smell, matters to alligators or is just an accidental effect. Their musk mainly travels on the water surface and makes a beautiful oily sheen, after bellowing, head-slapping, or aggressive behaviors. We smell its airborne molecules at five or six feet off the ground, but what use is that to an animal as low as an alligator? This is just another instance of what relativists from Einstein to Benjamin Lee Whorf have always said: We see what our senses allow us to see. From our "tall" bias, we imagine that alligators throw bouquets of scent into the air, when in truth they may just be painting their odor name and intention on the surface of the water, from which light particles happen to rise and evaporate into the musk we smell. To truly understand the features of an alligator's life we would need to perceive the world through its sense net, and this is where technology sometimes helps more than observing can. For example, we know a lot about auditory and visual communication in animals, because hearing and seeing dominate our human world, but much less about animals' tactile, electrical, sonar, or olfactory communication, because those ways of sensing don't "make sense" to us as profoundly. But once you have seen a bat echolocate or watched an alligator touch distant pond mates with its water dance, your idea of *seeing* and *touching* changes.

By midafternoon, we had rounded up the last of our alligators and felt about as bone-weary and nerve-jangled as we needed to. Alligator handling is not so much a skill as a willingness, but it's not to be wasted; so saying goodbye to Kent, I promised him that whenever I was in the vicinity, he could count on me to wade in and lend a hand. Many kinds of people end up handling crocodilians. Kent, a university-educated and trained zoologist, was one kind; the wild and woolly ex-poachers another; the good old boys of the Louisiana bayous were still another; and then there were old-fashioned naturalists, like George Campbell, who invited me to pay a call on him and his "treacherous" pet alligator, Spiro, named after a member of the Nixon White House.

Early the next morning, I flew to Fort Myers to meet George, who was head of the Southwest Florida Regional Alligator Association and was often called upon to remove nuisance alligators from people's backyards, swimming pools, and other unwelcome spots. A tall, slender man with long white hair, translucent skin, and a gentle manner, he'd loved crocodilians for most of his seventy years and at one point had had the largest collection of crocodilians in the United States—in fact, a collection second only to that at the Berlin Zoo. What had made this so unusual was that he'd had it in the basement of his house in Detroit. His son tells a wonderful story about his mother during those years. The family swore not to talk about their collection of crocodilians and other reptiles, as it was illegal to keep them in suburban Detroit. One day, when his mother had her sewing group over, the ladies all plugged in their portable sewing machines and suddenly thirty male crocodilians began to bellow from the basement. One of the machines must have hit a B-flat they found inspiring. Nonplussed his mother quickly collected herself and explained that the plumbing had been acting up for days, and to pay it no mind.

Now, George had only one crocodilian left from his famous collection, the stunted alligator Spiro, which was thirty years old and, as he explained, "the only alligator born in Detroit since the Mesozoic Era." However, he and his friend Ann did have over two hundred animals that lived with them, right inside their house or in various outbuildings, sheds, and enclosures in the backyard. Spiro lived in a pen with a big washtub for soaking in and rocks for sunning. Though small for his size—only about six feet long—Spiro, George explained, had "a very nasty disposition," and was "a better watchdog than a trained Doberman."

"What exactly is a *good* disposition in an alligator?" I asked.

"Well, not this," he said as he opened the tall fence and stepped inside. Sunning himself on a rock, Spiro began with a loud hiss, snarled, turned toward us, and shifted his weight, ready to charge. George kept a safe distance and backed out as smoothly as possible. George went to college, but he learned about nature the old-fashioned way, for the most part—by watching it. At one time he collected animals for the American Museum of Natural History in New York City; he started Trinidad's national zoo; he worked in conservation for many years; he used to travel the world collecting animals (Ann once smuggled a snake into the country in her bra); and they still led groups of people to the Galápagos, Kenya, and other far-flung places. "If anybody can find six people, we'll go anyplace in the world with them," he said gamely. George wrote about the animals, and Ann drew them, for the books they coauthored. Together, they kept their own version of Noah's Ark. Whenever possible, they acquired two of a species, a male and a female. It would take pages to list all the animals they lovingly tended, but among them were: bush babies, living in cages in their living room (one hung in a big gym bag); marmosets; flying squirrels; goats; donkeys; cats; cockatiels with red Pagliacci rouge spots on their cheeks; a big apricot cockatoo, which allowed me to stroke its sumptuous neck feathers; about seventy turtles living in a special turtle area; two burros from Death Valley; a Florida turkey, a knobbly-faced creature with scarlet eruptions on its throat, orange tail feathers, a speckled nose, a big black tassel down its chest, and an iridescent neck that shunted in the light from slate-green to orange (its face looked like the linoleum of a cheap motel); a Costa Rican squirrel, which had its own knitted blue hat to cuddle up in; male and female peacocks; an African puff adder; a Gabon viper; two diamondbacks; an albino corn snake; a Mexican pink-kneed spider; a black scorpion; a South American lungfish; two hedgehogs; Gouldian finches with vibrant purple swatches across their chests; an endangered red-chested parrot, which had a yellow tummy and a blue-and-green head; lovebirds; zebra finches; white-tufted sultan chickens; giant macaws; an African hornbill; and mynah birds, one of which seemed to live in a constant state of cajoling, as it repeated: "Come on, come on. Hi, baby. Come on, come on . . ."

In the kitchen of the main house hung a plaque with an ancient Egyptian spell to drive off cockroaches. On the fridge, held by magnets, "The Official Ronald Reagan Door Mat." A five-foot-long plastic snake floated in the pool outside the living room's sliding glass doors. Sassy, a green parrot, which lived in a cage on the kitchen counter, kept saying hello in various registers and with different intonations. "Hello. Hello! Hello?" A stone alligator basked on the patio. Animal carvings decorated the walls. Even the wind chimes had an animal motif. A spread of magazines on the living room table ran a wide gamut, from *Mother Jones* to *Science.* A van sat in the driveway. SOME OF US AIN'T ON VACATION said its bumper sticker.

Over dinner, at Sonny's Barbecue nearby, I asked George about his famous collection. "What kind of a house did you have in Detroit?"

"A red-brick colonial, in an area called Grosse Pointe. I had more baths in my house than Henry Ford had in his. I put them down in the basement, and I put the whole thing together and plumbed it. I kept the crocodilians in tanks, sinks, bathtubs—anything that would hold water."

"How many did you have there at once?"

"About forty. Well, you know, there are about two dozen species and subspecies of crocodilians in the world today. Over the years, I had all of them. I've had every living crocodilian in the world at one time or another."

"How could you tend them? How could you feed them? Did you have to change their water?"

"There was one important drain in the floor and if that ever got stuck, I would have been in trouble."

"It was the second largest collection in the world, I understand."

George set his knife and fork down onto a plate heaped with barbecued chicken and french fries. Despite his love of animals, he was not fanatical about diet. "There was a director of the Berlin Zoo whose name was Schröder, and he was the strangest man in the world." George smiled hugely. "I guess *I* was the strangest man in the world; he was the next strangest. Anyway, we had a rivalry going. I was in international trade, so I roamed around the world a lot in those days. We still do—don't we, Ann? And this guy would send me a cablegram—He knew how many animals I had and I knew how many animals he had—and say, 'I've got a this-and-such and you haven't.' And then I'd catch up with him and maybe get one ahead of him. Then I'd cable him.

"Well, I'd go see him in Berlin every once in a while. He lived in an upstairs apartment at the zoo. In Europe, zookeepers live on the property. The first time I went to see him, I walked into this apartment. On every lamp and all over the ceiling—above the doors, hanging on picture frames, curtains, and everything else—were witches, little doll witches. This guy was ape on witches. He had hundreds of them in his apartment. There was also a shrunken head. Dominating the apartment was a Ping-Pong table. So the first time I went to see him, I said, 'Well, your collection looks great; I see you've finally got a so-and-so. . . .'" And he says, 'First we play.' I had to play the damn guy at Ping-Pong! He insisted on wearing me out with Ping-Pong before we could even talk about crocodiles. He never would talk about the witches hanging all over. Very strange man. They tell me he is still alive but that he's in an institution now. I think he should have been in an institution then. Well anyhow, he and I shared the distinction of having the greatest number of living crocodilians. Sometimes he was one species ahead of me, sometimes I was one ahead of him. This went on for several years."

"Where did you get your crocodilians from?"

"Oh, they weren't hard to get in those days. It was perfectly legal, for example, if I was going through India, to pick up a gharial or a mugger, or if I was going through the eastern part of Asia, to pick up Siamese crocs, which are now extinct in the wild, or saltwater crocs. They had them in the marketplaces often. I remember in Calcutta I found a wonderful crocodile in the Hogg Market."

"How did you get them home?"

"In my briefcase. They had to be small, you see. If I stopped here or there for a day or two, I put them in the bidet or in the bathtub overnight, and then if I had to stay around another day, I'd put them back in the briefcase or suitcase and stash it someplace in the room, so the room attendant wouldn't be snooping around, maybe lock it or something. I've done that with lots of animals, not only crocodilians. Spiro is all that is left of that greatest but one of all crocodilian collections," he said wistfully, holding his fork as if he were going to launch it on some invisible river. "But to have had that collection was a kind of triumph."

"What was it you liked so much about crocodilians?"

"Oh, many things. Crocodilians are a hundred times older than human beings, older than dinosaurs, older than flowers, even older than the continent of Africa."

"What a thought. What happened to your collection?"

"What finally did it in was the growth of many of the crocodiles. Some grew so fast as to be dangerous. When a big Nile crocodile almost twisted my arm off, I figured I had had enough, and sold the collection to Ross Allen, who had a big farm here in Florida."

Because we were planning a drive to Lester Piper's Everglades Wonder Park in Bonita Springs the next morning, we headed back to the house and called it an early night. What with the raucous chatter of the bush babies, the chitchat of the parrots, and then the roosters crowing at first light, it was hard to sleep. In the morning, I stumbled into the kitchen, heavy-lidded, for organic granola and coffee. Sassy, the parrot, greeted me by screech-singing, loudly, "La Cucaracha." When it got to the second verse, he went into a falsetto "la . . . la-la-la-la-la-la." The air, redolent with the combined aromas of various animals, smelled thick and sweet, like the inside of a circus tent.

Ann appeared in a pair of jeans and a fresh white shirt. Her short hair was neatly combed, and she looked rested and ready for the day, which would begin, as each day did, with feeding the two hundred animals. It took about an hour and had to be repeated at night. And then, of course, there were the nocturnal animals, which were on a different feeding schedule.

"Don't you ever find looking after so many animals a burden?" I said.

"Oh no," she insisted as she cut up oranges and other fruits and prepared egg shells, store-bought feed, and various tidbits. "It's wonderful waking up in this house. The bush baby in the first cage there is particularly glad to see me, because he's my special pet. He wants to hold my hand. He holds my fingers, he wants to be petted, and I give him something to eat. And then Sassy sings to us the same way she sang to you a moment ago. Cyrano [another parrot] says, 'Hello,' and he'll say, in various tones: 'I love you, I love you, I love you.' Animals give you a lot of love. Not many people have that sort of beginning to a day."

George strolled in, wearing a well-worn bush hat that snapped up on either side, and set to the morning's chores, which he and Ann divided. By noon, we had arrived at Lester Piper's Everglades Wonder Park, and helped ourselves to tangerines and starfruits fresh from Lester's trees, which he offered folks free as they entered. In his eighties, a little deaf, and somewhat grizzled-looking, Lester came out to greet George warmly. They were old friends, with a common lifelong crocodilian passion between them. Some said Lester came to Florida in the thirties, from Chicago, to escape the mob, and began buying up every mile of land he could for pennies an acre. Though he was reputed to be worth millions and still owned large parcels of Florida real estate, he kept the alligator farm, his pet venture, in fine fettle, with the help of his two grandsons. For one thing, Lester owned almost all of Florida's American crocodiles in captivity. Through overhunting and the disappearance of their habitats to shopping malls, golf courses, and other forms of progress, they had become nearly extinct in the wild, an American has-been. But Lester's shallow-water enclosure was chock-full of them. Strolling through the lush tropical landscaping, where there were forty-foot-tall cacti, carambola trees, spiky-barked kapok trees, ficus, and other exotics, along with hanging moss (not really a moss at all but an aerial plant called an epiphyte), we passed cages of panthers, vultures, roseate spoonbills clattering their platelike beaks, and other animals that would have been more at home on the Orinoco.

"Well, look at this," George said. "Assassin's delight." At one side of the crocodile enclosure, a giant overhanging tree offered its long, upside-down pink flowers, whose throats were fleshy pastels. "Angel's-trumpet. *Very* poisonous. And just a little of it would send you into a dreamlike stupor. Look, some of the flowers have fallen into the water."

I looked down at the crocodiles, with their long triangular snouts, fixed smiles, and dreamy languor. South Florida's coasts were once full of them. Now they were reduced to this, a cement fortress at a roadside show, and lucky to have it. Most of them looked remarkably healthy. Full-bodied, with fleshed-out limbs, they had shiny, clean feet with all the digits, and no encrustations; their eyes looked intact, and their tails were pointed (not blunted off in fights). They lay on top of one another like rounds of pastrami, occasionally shifting their weight or lifting a tail or leg into the sun. As we drifted through the grounds, we came to a small enclosure filled with American alligators. *El lagarto* means "the lizard" in Spanish, which is where the word *alligator* comes from. Prompted by some private obligato, one pressed up on its toes and did a high walk.

"Looks like someone's idea of a coffee table, doesn't it?" Ann said. "You know, I saw one in Texas climb a nine-foot chain-link fence. A woman I knew used to go out to the water behind her house, lure this alligator out onto the land, and feed it big slabs of bacon. One day, all on its own, it just climbed over the fence and went right into her yard. They finally had to put barbed wire atop the fence."

How do you call an alligator? "Hey, alligator!" a young woman yelled across the pen. This is incorrect. George and I glanced at each other with a shared secret. Our eyes quietly conversed: *Do you want to do it? No, you do it.* He leaned toward the alligators and whine-grunted "Umph, umph, umph," in a swooping high pitch, with lips closed and throat warbling. Half the alligators turned and looked at him; some grew tense and ready. One left its basking rock and slid into the water. "Umph, umph, umph," George repeated, and the gator swam up close at speed, eyeing us fiercely. There are as many variations on the best way to call an alligator as there are alligator hunters. Some say they have most luck by holding their lips closed and oinking. I once heard the far-famed (and somewhat notorious) Amazon guide Moacir Fortes call caimans with a closed-mouthed strident grunt a little more tubalike than George's call. Crocodilians make a variety of sounds, depending on the season and their mood, and callers mimic their several sounds. But most callers have one thing in common: They are attempting to make the distress call of a baby alligator. Hatchlings make a characteristic sound, which tells the mother alligator that they are ready to head for open water, or, if they are in the water with her, that they are in danger and need help. Male and female crocodilians of all species will home in on the anguished cries of their young and fight anyone or anything to protect them. The adolescence of an alligator occurs when it passes from giving off distress calls to responding to them and trades the helplessness of the baby for the gladiatorial will to arms of the adult. Distress is the bugle call of their lives. We just assume, because reptiles are so low down the evolutionary ladder, that they don't look out for their young, but alligators become diabolically protective. To save their young, *they* would slay dragons.

Female crocodilians are also splendid mothers. This surprises most people, and for the longest time it just wasn't known, since crocodilians nest in out-of-the-way places, like swamps, and are terribly shy. But enough close observers now have seen females with their young, and even filmed it, to leave no doubt about their tenderness.

Mother alligators lay eggs in mound nests, which they build of mud, twigs, and whatever else they can find. Squatting over the nest to deposit the thirty-five or so porcelainlike eggs, they sometimes hold one foot underneath to break the egg's fall. Then they stand guard, to keep intruders from the nest. Average incubation time is about sixty-five days. Fact: crocodilian babies don't have sex chromosomes. A baby's gender is determined by the temperature at which the eggs develop. Humans have forty-six chromosomes, with twenty-two pairs of autosomal chromosomes and one pair of sex chromosomes. But about two or three weeks after a crocodilian egg has been laid, the mechanisms that will cause a male or female to develop turn on, cued by the ambient air temperature. Ninety-four degrees Fahrenheit or higher produces males; 86 degrees Fahrenheit or lower produces females. Most often, one finds an entire nest of one sex or another, entire clutches of male or female eggs, or the nest is female except for the top two or three eggs—because more heat concentrates at the top of the egg chamber, and those few become males. Many ingredients combine in the ultimate equation that will produce male or female offspring. For example: where the mother decides to lay her eggs within the nest and where she chooses to build the nest. She may set up her nest in the shade or in the sun or in equal amounts of sun and shade. It could be that the environment, the ambient air temperature alone, determines which sex will be born. Or it may be that the mother chooses in some way. The female might somehow assess the population ratio and decide where to put her nest. *There sure are a lot of males around,* she might decide. *I think I'll lay a cool nest and produce some females.* At the moment, no one knows. Much is known, however, about crocodilians' response to temperature. If you incubate them in a cool place, they will seek to live in cooler temperatures later on in life. Lighter-colored hatchlings emerge from cooler eggs and darker-colored hatchlings emerge from warmer eggs.

A baby alligator has a sharp tooth to break the shell, but sometimes the mother comes, hearing its calls, and gently lifts the egg in her mouth, cracking the shell by pressing it between the tongue and the palate but not damaging the baby inside. It must take unimaginable precision and control for her to pick up the egg in her massive jaws and crunch down delicately enough to free her young without harm. Then she leads the babies down to the water, sometimes carrying them there in her open mouth. It's not unusual to see a mother alligator with a squirmy hatchling or two in her jaws, ambling down to the shore. In the water, they swim around her and crawl right up onto her head and back, to sun and rest, or they trail along behind her like a brood of ducklings. Fussing with and nuzzling them, she keeps them close while they learn to feed on insects and small fry.

Sometimes a male and female will work together to build a nest and guard it through the gestation period. One often sees baby alligators sitting on the head of a giant male that is a holy terror to every other animal in the vicinity. Crocodilians have a whole series of vocalizations between male and female, female and offspring, offspring and adults, distress calls, etc. The young are playful. Alligators are oddly similar to penguins and other birds, when you think about it: They build nests, they indulge in intense parental care, and they call to their mates and their young. If they don't have songs per se, they do have tuneful outcries and yearnings.

The first year of life is especially tough for an alligator. Yearlings are only about two feet long, and three quarters of them die, because many animals eat baby alligators—fish, frogs, wading birds. Once they gain in stature, they don't have that problem, but then they have to start worrying about the adults. As the young become two- or three-year-olds, adult alligators start to chase them around, driving them off to find their own territories and families. A three-year-old may be only three and a half feet long when it begins its wandering. Sometimes people see them on the roads and in the ditches. Soon they grow to six feet, reproductive size. In most reptiles, and especially in crocodilians, puberty depends on size, not age. In the wild, they begin to reproduce at the age of nine or ten, though in northern populations (North Carolina, South Carolina) puberty might occur as late as fifteen years old for males and even later for females, who can be about eighteen years old before they start to breed. By thirty, a male alligator may show signs of senility and lose interest in mating, not replace its fallen teeth, develop mottled, rough skin, and even go blind. But a number of well-fed crocodilians in captivity are thought to have lived as long as ninety years.

In the wild, they eat every living thing their jaws can catch, from fish and insects when they're young, to turtles, dogs, and other small animals. Like their relatives, the birds, all crocodilians swallow what are called gastroliths—a kind of millstone to aid digestion. Usually they're stones, but they might also be pieces of metal or wood. Dinosaur skeletons have been found with similar gastroliths. Once, at a meeting of the London Zoological Society, a game warden from Tanganyika displayed the stomach contents of a saltwater crocodile he had killed. It included "three coiled wire armlets, eleven heavy brass arm rings, a necklace of glass beads, fourteen leg and arm bones from various animals, three spinal columns, several porcupine quills, and eighteen stones of various sizes." In 1950, when the Cincinnati Zoo's prize crocodile, Marc Antony, swallowed a Coke bottle, the zoo vet operated and found in its stomach lots of broken bottles, some marbles, bullets of various calibers, a porcelain elephant, and thirty-nine stones.

"George, what's the strangest thing you've ever heard of anyone finding in a crocodilian's stomach?"

George scratched his beard and thought for a moment. "Well, I know of one animal that died of starvation after eating a Styrofoam pillow that filled its entire stomach."

Once in a great while, white crocodilians are found, with milky-white skin and pink eyes. Campbell has a photograph of a small spectacled caiman, found in Venezuela, imported to the U.S., then exported to Thailand, where a fancier paid the incredible sum of $10,000 for it. It was a pure albino, with pink eyes and floury skin. Unfortunately, this extremely rare specimen did not survive long in Bangkok. (Campbell also has a photograph of an albino male Burmese python, draped around the body of a large, stout, mustachioed young reptile dealer who lives in Fort Myers, Florida.) Such animals are put to stud. Zoos and fanciers pay the amazing sum of $10,000 per service. Because he had pictures of an albino blackbird, an albino turtle, and various albino snakes—and obviously relishes albino animals—I recommended to him *The White Lady,* a charming memoir by Leonard Dubkin, about finding and raising an albino bat. Although I wanted to see a large albino crocodilian, I hadn't much hope of it.

My last question to George: "Do you think you'll ever collect that many crocodilians again?"

"No," he said, looking longingly at the collection of American crocodiles, which we had returned to. "Now I collect other—well, more manageable—animals. In fact, we've got a pair of miniature horses arriving real soon."

"Don't let them trample you in the knees," I said as we helped ourselves to more of Lester's sweet yellow carambolas, then returned to Fort Myers and said our goodbyes.

Back in Gainesville, I checked into a hotel on Bivens Arm, a lake that was connected to Paine's Prairie. In Florida, prairies are marshes, flooded grasslands, and Paine's Prairie is a state preserve that stretches seven miles long and two miles wide. A prairie is a wonderful place for alligators, and they were regularly seen moving back and forth between Bivens Arm and Paine's. I yearned to see them in the wild, going about their business. I had heard that many nuisance alligators had been set free in the lake by officials at one time or another. Islands of vegetation floated close to the shore. Small gators enjoy climbing up on them and sunning themselves, but at that time of year they would be elsewhere, in deeper water (which holds its warmth longer). At twilight, I walked along the swampy edges of the lake. Towering oaks, reaching out into the water, dripped Spanish moss from their branches. Tall grasses make perfect nesting sites for birds and hiding places for alligators, so I held a flashlight up against my forehead and shone its beam along the shore, but saw nothing unusual, no laser-red eyes. In the darkness, it was especially easy to slide off the present time and place as if it were nothing more than a sandy dune, and I tried to imagine what life must have been like in the days of Augustus, when, as Pliny records, gladiators once slaughtered thirty-six crocodiles for the amusement of the emperor. Herodotus chronicles the Egyptians' passion for the Nile crocodile and the sacred crocodile cult: "Each person has a tame crocodile; he puts pendants of glass and gold in its ear lids, and gives it a regular allowance of food daily. When it dies it is embalmed, and placed in a sacred repository." Archaeologists found hundreds of such mummified crocodiles in the catacombs at Thebes. But it was in the city of Crocodinopolis where the cult reached its glory: Priests worshiped a live crocodile god, feeding it mulled wine, roasted meat, and cakes. Today, there are still strong crocodile cults in some parts of the world. When an elder of an aborigine community dies, his kinsmen cremate him, take some of his long bones, wrap them up in skin, and go in search of a crocodile, which they persuade to eat the bones. At that moment, when the bones enter the body of the crocodile, the soul of the person enters, too. From then on the crocodile will carry the soul on all its journeys, protecting it. If the kinsmen were to kill the crocodile, they'd be killing the soul of their elder, who, along with their other ancestors, roams the world protected by tooth and claw.

The next morning, I sat on my balcony, a few yards from the water, and drank coffee as I watched the fog roll across the lake like a thick lager and then lift with the first hint of the day's heat. Alligators can live in unusual places if they have to. In theory, they could indeed, as the persistent street myth has it, live for limited times in the sewers of New York. It's warm enough, and there are enough rats to eat. They could get vitamin D from their food; they wouldn't need the sun. In the 1930s and 1940s, an inspector went down into the New York sewers and saw some alligators, as is well documented. But they couldn't survive for any length of time in the sewers, only a few months at the most, because they can't live long in salmonella or shigella or *E. coli*, organisms that one usually finds in sewage. Also, alligators live at temperatures between seventy-eight and ninety degrees, and caimans need temperatures between eighty-four and one hundred degrees. So if an animal is flushed or dumped into the sewer, it might well survive the spring, summer, and fall, and then winter's cold would kill it. Sewers would do in a pinch. But alligators do have certain landscapes they prefer. And the lake was a perfect habitat. No doubt about it. In the distance, a flock of gulls floating on the water looked like a letter torn into pieces. On a nearby tree limb, an anhinga spread its wings and stiffly arched them forward, as if conducting an orchestra. The anhinga stalks prey underwater, and I could see one close to the shore with just its snaky neck and beak sticking up. A cormorant posed on a live-oak branch with its big black wings outstretched. When it turned its neck sideways, it looked like the Prussian coat of arms. A black gallinule with a long scarlet stripe down its nose hopped among the shore grasses. Any one of these birds would have made tasty prey for an alligator. Lifting my binoculars, I searched the water for the > that might be a gator's wake. Then I searched the banks, where one might have been basking. A small tear in the surface of the water turned out to be only a leaf. Flocks of white egrets twirled slowly, parasols overhead. A reflection of passing clouds seemed to still the water, as if someone were smoothing out a rumpled fabric with one hand, and I seized the chance to scout the surface more carefully. A great blue heron floating near the shore started to flap, dragged its feet in the water for four touches, then finally took flight. It was a scene of gator-perfect serenity. As the day warmed up, birds perched on five fishermen's stanchions leading from the shore into deep water. Mats of vegetation floated together and drifted apart. The water began to glitter like a marquee. One small mat of vegetation suddenly turned on edge, and I saw three connected pads reel into focus . . . The nose, the head, the back. Sharp scutes led from the forehead to dark eyes ringed in yellow and a plump, round nose. Arching its back, it became a gently sloping pyramid, a symmetry of line from tail to snout. Sometimes it just hung in the water, only its nose and eyes showing. Not more than twenty yards from me, it cruised back and forth, parallel to the shore, which it seemed to be watching. Like a floating compass, it turned and pointed, first south, toward a Chinese restaurant overlooking the lake, then east toward me. My skin crawled with wonder. I must have earned some Brownie points in heaven to be allowed a vision so rare. Was it male or female? I wondered. And what was it doing up so early in the year? Without warning, it turned sharply and headed back into deeper water, probably to find a warm spot on the bottom again, where it would wait in suspense for all the powwows of spring. Then, along with the other alligators, it would pop up to the surface, with four or five inches of mud caked all over its head, and sit for a while in a sort of daze, until the world added up and it was time to eat and bask and look for a mate. Soon, the alligator was only a small wake in the distance, swimming straight on for the far shore, where there were no houses or roads, only moss-drenched trees and the inviting forest, remote and untraveled.

"See ya later," I called.

Chapter 3

THE MOON BY WHALE LIGHT

Roger Payne was not hard to spot at the airport on Maui that February day in 1990. He was the only person who looked as if he had just flown out of a war zone. His left eye bore a half-moon bruise below it, a small piece of gouged forehead had been pushed back together, and an angry cut was just starting to heal above his mouth. One evening earlier in the week, he had strolled across the lawn, hands tucked in his pockets, regarding the beauty of the Hawaiian night sky, forgotten about a low rock fence, and tripped squarely onto his face before he could pull his hands out to break the fall. His glasses fell, too, and cracked at the nose bridge. Repaired repeatedly with Krazy Glue, they now sat at several angles on his face, one lens tilted forward, the frame slightly askew. So it was an unlikely apparition holding a red-and-yellow lei of Plumeria blossoms that greeted me in the polyglot hubbub of the airport. But it was also someone I had waited a dozen years to meet, ever since the night in the mid-seventies, at Cornell University's Bailey Hall, when I attended his lecture on the songs of humpback whales, which he concluded with a duet for cello and whale song. He was clearly an expert and talented cellist, but it was the whale songs themselves—great booming ragas of creaking and moaning and seat-shaking bass—that captivated everyone with their beauty and mystery.

Leaving the overhanging shadows of the terminal, we strolled out into the sunlight and drove to the town of Kihei and an oceanside house owned by Ani and Jerry Moss, two whale enthusiasts. Over the years, Roger had traveled the world, recording and analyzing the songs of humpback whales and studying the habits of other whales. By his definition (derived from Melville), a whale is "a mammal in the sea that has a horizontal tail and spouts," so it includes both the large animals we usually think of as whales and also the small whales we describe as dolphins or porpoises. Whales have the largest brains on earth, brains every bit as complex as our own. They have culture, and they have language. They sing songs that obey the kinds of rules one finds in classical music. What does a creature with the largest brain on earth use it for? Why does it sing? What do the songs mean? Almost everything about whales is a tantalizing mystery. We ache to know about other forms of equally intelligent life in the universe, and yet here are creatures as unknown as extraterrestrials right among us, moving in a slow-motion ballet under the oceans, hidden from our view. Questions about mind and music had been plaguing me for some time, so although I had never met Roger Payne before, I had met some of his fascinations and questions and considered them old friends.

Turning onto a shore road, we found the Mosses' home, set among trumpet flowers and bougainvillea, sprawling on a promontory above the sea, with its own small sandy beach and ragged shoreline. Jerry, one of the founders of A & M Records, had just left for Los Angeles, but Ani was still there, along with her sister, Katy. Ani was a tall, thin, beautiful, fey, fawnlike woman of unidentifiable age who had once been a *Vogue* model (and still looked the part).

Her sister, also a thin, pretty blonde, was an accountant from Salt Lake City, who could, as it turned out, tell off-color, working-class jokes with such wide-eyed innocence that they packed a double whammy. The plan was for Roger and me to rent a Zodiac and go out to find some of the singers. Each day, we would rise at 5:00 A.M., phone the National Weather Service's general- and marine-forecast recordings, and even the pilots' Flight Service Station, then scan the ocean through binoculars, and see whitecaps too treacherous to risk. A trough had settled over the islands, bringing steady rain and high winds; the seas were eighteen feet, and the storm system was unyielding. So since we were housebound, Roger worked in the water, installing an offshore buoy to which he had attached a hydrophone; an antenna hitched outside the Mosses' house led to a receiver in their living room, and this would allow them to record whale songs for him continuously in season or tune in whenever they were just in the mood for a concert.

Roger was a tall, slender man with sturdy shoulders, enormous hands on which the nails were neat and trimmed, a long stride, and a slightly rocking gait, probably the result of a knee operation he had had the previous year. When he walked fast, his hips sometimes seemed to be balancing along a spirit level. Parted on the left, thinning a little on top, his slate-gray hair looked slightly windblown even when freshly combed. He had a large forehead on which four evenly spaced lines formed when he was concentrating, hazel eyes that more often looked brown than green, and a small, neat nose. Sometimes, in repose, his face was undisturbable and fifty-something, but when animated it often became that of a rompy, mischievious twenty-year-old. Although he spent many months out of doors, he had the kind of front-only tan that one acquires accidentally. His clothes were freshly laundered and ironed, his gray-green pants had a small constellation of holes on one leg, and both pockets on his blue shirt were frayed. He slipped into a Brooklyn accent from time to time in conversation, just to emphasize the silliness of something or other, but his normal speaking voice was unusually resonant and poised like a singer's, and indeed he was a madrigal singer. What dialect he spoke would be hard to pin down. In a cosmopolitan vernacular that shifted easily among classes and cultures, his vocabulary was peppered with scientific jargon, sixties lingo, literary allusions, musical terms, poetic images, casual down-and-dirty cursing, plus the verbal dressage needed for courtesy or protocol. A word like *groovy* or *bozo* mixed naturally with the down-home expression "right quick," such British TV sitcom exclamations as "Lord love a duck!"; a heartfelt "Bless you" by way of thanks; or an unexpected leave-taking like "Let's blow this Popsicle stand." "Well, that sucks the big one," he could say unselfconsciously, and the next instant utter a string of well-groomed clichés. In situations that required the delicate handling of people, he glided into a tone of casual high regard that was intense, warm, and smooth as flowing lava. His father, an electrical engineer at Bell Labs in New York City, had been every bit as absentminded as Roger freely confessed to being. His grandfather had been a logger, his mother a violinist and violist, beside whom he often sat when they played string quartets with friends. Before she married, she had taught music at the Mannes Music School in New York.

For days, telephone calls had been crackling back and forth between the house and a ship at sea. Roger, who was director of the Long-Term Research Institute, in Lincoln, Massachusetts (an affiliate of the World Wildlife Fund), had been trying to acquire a boat equipped with directional sonar. But the boat needed expensive and unexpected repairs. Now it seemed a smaller but more workable boat might soon become available. This new forty-six footer was built in Sri Lanka, had directional sonar, a directional hydrophone, ten halogen lamps built into the hull to illuminate the ocean, and other desirable fittings. Roger was also trying to coordinate trips to Japan, the Galápagos, Alaska, and Hawaii, and to review whale research from all over the world. The International Whaling Commission declared a moratorium on commercial whaling in 1982, ten years after the United Nations Conference on the Human Environment called for one. But the IWC moratorium didn't take effect until 1986, and it left a loophole: Countries could "kill, take and treat whales for purposes of scientific research." Japan had been especially unscrupulous about taking advantage of the loophole, and Norway was another offender. So much of Roger's time was also spent trying to save endangered whales. His days brimmed with commotion and he must have felt like he was living in the middle of a Charles Ives symphony. Most of his recent research efforts had focused on the humpback whale's songs and the family life of the "right whale," but all whales intrigued him, since scientists still knew so little about them, and nonscientists even less.

If you ask someone to draw a whale, she will probably draw a sperm whale, the bulbous-headed whale made famous in Melville's *Moby Dick,* a book that is as much a treatise on whales as it is a piece of fiction. But whales come in many shapes, sizes, and colors. There are two basic groups: the toothed whales (Odontoceti, from the Latin for "tooth" and "whale") and the baleen whales (Mysticeti, from the Latinized Greek word for "whale"). Toothed whales include the sperm whale, the dolphin, and the orca, or killer whale, and they have a single external blowhole, which in the course of evolution has migrated to the top of the head. They echolocate just as bats do, using sonar to scan their world, find their prey, and map their underwater landscape. And they have teeth, which they use to hold on to such prey as fish, squid, and shrimp. Whales swallow their prey whole, so the teeth are for grasping rather than for chewing.

In contrast, baleen whales don't have teeth but hundreds of tightly packed, springy baleen plates (made of keratin, the same substance as human fingernails), which grow down from the upper gums. Baleen whales have paired blowholes—nostrils, in fact— which are on the top of the head. Some baleen species graze peacefully as they move through the water, rolling slowly through the surface with their mouths yawning open. Because the baleen has a smooth outside edge and a bristly inside edge, water can flow freely through the whale's mouth, but krill, plankton, and small schooling fish get caged inside. Other species have pleats on the throat, so that they can stretch their mouths open even wider, like valises, and when they're feeding they roll on one side, take in a huge amount of water, expand the pleated throat, force water against the roof of the mouth, and press the water out, leaving the meal behind.

Those two large groups, Odontoceti and Mysticeti, include seventy-seven species of whales and dolphins—all that inhabit the earth. In a rather ghoulish twist, one of those species, the right whale, a Mysticete, gets its name because it was "the right whale to kill." Ignorant about whale species, new whalers would look out, see a whale, and ask if that was the right whale or not; in time, the name stuck. When right whales are killed, instead of sinking as most dead whales do, they float; they don't struggle much in battle, either, and their baleen was extremely valuable. Now the right whale is one of the rarest whale species, and it has a special distinction in the history of human affairs. Every species of animal that we have brought to extinction has occupied a limited area—an island, an archipelago, a continent. We have never in our tenure on earth brought to extinction a truly cosmopolitan species, one with a worldwide distribution. "The closest we've ever come is with the right whale," Roger explained over dinner, "and we came so vanishingly close. It would have represented a new benchmark, a new low, the lowest, the most careless, the most outrageous thing that humanity had yet done to the planet. The fact that our generation is now making the effort to prevent that extinction is evidence that we're waking up at last. In that sense, the right whale is an important bellwether of the human condition."

Another species of Mysticeti, the gray whale, became extinct in the North Atlantic by the end of the seventeen hundreds, at the hands of Basque whalers, the founders of seagoing whaling in the West. It was almost certainly those whalers, and the Vikings, who first discovered America, not Columbus. Roger quipped that what Columbus really discovered was "public relations." When the gray whale was formally "discovered" in the nineteenth century in the North Pacific, it was called the devilfish. Captain Charles Scammon, a naturalist, found its major breeding areas in the lagoons of Baja California, and furiously hunted it; the grays killed several men and smashed all his boats in very short order. This same species is now noted for what's called "the friendly-whale phenomenon." In 1977, a single gray whale in San Ignacio Lagoon, near Scammon's Lagoon, off Baja California, became "chronically friendly," as Roger put it, and allowed itself to be patted by passengers of all the whale-watching boats that could find it. During the next several seasons, the number of friendly whales soared, until anyone who wanted to pet a whale could do so. Though no one was keeping count, in the previous winter there had been hundreds of gray whales approaching boats for cosseting and stroking. Now it seems to have become part of their whale culture, something they've learned from each other. In the lagoons, where gray whales gather in high numbers in the wintertime, it can grow terribly windy. Tourists in a whale-watching boat near a gray whale may find the wind blowing them along the surface. The whale isn't borne along by the wind, and it will go through contortions to stay with the boat, presenting its belly to be scratched and rubbed. Many times a day, this will happen, with boatloads of people leaning out to touch a whale. Originally, the friendly gray whales drew tourists, but it soon was the other way around—the presence of the tourists drawing the whales, who actively searched for boats. The whales rush out and will even ram into a boat and then quickly roll over like puppies, belly-up, because they love to be patted and rubbed and scratched. To Roger, they were the classic example of how wrong our conceptions about whales had been: "Imagine, it was the devilfish, the malicious animal that had the gall to kill people who were attempting at that very moment to reach its heart or lungs with a spear so that it would bleed to death internally. Not a very strong sign of aggression, I should say. How could we have been so wrong to name this animal the devilfish when it turns out to be so friendly?"

One genus of whales, *Balaenoptera*, includes five closely related species—sei, brydes, minke, blue, pygmy right—which are essentially small, medium, and large versions of the same body plan. The minke whale is the smallest baleen whale. The pygmy right whale, a rare creature about which little is known, is so similar to minke whales that it's hard for scientists to identify in the wild. But the blue whale is easier: It is the largest animal ever to exist on earth. It can grow to as much as a hundred feet long. Its tongue weighs as much as an elephant. To execute the simple maneuver of putting its head down—that is, going from horizontal to vertical in the water—it first has to be in a hundred feet of water. When it does that or stands up on its tail, it experiences a difference in pressure from the tip of its nose to the tip of its tail of three atmospheres. The heart of a blue whale weighs several tons, and on a factory ship it often took six brawny men to drag the heart out with flensing hooks. The aorta leading from its heart is large enough for a child to crawl through, and the major blood vessels appear to be about the size of a sewer pipe. A salmon could comfortably swim down them.

The blue whale makes loud, low-frequency sounds that can travel enormous distances. The ocean transmits sound in strange and unlikely ways. There is a layer of water, known as the deep sound channel, in which sound waves can be trapped and spread great distances because they bend back into the channel over and over, without losing much energy. Under those circumstances, whale sound can travel as much as five hundred miles before blending into background noise. These days, the oceans are polluted by human sounds. But in the tens of millions of years before the advent of ships (during which about 99.9 percent of the evolution of blue whales took place), whale sounds might have traveled out to distances of several thousand miles, so that two whales could have sat on opposite sides of the same ocean and been in contact with each other. Those wouldn't have needed to be complex conversations. They would not have been chitchat, either, but simple exchanges of information about where food could be found. If a whale had been hungry, it might have remained quiet; if it had been well fed, it might have spoken. Then, all a hungry whale would have needed to do was swim in the direction of the loudest sound. If a whale had had too much to eat, it would have been to its advantage to share excess food with its kin; next year, its kin might have returned the favor.

Finally, there is the humpback. Although it has long, paddlelike white flippers and a huge tail with markings unique as fingerprints, its most arresting feature is that it sings—sings complicated, beautiful songs. A bird will sing a song, grow quiet, and then perhaps sing its song again; but a humpback will sing a long, complex, sustained song and then go back and start again without any break, singing continuously. When it dives, it flexes its back sharply and appears to have a hump on its back, hence the name. It is acrobatic when it breaches. Sometimes, it will roll onto one side and wave a long flipper out of the water. At others, it will stick its head out of the water in a "spy hop," to look around. When a humpback feeds, it swims in a tight circle, spinning a net of bubbles around a school of krill or fish, which become alarmed by the bubbles and clump together, whereupon the humpback swings toward the center, mouth open, and gobbles them up.

Whales are mammals: They breathe air, bear live young, nurse them with milk, and have hair. People don't think of whales as hairy, but they do have a few whiskers. And though we picture whales wobbling with blubber to keep warm, a whale's real problem is staying cool. A whale is like a house with a too-large furnace and too few radiators. When a whale exercises in warm equatorial waters, it can die of overheating. If it races hell-for-leather in pursuit of prey, it can become so hot it virtually blows up. After a whale is killed in the Antarctic, it is eviscerated with a long, sharp flensing knife. The entire length of the whale's body cavity is opened up so that the icy water can wash it thoroughly. Then it's tied tail first to the bow of the catcher boat and dragged back to the factory ship, where it will be hauled aboard and cut up. If the trip back to the factory ship takes too long or if the whale is left in the water for too long, even though it is lying in icy water, its bones will be charred by the heat of its internal decay. When that happens, it's referred to as a burnt whale. Imagine an animal generating so much heat that even though lying under icy water with its belly cut wide open, *its bones cook.*

Sperm whales, most of which live close to the equator, cool off by diving to unimaginable depths. Plunging down to where the water temperature is close to freezing, sperm whales feed on squid or large fish, sometimes swallowing sharks whole. In that strange realm of pressure and near blackness, a sperm whale swims like a spaceship through slowly moving galaxies of luminescent fish—a world difficult for us to imagine. Small wonder that whales seem magical.

As Roger sprawled on the rug, adjusting the receiver, whale songs filled the house with otherworldly music, produced by singers who had been his often invisible companions for nearly thirty years. Although he had a photographic "fluke record" of many humpback whales, and could also identify some singers by their phrasing of the songs, he had most often heard the songs without being able to see the singer or guess who it might be. In that sense, the songs were like those of the troubadours, who wandered through the Middle Ages regaling people with songs anonymous but unforgettable.

Why do whales sing? One theory argues that humpback whales use their songs as other animals use their horns. The whale with the longest and most ingenious song wards off competing males. Another theory has it that the songs are more like peacocks' tails—the whale with the best song is the one most attractive to females. But that doesn't explain why whales revise their songs. I wondered if whales changed their songs for the reasons humans do—for sheer variety, or to include new myths or folk wisdom, or out of a kind of mental fidgeting, or as a way to give the group a stronger sense of community, or simply as a form of play, or as a method for generations to set themselves apart, or to pass along new information about their changing environment, or for reasons as whimsical as fashion. They live at such great distances from one another. Maybe singing is their equivalent of shepherds' whistling or yodeling across valleys with news—or just so they don't feel quite so alone.

"Could they be changing their songs for the same reasons human beings do, in an intelligent way?" I asked Roger.

He glanced at me over the top of his glasses, then returned to a delicate soldering job and said, "Maurice Ewing, who was head of the Lamont-Doherty Geological Observatory, in Palisades, New York, and is one of those who really synthesized the details and facts that led to plate tectonics, spoke of what he called 'brutal facts.' A brutal fact is one that goes against your natural inclinations and beliefs, yet you're forced to pay attention to it and recognize that it's telling you something wholly unexpected and very powerful. Well, some brutal facts associated with whales make it very difficult to figure out what the songs are all about. Let me give you a few examples. The songs are incredibly complex. They change every year, and they're very beautiful. For us, they trigger many ideas and emotions—some people respond to whale songs by weeping. But another brutal fact is that they're monotonous. They repeat endlessly. It doesn't sound that way to a casual listener, but if you sit for an entire season listening to whale songs, you can get roundly sick of some of the variations you're hearing. A song won't be completely different for several years, so you must keep in mind that whatever it means, its message is bound to be very monotonous."

A long, trilling bass filled the house with sounds both haunting and subterranean. Creaking doors turned into ricocheted moans. Nothing looked out of the ordinary, but the air felt as if somewhere glasses were thinly rattling. How could this plunging, stuttering, and swooning be monotony? To a trained ear, familiar phrases reveal themselves as predictably as themes in a well-known piece of music. I thought of the variety imprisoned in an Indian raga or in a Bach fugue, which to some ears also sounds monotonous.

"Do you think their monotony makes them less aesthetically pleasing to the whales?"

"Oh no. Not at all. What could be more monotonous than a teenager's playing the latest heavy-metal tape three hundred times in a row, until it's worn out or demagnetized? No, if you tune in and are a regular listener to pop music, you'll hear the Top Ten songs played most of the day on many stations. That doesn't affect aesthetics. What I'd like to know is: What's the evolutionary advantage of this monotony? Of course, it's just as hard to say why people sing. In the case of rock musicians, you can see that it greatly improves their reproductive fitness," he said, laughing, "but not all of us are rock musicians." Roger unfolded his long legs slowly, one at a time, with the care of an afghan hound standing up, and ambled over to the electrical closet to test another receiver. There, among fuses,

wires, and electronics, sat stacks of New Age music, all published by
A & M records. With one hand he twiddled a knob on a control
panel, cocked an ear, listened intently, then returned to the spill of
wires, boxes, and screws on the rug.

"Suppose human beings evolved two forms of communication,"
I said, "one that is direct emotional communication—music—and
one that's analytical and verbal, which we call language."

"Now you're exactly on to what I'm suggesting. I like that idea.
It would be wonderful to be able to look at someone and make those
noises that are deeply evocative of a particular kind of emotion and
thus lock the other person to the emotion you're feeling. And we
do do that to some extent. If we see someone weeping, our urge is
to weep with him. Or if we see someone yawning, we may yawn as
well. Such things help to synchronize the behavior of a group. I've
done a lot of madrigal singing, and in some of my favorite songs
you're saying fa-la-la-la-la a lot of the time. Tiddly-pum, tiddly-pum.
It doesn't *mean* anything. But it's just right. It has tremendous
artistic importance and meaning, which people memorize and love.
There don't have to be words in these songs, or any direct meaning,
for the songs to be meaningful and selected by evolution. But then
there's that monotony. It would be almost as if you sat each day and
told the story of some terrible trauma—or wonderful love or deep
disgrace—over and over again, while everyone around you was telling the same story."

"Birds and other mammals get along perfectly well with songs
that don't change all the time," I said. "Why is it so important to
whales to change their songs?"

"I could make up a sort of half-baked answer. I could say, for
instance, that if one male comes up with a song that's attractive to
more females, the other males in the area will soon recognize that
Joe is doing a lot better than they are and change their tune to copy
Joe, so then Joe loses his advantage. And the others, or Joe, would
then try different versions that might give them an advantage over
the competition, even if it's just a momentary one."

"So we don't know why they sing. But it's only the males that sing, right?" I pictured an oceanful of cetacean Pavarottis.

Roger smiled. "There's some confusion over that. We have thirty-five singers of known sex and they are all males, except one. An adult and a calf were seen by a highly reliable observer, Graeme Ellis. Singing was coming from the adult. Graeme dived to observe them, and as he watched, the calf went down and appeared to nurse, and the adult released what seemed to be milk into the water. A puff of milk should be a pretty good indicator of sex. But the trouble is that even though Graeme is a totally experienced observer—and I completely accept his interpretation of what he saw at face value—I am an experienced observer, too, and I've been so badly fooled so many times by what whales were doing around me that I know how badly anyone can be fooled. For example, in Argentina, where you can sit on cliffs and look directly down through the water, I saw a female and a calf underwater with no other whale around for as far as I could see, and suddenly a male was there, underwater, right next to them. He messed around with them for five or ten minutes and then disappeared without blowing. To an observer on the beach or in a boat, as Graeme was for most of this time, he would have been invisible—no one would have seen him approach or leave. The only reason I knew he was there is that I happened to have a high and favorable viewpoint. I think it's possible that there was a male down underneath the female and calf Graeme saw. But Graeme says that as the female returned to the surface, the sound diminished in intensity, and as the calf approached the surface, the sound level remained about the same. That is an extremely important observation, because if you are listening with a shallow hydrophone to a whale singing, at the moment the whale comes to the surface, most of the energy from the singing is refracted downward by the warmer water near the surface and doesn't get to your hydrophone. The result is that when the whale is right at the surface, it sounds very feeble, then as it dives, the sound can travel directly to your hydrophone without being refracted away from it and the sound becomes louder. I'm still not sure that there wasn't a male singer that was out of sight down below or that the female didn't interpose her body between Graeme and a singing calf each time she happened to come to the surface. On the other hand, he may be absolutely right—maybe females do sing. If you take even a newborn chicken and give it enough testosterone, it will begin crowing like a rooster. You can make the female of many bird species sing a male song by injecting the right male hormones. So that might also be the case with whales. A female with enough male hormone might sing the male's song. Or another possibility is that it could have been the calf singing; it might have been a male calf."

No one has any idea how humpback whales make their sounds. Joking about how little we know, William Schevill, a distinguished elder statesman of whale biology, once said, "Perhaps they make their sounds by rubbing their vestigial hind limbs together." For all we know, they play their ribs like a concertina and their baleen like a pocket comb. I pursued the question with Roger.

"Don't they have a larynx or windpipe?"

"It used to be thought that whales didn't even have vocal cords. But now we know that certain Odontoceti have something very much like them."

"How about air pockets?"

"They have every kind you can name. They have an area of their windpipe that might be in some way involved. They have a plumbing system that's so fancy it could support any theory you like about how they generate sounds, but at present, any other theory would do, too. We just don't know where their sounds are coming from. The harmonic series associated with the sounds are certainly the kinds that would be made by a system based on air—closed pipes filled with air."

For a moment the creaking and moaning gave way to popping sounds and clarinet notes. "How about other passageways working like whistles or flutes?" I suggested. "The Aztecs had a large variety of whistles and flutes that could make many different sounds, depending on the air chambers or the chambers holding water and other fluids."

"Whistles, yes, but no flutes, because a flute is an open-ended pipe. But whales could be using any number of different sound-producing mechanisms, and some of their sounds are clearly just a train of pulses produced so rapidly that you and I perceive it as a tone. The tone A on the piano is 440 cycles per second, and we normally think of it as the kind of sound that might be produced by a flute, for instance. But you can also get a nice tone of A by taking 440 noisy soundbursts per second and listening to them. What you're hearing is the rate at which these little bursts of sound are being produced; and that rate is the note A on the piano. If you made it 238 bursts per second, you'd get middle C." Sweeping aside a row of invisible possibilities with one hand, he said, "One thing I can tell you is that when a whale sings, no air is released."

"What a mystery."

"It's one of the more intriguing little mysteries of our time."

Roger walked outside to adjust the antenna he had put up near a chunk of fused crystals, embraced by ferns, that sat on a block of lava on the grassy promontory just beyond the back porch. Ani said she had set a crystal down on the house's private beach out of respect for the wild dolphins, and it drew them. I did not pursue this. Two white rope hammocks hung between palm trees, and flowery terraces led to an open-air shower made of lava and other rocks. Thick white clouds churned fresh smoke above the horizon. One whale singer came on strong, like a yowling tomcat, while we fixed an impromptu dinner of mashed potatoes, broccoli, salad, and ice cream. Ani was wearing a new black sweatshirt with good drawings of a humpback mother and calf. Everywhere you looked in the multilevel, meticulously decorated house, primitive sculptures and paintings mixed with images of whales. There were whale sculptures, whale drawings, whale videos. Katy was wearing a silver ring on which two dolphins were entwined.

Roger took down his long, splayed-fingered antenna and found a better spot for it, at the side of the house, near a tree. It was a line-of-sight antenna, directed toward a buoy about three hundred yards offshore. With the buoy, worth only about $700, Roger was hoping that he could make a unique collection of a week's continuous recordings. When he returned, taking care to close the screen door snugly to keep out poisonous centipedes that rippled through the grass and could bite, we sat down to eat, serenaded by a concert both eerie and familiar.

One morning, though the seas were galloping and high, we stood on the promontory in back of the house, binoculars pressed to our eyes, searching the horizon for whales. Actually, all we were looking for was a "blow," the misty spout a whale leaves when it surfaces to breathe. This was not the only sighting cue we could use. Whale watchers have learned to look for a rolling animal and for a whitecap splash of flukes or flippers. A sperm whale throws its flukes very high into the air and their trailing edge has a big notch on it; humpbacks have multicolored flukes; a right whale has broad, lip-shaped flukes with a shallow notch. Whale scientists look for changing color under the water—say, the pale blue of humpback flukes near the surface. They look for "footprints" in the water, rings that look like slick footsteps, caused by animals swimming just below the surface. They look for a dorsal fin. The killer whale has a very tall, erect dorsal fin, whereas the southern right whale has no dorsal fin at all. But the most common guide is the blow, because it varies so much among whales and can be seen at such a distance. In the dry Antarctic air, the blue whale shoots up a thin column that can rise a hundred feet and stay visible for thirty seconds. The sperm whale has a forward-canted, left-sided blow, easy to identify. Right whales and bowheads make a misty, V-shaped blow from their twin blowholes.

"There's a whale!" Roger said, pointing to a wedge of ocean just off the southern end of Molokini, a crescent-shaped island across the bay from the Mosses' home. "It's moving north along the island."

A moment later I saw a low, bushy balloon of vapor, the signature of the humpback. Early mariners used to think that the exhalations of whales were poisonous, a caustic mixture of brimstone and sulfur that could strip the flesh from any man who chanced too close. Perhaps the blood entering the lungs of wounded whales sometimes tainted their last breaths, giving them a fetid odor. But scientists who have been drenched by the breath of healthy whales say that it feels like a delicate mist; some report a faint odor of musk.

The clouds had begun to swarm again, and to keep ourselves dry and warm, we put on many layers of clothing over our swimsuits, then took green plastic trash bags and cut arm- and head-holes. No one else was crazy enough to be at the marina when the sky was like clotted milk and a blue veil of rain hung on the horizon. Roger steered the Zodiac out to where the waves were heaving, toward Molokini, where we knew that at least one whale would be singing. And what a song it would be! It was said that the shape of the island created lovely echoes when the whale and his listener were in just the right position. The farther we got from shore, the higher the waves became. High enough that Roger paused suddenly to teach me how to restart the engine if it should fail; he gave me the throttle and rudder, making sure I could steer straight and in circles. He was not planning on being washed over the side, but the wind could get right underneath a Zodiac and flip it, and the current could carry one some distance. Then we continued at speed. Over my shoulder, I watched a faint blue drape of storm approach the north end of Maui. The winds had begun to pick up again, the lunging waves shook froth from their mouths like runaway horses, and after each crest we skidded down into the bottom of a bowl, the sides of which grew steeper. Roger cut across them obliquely, like a surfer riding the inside of a wave, angling smartly from one crest to another. Although I had been in Zodiacs in rough seas in South Georgia and the Antarctic, I had never been in one handled more expertly than this; we skidded across the sides of tall, muddy-blue waves to weave among the convulsive valleys where rising and falling waves met. Then water spumed over the bow, spumed a second time, and Roger turned sharply at a ninety-degree angle and headed straight back for shore. There was no use going on: It would be unsafe. If we hugged the coastline, the waters would be a little calmer. The suddenness of his decision to turn back surprised me, but then I realized that this small boat was one of the main tools of his trade and he had learned its limits and eccentricities, just as he had learned to read the many moods of the ocean. He could judge the difference between potential discomfort and potential danger. It is like that for me when I fly airplanes. On final approach, in a savage crosswind, you can reach a point where it is no longer possible to land safely, because you've used up the full travel of the stick and rudder. The oceanic sky has overpowered you, the limits of your craft have been reached, and there is no use going on. All you can do is search for an airport somewhere else.

"A whale scientist's work isn't always as balmy as I'd imagined," I said as we began the bouncy return to the marina, with the wind now against us.

"This is normal. You're always at the mercy of the weather, and storms seem to follow me." Roger had tied a panama hat on with a string under his chin, but the brim fluttered in the squall, and spray had thrown rivulets down his glasses. Running across the choppy waves, the boat bounced hard, and the ride jarred our kidneys and bones. But the ocean was a wild, beautiful tumult. I could understand why the painter J. M. W. Turner would have himself lashed to the mainmast of a ship and go out into the middle of a raging storm just to behold its color and fury. Below us somewhere in the gelatinous phantasmagoria of churning blue, the whales wouldn't be much aware of the storm. Their world, which has as much geography and real estate as ours, is distinctive. There are mountain ranges in their world, great gorges and rift valleys and sprawling prairies, and even hot springs and volcanoes. We forget that the ocean floor includes some of the tallest mountain ranges on earth—we just don't see them. And there are the magnetic features, about which we know so little. Because we don't steer along the magnetic web of the planet, we forget that other animals do. In some underwater valleys, the magnetic signals are polarized in one direction; in some harbors the signals are bound to be stronger or weaker, or perhaps even jangled by power plants and motorboats. Whales navigate through a rich, complicated landscape at a stately pace, slow as zeppelins, majestic and alert.

When we were at last back at the marina, cold, tired, and wet, we loaded the Zodiac onto a waiting trailer and headed for a nearby fast-food restaurant to get a hot breakfast. Roger ordered scrambled eggs and a rasher of bacon. Both arrived in nearly the same dull resiny color. The coffee was strong enough to trot a mouse across.

"What was it like the first time you heard whales singing?"

"I was in Bermuda, as a guest of the late Frank Watlington, an engineer who worked for the Lamont Geophysical Field Station. He used to go out towing hydrophones when the Navy was firing off explosives and record the sounds far away. But when he did this during humpback season, he often heard the songs of whales, which fascinated him. One April day, he played them to me in the engine room of a wooden minesweeper just like Cousteau's boat, the *Calypso*. And although the boat was very noisy and loud, out of his tinny speaker came incredible sounds. I had never heard anything like them. They riveted my attention as nothing ever had before. These were superb recordings he had made on bottom-mounted hydrophones that the Navy was using for purposes of listening to enemy submarines and that sort of thing. Later, he gave part of his tape collection to me. It's some of those sounds that the world has heard since on the record *Songs of the Humpback Whales.*"

"Why do the songs move you so?"

"Why is spending the afternoon standing on your feet and tiring out your calves in a museum to see great art worth it? Why do you spend thirty dollars in an evening to go hear music? I don't know. To me it's a marvelously evocative performance that comes from the most unexpected quarter. It would be the same as walking by your cat and having it start humming a tune to you. Humpbacks have been singing longer than human beings have existed."

"What is the most beautiful encounter with singing whales you can remember?"

"Oh, that's easy," he said, stretching his long legs out into the aisle and settling against the booth wall, a mug of coffee in his hands. Looking somewhere in the middle distance, he shed the present easily, as if it were nothing more than a light sweater. "Lying in the cockpit of a boat at night off Bermuda," he said, "with a faint gentle breeze and the mast sweeping across and clouds of stars above you, listening to the sounds of whales, which are sort of flooding up out of the ocean through the earphones you're wearing as you become part of the same rhythm that the songs dance to. The songs are set by the rhythm of swells in the oceans. If you listen to whales when you are being borne on the sea, you can feel that the rate at which they're producing a given phrase is about the same as the rate between the swells that are coming by. What an extraordinary, compelling experience that is! You never tire of it. The ocean is the greatest of all echo chambers—there's nothing like it on land. And when you listen over a pair of headphones to whales under perfect recording conditions in deep ocean, it's really as though you were listening from within the Horsehead Nebula, or some galactic space that is otherworldly, not part of anything you know, where the boat itself is floating. Once, for example, on an early fall night, I was coming back from the Arctic, where I had been working on bowhead whales in a boat at sea. As we flew down across the Canadian Arctic, we were beneath an arc of northern lights, which were pure green and bell-shaped. We and the plane were the clapper of this bell, with the green light over us. And for the first time in my life I felt that I was in the position of the whale that is singing to you when you're in the boat and just listening to it. That's the kind of space that is somehow illuminated, depicted, made sensible by the hydrophones. It gives you a special impression of the sea. We all love the ocean's beautiful sparkle blue, but beneath it, down deeper, whales are moving with slow, drifting currents, whales that are great, gentle cloudlike beings, not just some *meaty animal.* Everything the whales do is so slow, so deliberate, outside the normal time sense of the human world. When you watch whales for an entire afternoon, you don't realize what they're doing. You see things that look very slow and graceful. Only later, when you've looked at your day's notes, might you put it together and say, 'Oh my God, this animal was *playing.* That's what I was seeing, but I was seeing it at a speed much slower than I'm used to.' Whales teach us a new sense of time."

In a nearby booth, a young man wearing an electric-blue T-shirt on which the letters M-A-U-I were arranged in the rough shape of the island, was reading a local newspaper. The headline and a drawing announced yet another occasion on which a whale had saved the life of a human being: in this instance by reportedly driving off sharks that were heading for a fallen surfer. Do whales have emotions like ours? I wondered. How intelligent are they? Do they have minds of the sort that would be familiar to us?

After all, mind is such an odd predicament for matter to get into. I often marvel how something like hydrogen, the simplest atom, forged in some early chaos of the universe, could lead to us and the gorgeous fever we call consciousness. If a mind is just a few pounds of blood, dream, and electric, how does it manage to contemplate itself, worry about its soul, do time-and-motion studies, admire the shy hooves of a goat, know that it will die, enjoy all the grand and lesser mayhems of the heart? What is mind, that one can be *out of one's*? How can a neuron feel compassion? What is a self? Why did automatic, hand-me-down mammals like our ancestors somehow evolve brains with the ability to consider, imagine, project, compare, abstract, think of the future? If our experience of mind is really just the simmering of an easily alterable chemical stew, then what does it mean to *know* something, to *want* something, to *be*? How do you begin with hydrogen and end up with prom dresses, jealousy, chamber music? What is music that it can satisfy such a mind, and even perhaps function as language?

"Remember those 'brutal facts' you were talking about?" I said. "I've been thinking a lot about the mind of whales. How self-conscious do you think whales are?"

Roger turned his fork over and nudged his slices of bacon into a kelplike dune, cut off a section, and chewed it thoughtfully. "There are reasons to suspect that the brains of whales—and I'm including dolphins—are equal to or of even greater complexity than the brains of human beings. These complexities must serve some important role in the lives of the whales and dolphins. But nobody has a clue as to what that role is, not the slightest idea, not even a persuasive theory. I will go out on a limb and say that the most interesting question in biology today is what dolphins are using their complex brains for; I can't think of anything that would be more interesting to know. You can say, 'Well, maybe they just have a large brain; why not?' Well, I can tell you why not: It's because brains are extremely expensive to maintain and operate. For example, during the first few weeks of life in a human being, whose brain-to-body ratio is not very unlike that of a newborn dolphin, the brain requires about a third of the metabolism of the whole body just to run it. It's a very costly thing to have. So you don't just kind of end up having a fancy brain. You have a fancy brain because there's a very important reason why you need one. It is selected for, and as soon as the advantage that is conferred by having it is gone, you'll lose it and lose it fast. What this means is that there must be something that dolphins and whales are doing with their brains that's fundamental to their lives.

"Here's one of the standard unsupported guesses: They're using them for fancy acoustic functions—by making a few clicks, they can not only hear how far it is to the bottom in many directions but they can also figure out its structure and how soft it is and how many fish are hovering above it and which others are buried in the mud and so on. Yes, those are all very important functions. But equally complex tasks are done by bats with brains that are probably a thousandth the mass of the brains of dolphins. And I can't believe that dolphins' brains are so inefficient that they have to be so much more complicated just to equal what can be done in a brain the size of a pea or much smaller. So I don't think that's going to solve the question. No, there's something they're using their large brains for that, I suspect, is completely different from what we use ours for. Ours, basically, serve and interact with two things: one, our opposable thumbs and grasping simian fingers, which, with our brain, make possible eye-hand coordination; and two, language and all that language does for us. Do whales have a language? Well, as I said, if there is a language to the songs of humpback whales, it's very monotonous. They're repeating themselves endlessly, saying the same, perhaps very complex, thing over and over, for months at a time. So it won't do to say that they have a language that is in any sense equivalent to or similar to our language, if they use all of its complexity and structure to say just a very few things. You could say that the song is analogous to a carrier frequency in a radio and that basically it is the minor modifications in the song that carry the message. I somehow think that's unlikely, because whales tend to be alone when they're singing, not in social groups, not in contact with other whales. When a whale comes near a singer, the singer instantly shuts up, and often a fight will ensue. That suggests that the song is a simpler thing, either a challenge or a wooing call. But it doesn't explain the big brains. I think the brains of whales are being used for things we have no intuitive understanding of whatsoever, yet what they're used for is critically important to the life of the whales. It must deeply affect their reproductive fitness. It must be crucial to their survival. But we don't know what it is."

Turning sideways, he leaned back against the outer wall of the booth and propped one sneakered foot up on the bench seat. "You could ask, Why do human beings have such huge brains? There are lots of theories, but to me the one that's most appealing is that human beings dwell in long-lived societies in which they have contact for years with the same individuals and family groups, and these groups are constantly exchanging favors, with the idea that if you give a favor you will get one in return, then you have to wait around and collect on the debt. This process is sometimes referred to as 'reciprocal altruism,' and although nobody has found a means by which just plain true altruism could be selected for, reciprocal altruism could very well be accepted and selected for. A classic example of reciprocal altruism is that you are drowning and I reach down and grab a stick and hold it out and you grab it and I pull you to shore. I've done you the most important favor of your entire life, and you owe me a big one. All I had to do is bend over, pick up a stick, and extend my arm. And now, oh my gosh, what can I expect from you?"

A pink-and-white-uniformed waitress with a bouffant hairdo appeared suddenly with a heavy pot of coffee and poured something like crude oil into Roger's mug. He thanked her and continued: "Why, tremendous things, for a tiny investment on my part. But I might have to wait a long time for you to come up with a reward large enough to express the depths of your gratitude. You can get a social system going based on reciprocal altruism, but it will only work in groups in which associations last for a very long time. It doesn't work in groups in which you have a total despot at the head who will just beat you senseless if you don't pay up. It works in groups more like human groups, and may in fact be like whale and dolphin groups. The smarter you get the smarter you have to be, because eventually that kind of system invites cheating. So let's say, for example, that I discover a beautiful bush of blueberries as we are walking along together. And at the moment, I owe you. I say to you, 'Ah, Diane, look at this marvelous bush of blueberries. Because of what you did for me last week, these are yours, all yours. I'm not going to take any of them.' You begin eating them, with gratitude, and you're glad to have them all to yourself. But the reason I've really done that is that I've noticed another one in the distance that is better than this bush, and I want to keep you away from it. So I wander off until I'm out of sight and then quickly devour it, while you're left with the lesser meal. You have to be able to detect in me little signs that tell you I'm lying. And that requires some very sophisticated analysis of what my true motives may be. If reciprocal altruism invites cheating, then you must become a deft detector of cheating, and if you get good at detecting cheating, then I have to get better at cheating in more subtle ways. What you end up with is a brain racing in its evolution toward greater and greater complexity and sophistication to be able to detect and to employ cheating. You'll quickly end up with animals that have fancy brains. That could be true for dolphins. They certainly exist in long-lived social groups in which they have opportunity to repay reciprocal debts.

"But they may need their brains for reasons much more complex than that. Think of how important myths are in our cultures. Think of all the similarities that myths have, think how memorable those elements are, and how they control the lives of the people who hear them. There may be some kind of need for myth in the vertebrate brain, whether it's located in the head of a whale or of a person. Nobody really knows."

After breakfast, before returning to Kihei, we paid a visit to Spear Venus at his shop, Venus Electronics, where Roger ordered a special tape recorder with features he needed for recording whales. A whale enthusiast, Spear had worked with Roger in the past, observing and filming whales. His brother owned a local television station. Drifting into an alcove at the back of the shop, which was a small gallery of signed Salvador Dali prints, Roger discussed with Spear the possibility of a donor buying an FM radio station so that he could make ultra-high-quality stereo recordings from a bottom microphone in deep water, then broadcast the songs. People all over the world would be able to tune in to Whale Hawaii and hear nonstop singing.

"What would a station cost to buy?" he asked.

Spear adjusted one corner of a Dali print. "Oh, I would think around a hundred thousand dollars."

"You could sell it by subscription," Roger explained, "and scramble the signal. People could have it as background music in their house. Every now and then, a whale would come by and sit right on the mike and sing and blow everybody's mind. Look, I want to make long-term recordings of humpbacks," Roger explained. "But if you want to get into it commercially, I can't think of anyone better."

Spear stroked his mustache. It was an idea that appealed to him both environmentally and commercially, but he was getting ready to retire and hoping to travel the world with his wife and two small children. But he agreed to think about it and lend a hand setting it up, if the money became available. Whale Hawaii: a steady pour of whale songs streaming around the world above water, so that human beings could hear them, like neighbors picking up on a party line.

At last, we returned to the Mosses' house, where Roger continued work on the buoy. The winds were growing loud and unruly, but surely the next day the squalls would have moved on like a flock of migratory birds.

The following morning, when the winds ebbed a little, we went out in a Zodiac piloted by Colin, a young, fair-skinned Englishman with heavily freckled ears and sunburned neck, chest, and arms. At regular intervals, explosions came from the nearby island of Kahoolawe, where the U.S. Navy was practicing bombing. According to Hawaiian legend, the island looks like a humpback, which is why the whales keep returning. At Molokini, Roger dropped a white hydrophone into the water on a long black line and put on a headset. Smiling, he handed the headset to me. Painfully loud whale songs surged through both earphones. Three whales were singing the same song somewhere beneath us, their voices blending and mixing. A storm began prowling Maui. The ocean was cobalt blue, like an Oriental glaze, with gray clouds reflected in it. At times it was the color and texture of whale skin.

"I think he's starting back up," Roger said.

"How can you tell?"

"From where the singer is in the song—at *rattle, rattle, rattle,*" he said. "I think it's the coming-up section, but I don't know this year's song very well yet."

The apparently silent ocean filled with white curds as it reflected the plunging storm clouds. The hydrophone drifted below the boat on its long lead like an electrode in a heart. Molokini's structure created a natural amphitheater, which concentrated the sounds. A slow hooting began, like that of a barn owl. It seemed to come from every direction and reminded me that Roger's doctoral work, at Cornell, was on how owls locate their prey, which was as much through sound as vision, he discovered.

"What is that strange hooting?"

Roger smiled. "A singer. It's very close by."

"But in which direction? It seems to be coming from all over."

"The boat transmits the sound to you from all its interior surfaces. It's as if you were sitting in the center of a loudspeaker."

Now I can understand how Greek sailors of the ancient Mediterranean, bewitched by eerie singing, thought it came from Sirens. Although there are no humpbacks reported in the Mediterranean today, an intriguing possibility is that humpbacks once thrived there, among other whales, and were indeed the Sirens of Greek myth. At night, far from land, under a mantle of stars, lonely sailors could have heard the plaintive songs of the humpbacks but would not have been able to tell where the music was coming from as it swirled around inside the wooden hull of their boat, wrapping them in a cocoon of lamentation and desire. Whale songs can continue for many hours, even days, so the becalmed sailors could have grown unnerved and then drowsy, as the singing both bedeviled and enchanted them, and could have fallen asleep with Siren voices tugging at their dreams. Whales may well have been the mythic unicorns, too. Narwhals, which live in Arctic regions, grow long, tapered, spiraling tusks that exactly fit the description of unicorn horns.

Not only have whales generated two of our most beguiling Western myths, they frequent the myths of far-flung cultures, from the aborigines of Australia to the Quechua of Peru. The Inuit consider themselves the "people of the whale," an idea that figures in their creation myths and religious life. In *Whales*, Jacques Cousteau reports that "the Koryak people of Siberia . . . hold astonishing meetings during which they confess to whales any sins they have committed, any taboos they have broken, any evil thoughts they may have had." Throughout history, Leviathan, as the whale has often been called, embodied the monstrous grandeur of the unknown, nature at its most primeval and unplumbable, the rampaging beauty of the oceans, the magical realm where the ordinary and the sacred meet. When Melville describes a whale breaking the surface, a figment of fused grace and power, bursting from its cryptic world into the world of humans, he writes with unashamed worship: "Rising with his utmost velocity from the furthest depths, the Sperm Whale thus booms his entire bulk into the pure element of air . . . . In those moments, the torn, enraged waves he shakes off, seem his mane." Whales live enigmatic lives, in that realm impenetrable to our gaze. Small wonder they've seemed magical and strange. Until recently, we couldn't even enter their world long enough to see them completely. And scientists still aren't able to travel with them sufficiently to learn of their wanderings and relationships. Almost everything we know about whales we have had to learn from dead animals or from the occasional stranding of confused or sick ones. In rare, privileged moments, we enter their world, and then only briefly and shallowly, to watch through the murk or to eavesdrop.

Colin leaned over the side of the Zodiac and put his head underwater, holding his nose, then came up dripping, his short blond hair swept into a punk style. Momentarily disturbed, the water surface went back to being slick as whale skin and mottled by reflected clouds.

"Sounds close," he said.

But close might have been a mile or more away. Turning a slow circle, I scanned the horizon. Somewhere a whale was singing, and would surface to breathe, but I saw no sign of it. "How do they arrange their bodies when they're singing?"

"Most of the time they're head-downward," Roger explained as he untangled the hydrophone wire. "But when they're at the surface, breathing, they're horizontal, and they don't interrupt the performance of the song to breathe. They pace themselves the same way a human singer does, catching their breath between phrases. A whale normally breathes at the same point in the song. But sometimes one will breathe at an inappropriate moment—catch a breath in the wrong place. When that happens they don't stop the performance, and so songs with and without breathing in inappropriate places will sound the same. I don't sing, for example, 'Glory, glory [breath, breath] hallelujah.' I manage to breathe while producing the song, so as not to interrupt it. Whales do the same thing, and to me that suggests their singing is a conscious performance. They're good singers who don't mess up a song with awkward breaths. When they reach the surface, they often make a surface ratchet sound, sort of like a slowly opening creaking door; and I suspect that most of the time they start singing right after the surface ratchet, when they throw their tail into the air—'peak their flukes,' as it's called—and make the first phrase as they dive. Sometimes singing can last for periods of several hours, or even for more than a day. Once, off Hawaii, in a place where one seldom encounters whales, my former wife, Katharine, and I found a singer who was already singing when we began recording, and when we quit, deep into darkness eleven hours later, it was still going nonstop. Here, around Maui, where the whales are always interacting—getting into fights, chasing each other—a song rarely lasts for more than two hours, because another whale comes along and cuts it. A song stops when the singer is interrupted by another whale, a boat, a swimmer—any kind of stimulus that is curious or threatening and needs the singer's attention."

Roger was covered in bruises and Band-Aids. One fingertip was still shining from a patch of spilled Krazy Glue. As he recorded a song, he closed his eyes and his mouth fell open, as if he were asleep. A straw hat with an Hawaiian-print band kept the sun from his eyes. His unbuttoned shirt revealed a freckled chest; his legs were lightly freckled, too, and he was wearing maroon shorts. A pair of reading glasses dangled from a cord around his neck. A speedboat cruised by, playing loud rock music, its partying crew unaware of the concert in full swing below them. After it had passed, we moved to the windward side of Molokini, where its coral-covered wall drops six hundred feet.

I put on a snorkeling mask and fins and slipped over the side, into a school of fifty Moorish idols—a black-yellow-and-white fish with a small puckered mouth and a long spear trailing from the top of the head—and swam toward the wall, where brain coral ribboned like disembodied minds and parrotfish flashed blue-green spangles. Taking a gulp of air and diving a few feet, I heard the moaning of whales again, but this time louder and accompanied by gurglings and creaks. Then a trumpeting sound—half elephant, half monkey—surged into a two-stage grunt that started low and swung high, followed by a stuttering lawnmower that changed to a finger being dragged across a taut balloon, then a suite of basso groans and a badly oiled garden gate creaking open. Turning a slow circle, I looked for the singer, whose voice was everywhere, but saw only raccoon butterfly fish (bright yellow, with black masks) and a blooming garden of coral. I felt as if I'd fallen into the middle of a millefiore paperweight. This singer, warbling with such panache, was most likely a male. I could not see him, but his eerie song sent shivers down my back and made my ribs gently chime as it filled the waves with waves of music. Linda Guinee, of Roger's lab, and Katharine Payne, now a researcher at Cornell, had recently discovered an astonishing new fact about humpbacks: They use *rhyme* to help them remember their long songs. Floating in what might be a whale's epic poem, I marveled at its strange embroidery. Each time I dove a few feet under the surface, I heard and felt the radiant booming again, and wished I could hold my breath for hours, stay down and listen with the whole ocean cupped to my ear like a single hand.

But at last, too tired to keep diving, I climbed into the boat, and we cruised back to Maui. Rainbows formed in the spray at either side of the Zodiac. The siren song followed us for some distance, then vanished among shore sounds as we approached the marina. Thrilled to have felt the singing wash over me, I yearned to be near a whale in its own element, to watch its habits closely. Though that would be difficult with the shy humpbacks wintering at Maui, would it be possible elsewhere?

Half of Roger's whale study revolved around humpbacks and their songs. Studying them in Hawaii, hemmed in by the constant jangle of tourists, speedboats, and hotel chains, made relentless demands. The other half of his whale study took place on the coast of Patagonia—at an outpost far from noise and society. There, mother right whales raised their babies, eager males came courting, and it was possible to observe whale families going about their daily routine. When I said goodbye to Roger in Hawaii, I knew that we would meet again—first at the Long-Term Research Institute, and then in one of the wildest and most remote places on Earth.

· · ·

In the tony suburbs of Boston near Walden Pond, cedar-shake houses displayed their vintage on a chimney or gate and the pious fiction we call history could be read on markers and mileposts and in street names. Stone walls edged most yards, where peonies, poppies, and tea roses spilled from groomed flower beds. Orange daylilies grew wild in the culverts. At noon, shadows marched like militiamen along the thickly wooded roads.

On one lane, a driveway led to a white farmhouse and two large red barns. There were only wildflowers on this property, and a great press of wild and unruly trees, brush that had begun creeping close to the buildings and thickets barely held back by stone walls. The sense of sheer green abundance was overpowering. Nature may once have allowed this small human clearing in its midst, but it had obviously begun to reconsider.

The first red building, which housed the Long-Term Research Institute, looked typically barnlike from outside. But inside, it resembled a ship, with arched ceilings and exposed beams and other timbers. Three fans spun like propellers overhead. An open-backed flight of stairs with a white dowel-railing along one side led to a widow's walk with a porthole window in one alcove. Two offices were off that narrow landing, and another small staircase wound its way up to the attic rooms where Roger lived. On the first floor, a black cast-iron stove stood in a bricked corner of the otherwise wooden-walled room. Windows looked out onto the woods. On one window-sill a long heft of baleen lay like a tusk. Just below the window, a small draftsman's cabinet held twelve shallow drawers full of calipers, course converters, and other seafaring instruments. In photographs, two humpback whales patrolled the walls. Below them, on top of a long, low bookcase, whales done in bronze, brass, or soapstone were caught in mid-swim. A vibrantly colored globe of the world, on a dusty black stand, shone in the sunlight. A rind of Lucite, stretching down one side of the globe, helped to measure distances. At the moment, the Lucite rind was over the Atlantic coast. On the floor next to the bookcase sat a white whale vertebra that looked and felt like pumice. In the center of the room, a large wooden table and four screen-backed chairs invited the visitors to sit down. A basket held three Granny Smith apples, whose light fragrance wafted through the room. A viewing table for slides stood against one wall, and a reel-to-reel tape recorder, for the playing of whale songs, leaned against another. A dinner fork had been bent in half and attached to one tip of a twelve-foot-long gray plastic tube with rope and glue. Roger used it to reach the ceiling fans, catching their chainlike pulls between the fork's tines and yanking down to change the fan's speeds.

One had the overall sense of being able to see through every wall and partition into what lay behind it. You could see between the steps and through the white railings of the staircase to the rooms beyond. The balcony rails were set low and far enough apart so that they seemed to measure the space, not cage it. Windows at ceiling height revealed the sky and the treetops. Windows at waist height framed the red barn next door and the stone wall, the woodpile, and a monarch butterfly that was hovering in a chokecherry bush.

The lab was not yet finished; pipes, light bulbs, and switches dangled from the walls. In one room, a white electrical wire that would ordinarily have been looped up had been twisted into the shape of a treble clef. A tiny, galley-size kitchen, a bathroom, and a receptionist's desk sat out in the hallway. The letter trays were jammed with unopened mail, a heap of notes about phone calls to answer, Federal Express envelopes that had been left to sit for days after their arrival. Down the hall were the four small offices where Roger and his crew worked. In one of them, on a desk, was a scrapbook, photographs of markings on the heads of right whales. The Institute knew them as individuals. On another desk sat a stack of shiny black vinyl records. For a small membership fee, subscribers received the Institute's newsletter and a recording of humpback-whale songs. I picked up a record and carried it to the turntable in the other room. How could something as small, manageable, fragile, even, as that one record contain the huge voices of whales? But when

I turned the player on, beautiful whale songs fillled the dimly lit room with magic.

After a while, I returned to Roger's office, where overflowing bookcases reflected the many facets of his curiosity. Poetry books were lined up beside books on whales, music, Kipling's *Just So Stories*. Holding a mug of Morning Thunder tea, he stood at his desk, poring over a terminal moraine of papers—letters, schedules, journals, reminders. His diary and phone book were thick palimpsests of changing lives. Even he wasn't sure which numbers to use for which people or which appointments were definite. That was undoubtedly why he preferred to write only in pencil. In pencil, on a white lined tablet, were notes for a brochure that would explain the workings and goals of the institute to potential donors, when they visited the Institute's new ship that would be sailing up the Atlantic coast and docking at various ports along the way.

When Roger had purchased the ship, it was already named *Morning Watch*, but he was happy about the accidental felicity of that name. "It's everyone's duty to take the morning watch," he explained as he sat down on a low couch beside a potted Plumeria he had brought back from his recent trip to Maui. "Of course, it's much easier to sleep through life. But then you'll miss an incredible spectacle that's waiting for you. In the morning, dew lies heavily on the decks, you sometimes find flying fish that have leaped aboard by mistake in the night, their scales still shuddering with color, and the ocean is full of so many fascinating things, including whales."

"Did the Save the Whales campaign of past years help?"

"The Save the Whales campaign was a big victory for stopping a lot of the renegade whaling that was going on. But whales have survived into a time of high technology, and because of it, they are dying in numbers that make the days of all-out whaling seem trivial. More whales are killed every year from drift nets than by whaling ships. But even that is minor compared to how many die from the poisons being poured into the seas. We need to save the whales in their own right, because they are peaceful, intelligent creatures who have been our companions on this planet for thirty million years. But they are also guardians of our conscience, which remind us that the oceans themselves are endangered.

"We may be the biggest flop that ever came on earth," Roger said. "People often wonder just how intelligent whales are. But I could argue that there is no intelligent life on earth, that all we do with our brains is commit a series of the greatest mistakes . . . that the human brain is the most unsuccessful adaptation ever to appear in the history of life on earth. Neanderthal man only lasted for maybe seventy-five thousand years. We have lasted about a fifth of that time; what are the chances that we'll last another fifty thousand years? Whales have an important lesson to teach us. Whales have a large and complex brain but show no signs of threatening their own destruction. They haven't reproduced themselves into oblivion, they haven't destroyed the resources upon which they depend, they haven't generated giant holes in the ozone, or increased the earth's temperature so that we might end up with the greenhouse effect. The lesson whales teach us is that you can have a brain of great complexity that doesn't result in the death of the planet. And also that we shouldn't necessarily admire intelligence for its own sake. Most of what we will have to use our clever brain for in the next few hundred or thousand years, if we live that long, is undoing the effects of what we used our brains for in the last few hundred or thousand years—cleaning up the environment, for instance. One insult to the brain of a whale is to call it intelligent in the same way ours is. Intelligence may not be something we would wish to foist off on some other species like a whale. What we call intelligence may be only a kind of vandalism, just mischief on a grand scale. It might not be the only form mind can take, and it might have little to do with real wisdom."

A phone call interrupted him. The Voyager spacecraft was getting ready to leave the solar system on its journey to other stars, and a caller wanted to know about the whale greetings it carried. There were sixty-two different human languages and also singing whales. Now that human beings were able to leave the gravitational jacket of their own star and send an emissary out to spend the rest of its mechanical-electronic life wandering through space, how mature of us to devote a little bit of room on board to the culture of another species.

Roger gave the caller the references he needed, then returned to his seat by the window. The idea of whale songs traveling through the galaxy clearly thrilled him, too. "Some other extraterrestrial, space-faring civilization," he said, "will be able to realize that we talked in one way, and this other species that's also on the record talked another way. In some sense, we have begun to put the house of our own species in order. Now we have to recognize that other species have rights, that other mammals—like whales—are endowed by their creator with certain unalienable rights. This is a truth that may not be self-evident to all of us yet, but think what a revelation that same truth was to our forefathers in 1776. Pretty soon we'll realize that it's not just mammals that have rights—birds have rights, and so do amphibians, and so do lizards, and so do insects, and so do plants and planktons, and so on all the way down, until finally we become at peace with the rest of life on earth and recognize that we are just one species among many. That's a wonderful thing to be. . . ."

As evening deepened, a whippoorwill threw the boomerang of its voice across the summer woods. Roger smiled. He said that it reminded him of his childhood, and of his first inquiries into the sounds that animals make, long before he knew he would spend his life traveling the oceans with the steady companionship of whales. I had to leave, but I knew that the next time we met, it would be in an unworldly landscape, where one didn't expect to find anything so robust as a whale.

In mid-October 1990, I flew to meet Roger Payne again, this time on the wind-scoured slice of Argentina known as Patagonia, a land renowned for its blustery deserts, unusual wildlife, and rugged, self-reliant people. From the airport at Trelew (named after one of the many Welshmen who settled the region), we drove three hours northeast, to the Valdés Peninsula, a bludgeon-shaped piece of land separating two bays. Because both bays have a small mouth, their waters are much calmer than those of the galloping Atlantic, and migrating right whales stop there every year to raise their babies and engage in courtship, before continuing on south to the krill-rich feeding grounds of Antarctica. Twenty years before, when Roger had realized that the highly endangered right whales were pausing in the bays, he established a study site on the inside curve of the northern bay—on a somewhat hilly, scimitar-shaped beach below two cliffs—and the New York Zoological Society built a field station there. Technically, its address is Lot 39. But Campamento Ballenas is what most people call it, pronouncing the double *l* as a "zh," as Patagonians do, filling even their language with the sounds of the wind.

A drive north through flat scrub desert on a road dusty as a mineshaft led us past a shrine of Coca-Cola bottles. Many years earlier, a woman had died of thirst in this desert, but her infant miraculously survived. Legend had it that the Virgin Mary appeared at the spot where the baby was found. Now Argentinians stopped to leave a tribute of old bottles. Finally, we reached a gate in a wire fence. Roger opened it by fiddling with a lever system made of pipes and wires, and we proceeded down a bumpy, wind-gutted, water-eroded road. On a rise overlooking the camp, we paused a moment. Below us, dwarfed by ancient, fossil-peppered cliffs on the rim of the ocean, surrounded by thorn bushes and ice plants, sat a small, one-story house of white stucco, plus two Quonset huts and an assortment of tents. On the two cliffs—one right behind the main house, the other about a mile away—were small corrugated-metal huts. Night was falling fast, and the ocean had begun to darken, but here and there a small burst of white floated over the water, as if shot from an atomizer, where a whale was surfacing to breathe.

Continuing down to camp, we pulled up to the house. On its cement porch, tripods, cameras, and telescopes were roped to the roof beams to keep them from hitting the ground when they blew over, as they inevitably did. A whale's large weathered jawbone, attached to the wall by chains, made a cozy bench. A wooden swing, hanging from one rafter, rocked gently back and forth as if occupied by a ghost. A handmade birdhouse tucked up against the porch roof held a brown wren-sized bird, a nesting plain-mantled tit spine-tail. Lying next to the front door, part of a whale's skull—four feet across and about three feet wide—served as a table, on which someone had left a windbreaker. The house's windows were made to open and tilt down, to balance binoculars.

Inside the house there were four bedrooms, a kitchen, a sitting room, a photographic darkroom, and a main equipment room. The house was divided into two self-enclosed suites, and one had to go out onto the porch to get from one suite to the other. However, a crawl-through door, just big enough for a child, led from a bedroom wall to a second bedroom; Roger had designed it for his children when they were small. In the equipment room, a thick hodgepodge tumbled from shelves or lay across beams or was stored under tables or hung on the walls. So many people had come and gone over the years—bringing their equipment, supplies, and personal items—that no one knew what could safely be thrown out. There were many pairs of wading boots in an open closet. Orange exposure suits, yellow fishermens' suits, rain slickers of several colors, and red-and-white peaked hats marked EVERREADY hung around the room. On a high shelf, a wooden crate said: "Next Trip to Town Box." Roger's cauliflower-shaped straw helmet (with a gold cord he tied under the chin) was suspended from a nail; his head was so large that it was the only sun hat he'd found that fit. Propane lamps sat on a tall table, beside which tripods nested together in a wooden corral. Scattered on shelves were bottles and cans of everything from auto polish to Sno-seal, along with bobbins of wire, half a dozen tape recorders, old blue cans full of nails and screws, a collection of saws and other tools, and an extra toilet seat. An alcove, with a window looking out onto the porch and the sea, served as Roger's study; behind his desk and chair, shelves lining the walls held skulls of animals found in the area, preserved specimens in jars, field notebooks, and other paraphernalia.

There had been an attempt to make a yard in front of the house by edging an arbitrary area of blowing dirt and debris with fossil shells, but the wind had all but blasted it away. One shell hanging on a wire on a bush in front of the house was a reminder, perhaps, of some Christmas past. The cracked earth looked like pudding cooked dry in a pot. Despite the harsh conditions, flowers bloomed. Ice plants sent up bright pink-cupped flowers with yellow centers. Another low, sprawly succulent was covered with hundreds of daisy-like flowers. Tiny pinks nestled among tufts of tawny grass. All the plants of the region, either thorns or succulents, had evolved to preserve water. Sheep fences wove in and out around the camp, and low "snake fences" ran downhill to the beach. Graham Harris, a New York Zoological Society naturalist who lived in the nearby town of Puerto Madryn and had virtually reared his two children at camp, built the snake fences to keep out local pit vipers—a poisonous, rattleless rattlesnake—but the fences had been buried in places by wind-driven sand, and in hot weather the vipers got into camp anyway. In front of the house, across the dirt yard and beyond the sheep fence, was the boathouse—a corrugated-metal Quonset hut that held the Zodiacs and a pungent whale skeleton. To the left of the house was a Quonset-hut dining hall, and beyond that the outhouse. Made from slats of now-gray wood, the outhouse had a plank to prop the door closed. Attached to the plank, a flagpole whose flag had long since blown away signaled when the outhouse was occupied. If the pole was up, someone was inside. If it was down, pointing like a dousing rod, then the outhouse was empty. A plaque on the door identified the building as THE TEHUELCHES' REVENGE, which referred to the Indians who had originally settled the region and were brought to extinction by the Spaniards, leaving their myths and arrowheads behind. Inside, someone had scrawled on the wall: "Darwin's rhea was here."

Tents were tucked in among the thorn bushes, either near the ocean or on a rise near the main house. Mine was a khaki tent billowing at the edge of the beach. After I zipped the tent closed, horizontally and vertically, I crawled into my down sleeping bag and tried to sleep. The wind, swiveling smartly through the thorn bushes and gulleys, sounded like wet sheets blowing on a line. A snuffling, gargling noise seemed to be right outside the tent. Then a loud snort startled me, and I unzipped the flaps and looked out. There was no wild animal lurking beside my tent or on the beach. A huge moon floated low in the sky. The night was drenched with stars. It was like looking up at a planetarium. Two large cottony blurs hovered over-head, and to my delight I realized they were the Magellanic Clouds—neighboring galaxies of countless stars visible only from the Southern Hemisphere—which I had never seen before. In the moonlight, the ocean poured its black satin, and then a small white cloud appeared, like a corsage just above the water. A loud snuffle followed, and I realized: I have been listening to the night sounds of whales.

In the morning, I woke to loud soughings and raspings, and I looked out and saw four whales lolling close to shore. Rolling and blowing, they waved their flippers in the air, turned lazily, peaked their flukes. I could see, farther out, three more whales blow as they surfaced. Farther still, a lone whale breached, hurling itself high into the air, shattering the water when it hit, sending up great columns of spray; then it breached seven times more. The bay was full of whales. It is as wonderful as discovering dinosaurs in your garden. Petrels, sooty shearwaters, and black-browed albatrosses soared along the beach. Oystercatchers triple-chimed like a doorbell as they pa-trolled the waves. The air was cold and damp, and I dressed quickly and walked down to the dining hall, just in time to see a hairy armadillo (which Argentinians call a *peludo*) scurrying away from the front door with a crust of bread in its mouth. PELUDO PALACE, a plaque said at the front door. In front of the building, a wooden bench was held up by two perforated cans used to ship snakes. All the antivenin for the local species of pit viper came from snakes captured in camp. Next to the bench, the vertebra of a right whale lay in the sun beside several old anchors.

Laughter seeped from inside the dining hall, and when I opened the door, I found a long table with benches and chairs around it, at which eight people were sitting and drinking coffee from metal mugs, or maté from a small gourd with a fluted silver-colored straw sticking out of it. The "chicos"—Roger's affectionate name for the university students Juan, Gustavo, Minolo, Gaby, and Anita—were spending the summer in camp to do whale research. Gustavo, who had lived at Roger's lab in Massachusetts for four months the previous year, doing research and perfecting his English, was built like a soccer player; his friends sometimes called him Nono ("grandfather" in Italian) because of his balding head. His fiancée, Gaby, was slender and dark-haired, with a buoyant, rompy sense of humor. Tall and bearded, Minolo looked a bit French; he and his girlfriend, Anita, were college students at the University of La Mar de la Plata, along with Gustavo and Gaby. Juan, a tall, brawny student from the University of Buenos Aires, slept on a bed in one corner of the dining room, which meant that he did not go to sleep until the last person left after dinner, and he woke whenever the first person stumbled in for breakfast. Kate O'Connell, a petite, short-haired woman of thirty, a conservationist and an expert translator, was also at the table, speaking Spanish with animation and verve. Beside her, Tom Ford, a dentist from Massachusetts, began doing an impression of Sylvester Stallone as Rambo that needed no translation and sent everyone into howls. Tom was studying the bacteria in the exhalation of whales. This meant attaching a petri dish to a fishing pole and dangling it over a whale's blowhole just as it was exhaling. Thus far, he'd had good luck. In his checked jacket and two-week-old beard, Dr. Tom looked like a lumberjack. Judy Perkins, a blond woman in her forties, also a member of the lab, was in camp to collect skin samples from whales so that she could map their genealogy. In her work, she used a small crossbow to fire an arrow tipped with a biopsy dart, specially designed to collect small pieces of skin. Then, when she returned to the States, she would study the whales' DNA, to seek answers to questions about sex, lineage, and family groups.

Gustavo passed around cereal-crackers and cheese; Kate opened a cardboard carton of orange juice; Tom got out the French bread and butter. Marmalade and the local delicacy—a caramel-like *dulce de leche*—were already on the table. Gaby held the brown gourd full of maté in one hand as if it were a leather purse filled with gold. She offered me some, and my face twisted as I drank.

"Te gusta?" Gaby asked, laughing.

It tasted like strong, bitter spinach. With elaborate thanks, I handed the gourd back to her. She poured hot water into it, then passed it to Gustavo. When the liquid was gone, he handed the gourd again to Gaby, who refilled it with water and handed it to Anita. In this way, the maté always returned to one person to fill, according to custom, and then it gradually made the rounds of everyone at the table. It was not yet ten in the morning, but the day's bilingual slang lessons had already begun. This aspect of camp life had a practical side. It prepared everyone for the serious dramas of whale research, which could be dished out by unexpected weather, currents, or animals.

"How do you say it when someone is like this?" Gustavo asked, pushing his nose up in the air. Judy offered him the words *snooty* and *stuck-up*.

"What does it mean exactly when someone says *ecco*?" Roger said, stretching out and emphasizing the first syllable of the word. Minolo explained that it was the rough equivalent of saying "I see" or "I understand."

When Gaby referred to *la tormenta* of yesterday, I asked her what the word meant, and learned that *la tormenta* was a thunderstorm.

"Can a person also be *tormented*?"

"Oh yes," she said, "pouring hot water from a thermos into the gourd and passing it to Minolo. "Someone can be *attormentado*. How did you say? . . ."

"Tormented."

"Tormented," she said firmly. "They feel so bad all the time, like they have a thunderstorm inside of them."

Juan heated a cup of milk and dissolved squares of chocolate in it. A scuttling in the dirt outside caught our attention, and through the open door we saw a small, strange, guinea-pig-like animal run toward the beach, followed by three babies.

"What on earth was that?" I asked.

"Cuis," Juan said, a word pronounced as *"quees."*

"Do the locals eat them?"

"Oh sure," Tom said. "They make *cuis* lorraine."

Pulling the large round of red-rind-covered cheese toward me, I cut a few chunks out of it, leaving it crumbly and untidy. "Sorry about chavelling the cheese," I said.

"Chavelling?" Gustavo asked. "What means chavelling?"

"Beats me," Roger said. "I've never heard it before." Judy and Tom shook their heads.

"It's a British word," I explained, "for cutting something—like a piece of bread, cake, cheese, or pie—in a sloppy way." Roger translated into Spanish, with a pantomime of someone cutting a messy slice of pie. I gouged another wedge of cheese loose.

"Stop chavelling that cheese!" Gustavo demanded melodramatically.

"Have you heard about the chavelling salesman?" Roger asked.

"Yes indeed," I said. "Hide your young cakes."

As the day brightened, filtered light poured through a skylight overhead. The rest of the curved ceiling was covered with long white Styrofoam squares. A sink, refrigerator, and gas hot-plate were at the far side of the hut, next to open crates filled with fresh tangerines, apples, cabbages, potatoes, and onions. A net bag held carrots, cucumbers, and squash. Sausages hung from a string. Finishing his coffee, Tom took two cutting boards from the sink and handed them to Minolo and Juan, along with half a dozen sausages for them to skin with paring knives. It was Tom's turn to cook, and he was planning a kale-and-sausage soup, which was to simmer all day.

After breakfast, we packed sandwiches for lunch, put on exposure suits and fishermans' oilskins, and climbed into the Zodiacs. There were many experiments to conduct, and the blustery day was just calm enough to launch the boats. My Zodiac included Tom, Juan,

Kate, and Roger, who was at the helm. When we saw whale tails and a lot of spray and movement in the distance, we headed straight for them, slowing down after fifteen minutes as we spiraled close. A confusion of flippers and tails slid across the surface of the water, where a number of whales were rolling. One whale in the middle of the group suddenly rolled upside-down.

"How many whales are we looking at?" I asked.

"That female," Roger said, outlining her body in the air, "is belly-up at the surface, trying to avoid mating. There's a male on the near side of her"—he pointed out a long, dark shape—"and also one on the far side of her." Now I saw the two males surfacing and blowing. "But if you look down, you'll see that there's a third male holding his breath underneath her, waiting for her to turn from the belly-up position, in which her blowhole is underwater and she can't breathe, to a belly-down position. She has to roll in order to breathe. Sooner or later, she's got to roll toward one of the two males flanking her. But when she's on enough of an even keel to be breathing air, she's accessible to the male who's underneath her. A mating group often includes this many males. If one of them leaves the group after he's mated with the female, then she can easily avoid the other two, and that means they won't get a chance to mate with her. If there are four males, though, and if two mate with her and leave, the other two won't necessarily get a chance to. So you get into very complicated situations, in which some males have no opportunity to mate with a particular female."

"This doesn't sound very cheery from the female's point of view," I said. Rolling over to breathe, the female whale gave out an aggressive growl as a male put a flipper across her back. With a twist, she pulled a few yards away and the three males followed her. She rolled onto her back again.

"Okay. Let's look at it from her point of view," Roger said. "If you are a female coming into this area, you don't have any means of choosing a mate, and chances are you're going to be raped repeatedly by males in a group. But there is one way you can favor a particular male. You can wait until you're mated with by the male

you wish to be mated with and then just leave the area. You get the
hell out as fast as you can. I think that's what's happening here."

As we watched the melee of mating, it was tough to tell which
parts belonged to which whale. A shadow climbed the female's belly,
and she flailed and swerved. Being upside-down did not protect her
from mating, because a male whale's erect penis, which is tapered,
can be as much as nine feet long. And it is controllable. A human
male cannot voluntarily move his penis by more than a few millimeters, but a right whale can move his all around like a long finger. It's
stored inside the whale, and when he's swimming around, it is
invisible. He also has internal testes. Human males have external
testes, because the testes must stay cool or the male won't be fertile.
Nobody really understands how whales can have their testes inside,
for streamlining, and not have their fertility affected. When a
whale dies, the penis is extruded. All European woodcuts depicting
dead sperm whales on a beach show a whale with an extended penis.
Every sperm whale north of forty degrees north latitude is male; so
every sperm whale stranded in Europe was a male.

Half a mile away, a whale's tail hovered in the air, splashed down,
then hovered again, this time for quite a while. He was only indulg-
ing in a favorite whale pastime; they entertain themselves by balancing their tails in the air. It is like someone holding a stick on the tip
of his finger.

Hours had quickly passed, and Kate broke out a sack of ham-and-
cheese sandwiches and small, sweet Argentine tangerines and passed
them around. Roger unwrapped a camera with a telephoto lens,
stood up, and photographed the fine display of mating and balancing
whales. Then he carefully wrapped the camera and stowed it in a
watertight trunk.

"In right whales, you have a very curious thing," he said, sitting
down. "The testes of a male blue whale, the largest whale in the
world, weigh about seventy kilos—a hundred and fifty-four
pounds—combined. You might ask: 'What do the testes of a male
right whale weigh, since it's a much smaller animal?' The answer is

one metric ton—twenty-two hundred pounds! These are the largest testes ever recorded in any animal."

"Why should there be such a difference?"

"For a very interesting reason, which has been most clearly demonstrated among the primates," Roger said. "Thirty-three species of primates have been studied in which something is known about both the weight of the testes in the male and their techniques of mating—whether a given female mates with one male or with several males. If you plot a graph of testes weight versus body size, you discover that those primate species in which several males mate with the same female have testes that are much larger than those in which only one male mates with a female. The classic example is the difference between a chimpanzee and a gorilla. The chimp, a species that has multiple matings, has testes much larger than a human being's, and they're very visible. Now consider the great, big, brutish gorilla male, which has total dominion over a group of females. Someone may eventually challenge him for his position, but until then when he mates with a female, he has no doubt that he is the father of her offspring. He therefore has to produce only enough sperm to fertilize an egg in each of his females. The result is that he has such small testes that when you dissect a male gorilla, you can hardly find them. The reason a chimpanzee has such large testes is that when he mates with a female, she has probably just mated with another male, and if he is to have any hope of success, he must produce enough sperm to wash out the contribution of sperm from the previous male and replace it with his own."

"And in the case of human beings?" I asked.

Roger laughed. "Yes, that's the tantalizing question. If you look at the chart, everything with outsized testes is several males mating with a female, and everything with small testes is a monogamous species in which females and males are faithful to each other. Human beings lie right on the borderline, and it's hard to predict which side they're going to fall toward. That may partly explain our marital ambiguities and the problems we cause ourselves socially.

Consider whales and their mating systems. Right whales are the supreme example of incredible sperm competition. A male who is going to mate with a female is competing with a whole series of males. When you watch the mating groups here, for instance, you see that a single female mates with several males in the course of an afternoon. If you are a male, probably your best strategy for any given mating session is to be the last, not the first. The male that mates last is the one that has the most sperm of his left in the female. He is presumably producing colossal quantities of sperm and flooding it into the female's reproductive tract, trying to fill it as much as possible with his sperm and, again, trying to wash out the sperm of the previous males."

"Ballenas!" Juan called, pointing a few hundred yards behind us, to where three whales were swimming in tandem. A mother and baby were being followed at a short distance by an adolescent whale.

"That's probably her calf from the previous year," Roger said, and went on: "One of the things I've noticed over the years is often when several males are trying to mate with a female, one of the males will try to push the female under the water so that he can mate with her, and it's always a failure. And I thought, what a bozo this whale is, until I finally realized that I was the one who was a bozo. What I was watching was one male pushing a female under for the purpose of letting another male mate with her. That's not a bad strategy if what you want to do in a few hours' session is be the last to mate. But it's the kind of strategy that would also invite cheating. The best way to get around cheating would be to be in a group of males that included male relatives of yours. Then even if it's another male who gets in the successful last mating—the mating that will result in fertilization of the egg—the sperm that won would at least have most of your genes in it. But now you've got a problem. You can't identify your father, nor can he identify you. You haven't got a clue who he is. So you can't go join your father's mating group. But there is a male relative that you *can* identify, and that's your brother. You know who your mother is—you lived with her for a year or fourteen months before you were weaned—and if she comes back with a young calf and if it's a male, it's your brother and you know that.

"Well, here's where a truly fascinating thing comes up. The females with calves in Argentina are spread out along the same section of coast. They move together as a group, but their interactions at very close range are fairly infrequent. For the most part, they're strung out like beads on a string. They seem to be aware of where the others are, and they avoid one another in some ways but stick together very strongly. A female with one calf might swim up to another female with a calf, and everything is fine until the calves begin to play. The second the calves begin to play, the mothers break it up, working hard if necessary. They will swim assiduously between the two calves until each one gets her calf to swim off with her. Why? Because at this time of the year, the mother is starving. She has swum up from the feeding grounds, which are maybe a couple thousand miles away, without eating; she has given birth to a calf without eating, and has pumped a blubber coat onto it and increased its size enormously without eating; and she must return to the feeding grounds without eating. So she has been starving for several months. Every single motion that her calf makes she pays for, so what she does is lead it away from any kind of play—except the one kind she tolerates—she appears to tolerate play with an adolescent.

"Now, here comes our big frustration. We can identify whales best when we're looking directly down on top of them from a plane, because of their callosities [the bumps on their heads], whose pattern, placement, size, and form are different on every whale—we can easily tell them apart. But to follow the whales that way means paying two hundred dollars an hour to fly, and that's ruinously expensive. We can't afford to hang around long enough to watch much behavior, so we really don't know who these adolescents are that the females allow to play with their young. My suspicion is that they are older brothers and that what the mothers are doing is allowing brothers to get to know each other, so that later on they can become a more effective mating group, which in turn will ensure that her genes have a better chance of being passed on. We have one example of a mating group that stayed together for almost six weeks and traveled together for 185 miles. That means that there would be a chance for reciprocal altruism to go into effect. One male could help another today, and the other returns the favor tomorrow."

The adolescent whale drifted away from the mother and calf and began swimming slowly toward us, curious, no doubt, about a black rubber fish with many moving animals inside it. Then, blowing and tossing its tail, it dove directly under the boat. A long shadow, spotted with white at one end where the head's callosities glowed, floated underneath us for what seemed like minutes. It surfaced with a blow, rolled onto one side, and curved back toward us. Its tail had a slightly ragged line of notches, probably orca bites.

"Watch the tail," Roger warned. "If you ever see the tail coming down on you, leap fast into the water. Don't even think about it. Just jump. You don't want to get crushed between the boat and the tail." But the whale dove back underneath the boat, rolling onto one side, apparently so it could look at us, then surfaced on the other side and blew a fine mist, which poured over us, smelling sweet, like wet fur. The whale circled back again and this time swam right alongside the boat. Its huge head, floating on the surface, came so close I could look into the blowholes, opening and closing like two hands held palms-together and pressing wide apart like a bellows at fingers and thumbs. A few hairs sprouted around the blowholes. Still quite young, the whale was only about thirty-five feet long. It had thick callosities, with whale lice clinging all over them, and the black skin was streaked with fine lines of the sort one sees on a window after rain. Males tend to have more callosities, as well as scrapes along their backs from fighting; and we thought this was a male. It brought its mouth toward the boat and nudged it. Stretching over the gunwale, I touched its head delicately with one finger. Its whole body flinched. How can it be so sensitive that it can feel a human's slightest touch? I wondered. And it's skin was startlingly soft, like oiled chamois.

The sound of light artillery in the distance drew our gaze to two breaching whales, hurling themselves into the air, half-twisting, like a top running out of momentum, and splashing onto their sides in thick geysers of spume. By then, the adolescent had returned to the other side of the boat and was languidly rubbing one whole flank along the gunwale, as a cat might twine between someone's legs. After several passes, it swam away, leaving "footprints" behind it—large pools of smooth, calm, glassy water. The afternoon had already dwindled into the short hours of twilight. The falling sun had lost a lot of its heat, and we were all starting to feel chilly, so we headed back to camp. Near shore, we watched a whale roll over and over; there were many shells and pebbles in the shallows, and it could have been scratching the way a dog enjoys rolling in the dirt. It waved a flipper in the air, followed with the semaphore of its flukes. At last we landed on the beach and dragged the Zodiac into the boathouse.

At sunset, an orange fur lay along the horizon and the sea grew blue-gray. Areas of wet sand, exposed by the withdrawing tide, shone like an array of hand mirrors. Venus appeared overhead, bright as a whistle blow, with the small pinprick light of Mercury at its side. As night fell, the shallows shimmered like ice and the frantic winds began to sound like freight trains. The wind has a large vocabulary in Patagonia. It shushes through the thorn bushes, it rattles the corrugated-metal walls; it flutes through the arroyos; it makes the cliffs sound as if they are being scoured by a wire whisk. A night heron cried *owow*. A whale sneezing loudly sounded as if an iron patio chair were being dragged across a cement floor. In the distance, three whales blew bushes of mist. Over the apricot horizon, the sky billowed upward, pale green to thick teal to a translucent wafer of azure blue.

Dinner began late by American standards. Around 10:00 P.M. the camp gathered in the Peludo Palace, where a gas lamp at one end of the table coated the room in a dusty glow. The wind howled now like a banshee, and everyone joked heartily in Spanish, English, and pantomime. Tom, a born comedian, told us some of his April-first escapades. One year, dressed as Darth Vader, he went door to door in Concord, Massachusetts, pretending to sell roofing. Another time, he dressed as Captain Hook, his wife dressed as Peter Pan, and his children dragged an *Exxon Valdez* oil spill (brown plastic garbage bags) as part of a family skit. While Tom ladled up the camp's favorite dinner—his kale soup, with garbanzo beans, kidney beans, onions, carrots, spices, and two kinds of sausage—he did a small cavalcade of impressions, ending with his forte, an exaggeratedly Germanic entity known as the Angstmeister. Each time Tom said *Angstmeister,* his eyebrows twitched and he went into pure Dr. Strangelove. The kale soup was so good we decided it deserved a formal name, but in the end we couldn't decide between Sopa Perdido and Angstmeister Stew. Gustavo pulled a plastic bag filled with dozens of baguettes from behind the refrigerator and began breaking off hunks. Tom leapt to his feet and became Bruce Lee attacked by six savage loaves of French bread. His shadows, leaping around the Quonset hut, mixed with those of diners animated by laughter. The propane lamp flickered. The winds caterwauled and whistled. We could as easily have been sitting in an Antarctic station, pegged out against the elements, or in a Neanderthal cave, drawn to the spectral glow of a fire. Minolo poured wine, beer, and Coca-Cola. Anita passed a salad of raw vegetables dressed with mayonnaise. Talk turned to sports. Judy, learning that I had once taught in Pittsburgh for three years, asked if the town was sports-minded. And I explained that the town was so besotted with football that when I left, I suggested to one of the deans that the signs on bathrooms in the university be changed from Men and Women to Tight Ends and Wide Receivers. The English speakers tried to translate this conversation into Spanish and only managed it when Tom jumped to his feet and did a Knute Rockne play-by-play explanation on the side of the refrigerator. Minolo told a joke about a man who encountered a friend of his whose job was at a sawmill, and Kate translated it phrase by phrase: The friend has many large scars across his face. "What happened to you?" the man asks. "Oh, we were betting on who could get closest to the saw," the friend answers. "I presume you won," the man says. "No, actually," his friend replies. "I came in fifth."

When at last we finished a dessert of *dulce de leche* poured over bananas, it was nearly midnight. We all piled plates into the sink. There was no running water, so the next day we'd wash them in the ocean. With a flashlight, I hunted my way back to the tent, behind a sheep fence and among a clutch of thorn bushes, on the ledge of the beach; zipped my tent shut; and crawled into my sleeping bag.

Fifteen minutes later, I heard footsteps outside. "Asleep yet?" Kate said. "I think there's an orca calling. Come on down to the beach."

At the shoreline, Tom was holding a tape recorder attached to a hydrophone line running out into the bay. Over the years, Roger had produced a library of right-whale recordings. Right whales make many different sounds: funny, serious, strange, underwater, in the air. Probably, they mean a variety of things; it's more mystery that remains to be solved. Despite the full moon, the sea and sky blurred in a creamy fog both eerie and radiant. Small green bioluminescent creatures flashed from the shallows. Whales glittered as they surfaced, and the moon seemed only their reflection. Close to shore, a right whale blew loudly. Another whale sneezed. The hydrophone picked up a stretched meow. No orcas were calling, but many right whales sighed and bleated through the pallid fog under the brilliant moon. Shivering, we decided to call it a night and returned to our tents and huts for a chilly sleep.

Over the next few days, camp life continued on its routine of hard work by day and antic bilingual meals at night. The ocean was too cold to bathe in, and people took turns driving an old pickup truck into Puerto Madryn to fill up the drinking-water jugs and buy fresh food. Inflation had skyrocketed in Argentina, and a truck bought for $2,000 ten years before was now worth several times that. But no one could afford to sell his truck, since new ones were much more expensive, whereas repairs were relatively cheap. All machinery— cars, generators, pumps—was in a perpetual state of mended dereliction. The camp's generator wasn't working, and the water tanks behind the house were also broken. Sometimes, dead rats were found floating in them, and we joked about passing out drinking water *con rata* or *sin rata*, as if they were just hairy ice cubes. Luckily, a workman was putting things back in order.

Although a core group of researchers remained in the camp, dozens of new people arrived and others departed. Doug Allen, an underwater photographer, who had curly red hair, a sunburn, and a thick Scottish accent, dropped by regularly and charmed us with his stark independence and gentle gregariousness, a combination very Patagonian. We adopted his word *suss*, which means to spy out something. One day, he casually reported that when he was in the water that morning, filming, he got too close to a calf and was walloped on the back of the head hard enough "to see stars." He believed that it was an accident, but he was clearly shaken; nevertheless, he would go out filming close to whales again the next day. A British filmmaker, John Waters, and his wife and their six-week-old baby, who had been born in a nearby town, came to live in camp for a while. A Japanese film crew stopped by for two days of filming. Whale researchers from Puerto Madryn came and went, as well as two game wardens. The New York Zoological Society, which ran and supported the camp, in part, had arranged for members on a guided tour of Patagonia to drop in for an hour or so. Another, similar group, we were delighted to discover, included John Emlen, the now-retired field biologist who had inspired Roger, George Schaller, and many other scientists to go out and study the ways of animals in the wild.

What drew researchers, film crews, and tourists alike was not just the abundance of whales in the bays but the continuity of Roger's work. Just as the callosities on right whales' heads made individuals easy to identify, so did the markings on the tails of humpbacks. But humpbacks are difficult to study. They have never been observed mating, for example. At the whale camp, researchers could live and work very close to right whales and watch their social behavior and record their sounds. Roger felt lucky to have found a species of whale that could be conveniently observed from shore. The camp was conducting the world's longest whale study based on known individuals. Each year researchers flew over in a plane, took photographs, and compared them to a file of known individuals. As of the most recent count, 960 whales had been identified. There were some right whales near South Africa, some off Australia, but only a total of about 3,500 left in the world. In the bays we explored, there were said to be about 1,200. Roger studied humpbacks in many areas, but right whales only in Patagonia, from this remarkable site.

One day, after the Japanese film crew packed up their gear and disappeared down the road in a tornado of dust, Roger and I sat on the porch steps and talked about Japanese whaling. If Roger had been especially generous with the film crew, who were making a two-hour documentary to be shown on Japanese television, it was because Japan desperately needs to change its attitude toward whales.

"The world has whales that appear to be intelligent, that can sing songs, change those songs, and use rhyme and human laws of composition," Roger said. "They form bubble nets of great intricacy and complexity and cooperatively feed together in clever ways. This is not the sort of animal you should turn into fat and oil and lipstick and margarine and cat food and corset stays. Whaling isn't something that has ever improved people very much. I'm going to Japan later in the year to talk with the Japanese people about whales. Once the people learn about this animal, their indifference, which is always based on ignorance, will be replaced by fascination, which is based on knowledge. I haven't the slightest doubt that their feelings about whales will change, and of course, they'll decry whaling, just as other peoples of the world have."

"The Japanese people have been good at protecting cranes, albatrosses, and other endangered animals," I mentioned.

"I have no quarrel with the Japanese people, only with their whaiers—ruthless hunters who have no future," Roger said. "I had a grandfather, a lumberman, who cut nothing but walnut trees, sometimes for whole years at a time, and that excess on his part, and on the part of his contemporaries, ensured that I would never have walnut except as the most exotic of woods. He was shortsighted. Was anyone warning him? I bet there was. Going on with the destruction of a species until it's brought to the point of extinction is madness—not just a little mad or slightly mad. It's authentic madness."

A sudden wave of laughter poured across a slope near the house, where six people were holding what appeared to be golf clubs. Some of them were wearing sunglasses and golf hats. Nine small numbered orange flags marked holes, and each person carried a bright-orange ball. Roger and I shook our heads in disbelief at the sight.

Unlikely as it may sound, the whale camp was home to the toughest—and most remote—miniature-golf course in the world. Patagonia's only miniature-golf course, in fact. Tom built it for Graham Harris's children and brought the clubs all the way from Boston. As another burst of laughter came from the fairways, we left the porch and moseyed over to the tournament.

"Yes," Tom said, chewing a big cigar, his green sunglasses flipped up at a right angle to his prescription glasses, "Golfito San José welcomes you." He handed me a putter and an orange ball. All around us, nestled side by side among the bushes and gouges in the earth, were the nine almost invisible holes of golf. The edges of the holes were lined with fossil oyster shells and miscellaneous bric-a-brac, including a whale tail vertebra, the keratin part of a horse's hoof, and chert (gemlike pebbles that cover most of the peninsula). Prickly quilimby bushes were everywhere. The holes themselves were rusty cans dressed with beach sand. The hazards were the arroyos, as well as live lizards, which sometimes darted into the open, guanaco droppings, seal bones, tufts of grass, splintered shells, dried ice-plant roots, and blowing dust. On the second hole there was also a "tarantula hazard"—the burrow of a trap-door spider that sometimes scrambled out to see what all the commotion was about. The fairways, also lined with fossil shells, made dog-legs and ran along cracks in the earth. One hole included a ski-jump rail from a salt train that used to provide one of Patagonia's few exports. Another hole required shooting down a spout made of an old stovepipe. Rather than a rusty can, the final hole was a deserted hairy armadillo den. The flagpoles were made from rods that once held up the snake fence. The flags themselves were ragged scraps of orange fabric, flown at one time as aerial guideposts. The "clubhouse" was an old gray wooden packing crate. Nothing was ever wasted in Patagonia.

Gustavo putted, missed the hole by inches, swore in Spanish, "Oh, the whore that gave birth to me!" and lifted up his ball, marking its final resting place with three sheep droppings. Gaby had her hair tied back with an orange bandanna. She stepped up to her ball, which was resting on an upside-down beer-bottle cap, swung her hips in an exaggerated golfing move, and chipped her ball past an eroded guanaco vertebra and close to the hole. Anita, in a blue surfing T-shirt, got ready to putt.

Tom put his hand out and said, "Nope. One of the laws of this game is: When a burying beetle crosses the fairway, you don't shoot. It's a beetle hazard." We watched a glossy black beetle run across the dirt and disappear under a bush.

"Ah yes. Silly me, I forgot," Anita said. Then she took her shot, sending the ball over a bird skeleton and down a drop into the center of a thorn bush.

Suddenly, a whale breached about half a mile offshore and we stood, clubs hanging idle, and watched in wonder as it breached again and again. What power it must have taken to lift fifty tons of solid animal out of the water and twirl it around in the air. Still, the motion looked balletic—floating, graceful, and controlled. A few hundred yards south, another whale got in the mood like an evangelist at a tent meeting, leapt into an aisle of air, and started breaching, too.

In the evening I shifted my gear to the corrugated-metal hut on top of the hill behind the house, from which I'd have a panoramic view of the bay. This meant climbing a steep, skiddy winding path for three hundred feet whenever I needed something. But the hut rattled wonderfully in a dozen registers of metal and wood, and became an instrument played by the Patagonian winds. The walls gyrated like a rocket during lift-off. The wind slaloming through the dunes made an hallucination of footsteps outside. Quite often, the roof banged so hard at opposite corners that it sounded as if a hand were ripping it straight off. Inside, a narrow bed attached to one wall had a small window beside the pillow, cut there at the request of a young woman who wanted to see the moon rising as she fell asleep. On another wall, a window looked out over camp and the sea. A third wall was a bookcase with peeling shelves. The fourth had nails as clothes hooks, with a warped table beneath. The entire hut was only about six feet by eight feet, and perhaps seven feet high. A candle sat in a wobbly three-legged holder, and poured wax down its shoulders as it guttered in the draft. Although the hut got hot during the day, it was not wise to leave the door open, because sheep or guanacos or pit vipers might wander in.

At sunset, Roger and I sat on the jawbone bench on the porch of the main house and watched the horizon's simmering cauldron of red. Enthralled by Doug's account of swimming close to whales, I was puzzled by how few of the people in camp had been tempted to do the same.

"It's those last ten feet," Roger said, leaning against the wall that had grown warm from the late-afternoon sun. "That's where most people find their nerve breaks down."

"But that's what life's all about," I said. "That's where you find all the intimate details. How awful it would feel, at the end of your life, to look back and know that if you had just stayed in there a few more feet, you would have witnessed something truly astonishing."

Roger nodded. He had spent his life walking the narrow corridor between the whale's world and the human's world. "I think you can know people quite well by the distance at which they drop back. Think how many miles all the people here had to fly, how many hardships they had to endure, how many hours they had to wait, how many people they had to deal with, just to get down here. It's like that every year. Some people drop out before they ever leave the States. Some are fine doing research on the shore. Some can even tough it out in the boats, but they panic at the thought of being in the water with whales. Some can get into the water and watch at a distance—but the last ten feet horrify them. Despite all the rigors and turmoil they've gone through to get here, despite their fascination with whales, which they spend their lives studying, they just can't face those last few feet. I don't think this is limited to whales. It has to do with the way a person needs to know life."

At the south end of the bay, a whale lifted its tail into the air and held it there, drifting downwind for five minutes. Then it swam back upwind, turned around and put its tail in the air, and drifted downwind again. Roger slapped his knee in delight. The whale was "sailing," using its broad tail in place of canvas and catching a stiff breeze to blow it across the bay. Right whales sometimes practice sailing for half an hour at a time; it appears to be one of their favorite sports. You'd think many animals would sail, since it saves energy and is probably fun. But the only other animals that do it are three species of jellyfish. When you get into the upper latitudes—the roaring 40s, the frantic 50s, and the screaming 60s, as scientists refer to them— you have perfect conditions for sailing. Why waste all that time and energy wiggling your tail violently back and forth to swim if you can just put it up in the air and sail?

As evening deepened, we sat quietly, watching the upside-down whale, the wind behind its broad tail, still sailing merrily across the bay. Close in, the ocean seemed to be moving fast from right to left. But on the horizon, it didn't seem to be moving at all.

"The whole thing is a giant wheel," Roger said, holding an open hand up and tilting it slowly, "turning just as the planet is turning." Three oystercatchers flew low across the sand in front of us, scolding a petrel until it flew out of their territory.

"No time to dawdle," Tom said as he and the chicos bustled in and out of the house, busily constructing things out of cardboard, coat hangers, duct tape, and scraps. That night was Halloween, and everyone had been invited to the fiesta, but they had to come in costume—a challenge to those of us living in camp with limited resources. Soon whale researchers from Puerto Madryn began to arrive with their families, bringing food and costumes, and everyone was eager to see old friends and talk shop with colleagues they hadn't seen for many months. A brass bell summoned us at last to the Peludo Palace. Our normal squadron of twelve had swollen to twenty-five, with children dressed as ballerinas, clowns, and pirates racing about, fake daggers drawn.

At last, the costume parade began. Juan had built himself a large guanaco head out of cardboard. John, disguised as a mosquito, wore a pair of welders' goggles on his head and a boat propeller lashed to his back. Rubén, a visiting airplane pilot, stomped in as Rambo, complete with fake muscles and fake bombs. His wife, Yvonne, shuffled along as an armadillo, covered in corrugated roofing. I arrived dressed as a weather system, *la tormenta,* wearing silver asbestos flame-proof boots, a fake-leopard-skin jumpsuit, and a silver collar, with my long, thick hair attached to a trellis of coat hangers. I carried a lightning bolt cut out of cardboard and covered with silver-foil liners from chocolate bars. Tom and three of the chicos paraded in last, dressed as a long, sprawling right whale, made from black plastic garbage bags stretched over a skeleton of wire, baleen made from long grasses, a cardboard tail, and cut-up plastic-foam cups pasted on the head as callosities. With a tank of compressed air, Tom made the regular sound of blows, and the four-man-whale lurched around the room like a Chinese dragon, to the squealing delight of the children. Later, as we ate our dinner of cold cuts, hot dogs, and cake, a loud racket of artillery fire began. This time it was not breaching whales we heard but genuine artillery. Outside the hut, I saw red rockets flash along the horizon, followed by explosions of white. The Argentine Navy had begun target practice over the ocean, no doubt to the terror of the whales.

After dinner, I sussed my way up the hill with the aid of a flashlight, closed the door with a clang, and climbed into my sleeping bag on the cot. Orion was just starting to rise and I could see it through the window beside my head. Up north, Orion tossed one leg over the horizon as it rose, but it appeared to rise upside-down, feet first, its sword stars gleaming. Of course, it was not Orion but I who had changed position. Still, it was strange to find the sun rising and setting in unfamiliar directions, and the constellations leaping skewed out of the blackness. Venus, *la lucera*, rose early and stayed late; steady as a pinhole, it shone hard and white, with the small bed-light of the planet Mercury beside it. I had brought along a Whitney's star-finder and a "pop-up sky," and when I held them overhead, I spotted Cetus, the whale, slithering out of the north, and Delphinus, the dolphin, arcing directly overhead. According to Greek myth, the sea god Poseidon was lonely without a wife and sent a dolphin messenger to court Amphitrite, one of the sea nymphs. The dolphin was so persuasive that she agreed to mary Poseidon, who in gratitude set the dolphin to swim forever among the stars. In another story, Ovid claims that Delphinus is the dolphin that saved the life of the seventh-century poet and musician Arion. According to this tale, Arion was returning home to Greece from a tour of Sicily when some of the sailors plotted to rob and kill him. Outnumbered and apparently doomed, he asked to be allowed to sing a final song. So hypnotic was the music that it attracted a group of dolphins. Seeing them, he dove into the water, and one of them carried him home safely to Greece. In this story, it is Apollo who adds a dolphin to the constellations, along with the lyre of Arion.

Throughout history, dolphins have been credited with acts of intelligence and generosity of spirit. Indeed, many cultures have stories of dolphins saving people's lives. Karen Pryor, a longtime researcher, was once asked about dolphins pushing people to shore, and she said: "Well, you never hear from the drowning people dolphins pushed *away* from the shore." For all we know, there may be some truth in that. But dolphins do seem to enjoy playing with humans, and they do so in many bays around the world. One of the strangest dolphin stories emerged in 1989, when the Iranian government accused the United States of using "kamikaze" dolphins to mine harbors and boats. A similar scenario was proposed by the seventies film *The Day of the Dolphin*, in which a dolphin researcher, played by George C. Scott, finds his dolphins nabbed by thugs hoping to use them to deliver a bomb to the president's yacht. In his memoir, *Behind the Dolphin Smile*, dolphin trainer Richard O'Barry confides that he was once approached by the CIA to train dolphins for military use. The Navy consistently denies that it is doing any such research with dolphins. But insiders have described a Navy technique of training dolphins to ram a person in the abdomen, an adaptation of the dolphin's natural strategy of killing a shark by ramming it in the gills. What disturbs many people is the idea that dolphins—peaceful creatures that since the time of Pliny the Elder have been observed befriending human beings—are now being trained to kill. Dolphins are the most intelligent whales; and they can transfer information among themselves. Chimps can learn sign language, and one was observed teaching the language to her offspring. Suppose dolphins, which may be even more intelligent than chimps, started training their young in the techniques of killing humans? Consider how fast the "friendly whale phenomenon" swept through the gray-whale population. It wouldn't be long before the oceans were full of killer dolphins. Instead of our having a friend in the sea, we would have a deadly new enemy, specifically trained to kill us. When people complain about using animals for warfare, the Navy sometimes counters that the Canine Corps, used in WWII, saved many Allied lives. But they neglect to point out that those dogs went through long, arduous periods of de-training before they were returned to society, precisely so that they wouldn't kill people. If the Canine Corps had escaped or been released before they were de-programmed, they would have savaged civilian populations, preying especially on children, who are drawn to dogs as friendly playmates. With such ominous thoughts, I closed my eyes under the gaze of Delphinus, let my mind fill with the tumultous sounds of the wind, and fell asleep.

We say dawn breaks, as if something were shattering, but what we mean is that waves of light crest over the earth. The next morning, rinsed by those light waves, I walked along the beach, beside overhanging cliffs, and realized what an ancient place the camp was based on. The cliffs were almost solid fossil—uplifted prehistoric seabeds. Fossil oysters large enough to have held more than a pound of meat jutted out from the top, and fossil sand dollars perhaps seventy million years old lay at the base. Fossil sea lions, crabs, and whales littered the beach. There was an array of dead penguins and other birds on the beach, too. In the tide wrack were feathers, flippers, mummified animals, and countless shells. Dunes of stones led down to the water. One thing the ocean does exceptionally well is sort according to size. There were fields of large stones, then ridges of medium-size ones, then areas of even smaller stones. Looking out at the water, I saw a mother and baby whale lolling in the shallows. When had they arrived? Rolling on her side, the mother whale swung her flippers up and nursed the baby. When a pack of seals appeared, and began playfully to pester them, the baby snuggled up to its mother and cupped its flipper around her. The whales appeared to have stopped in the water, but the faster I walked toward them, the more they seemed to be just another yard ahead of me. Finally, I left them and headed for breakfast at the Peludo Palace.

After coffee, cheese, and cereal-crackers, Roger, Judy, and I climbed into a car with Rubén, the pilot, and set out for the airstrip half an hour away. Roger pushed the windshield-washer button, but nothing happened. "No skunks," he said in Spanish to Rubén. Patagonians call the squirting washers "skunks." As a car passed us from the opposite direction, its driver put a hand against the front window. Roger did the same. In Argentina, car windows are made to shatter utterly on impact, so that someone thrown through the window in an accident won't get slashed by glass. Unfortunately, a sharp flying stone can shatter the glass, too, so locals mistakenly think they can hold the windshield together with one hand. Whenever they pass an oncoming car, they prop a hand against the windshield.

Rubén's Cessna 182 was hangared at a nearby *estancia,* next to a long dirt airstrip. Each year Rubén flies Roger and other camp people out over the bays, to photograph whales. Because the plane's tail letters are LV-JCY, Roger's children used to call it Love Juicy. We climbed aboard and headed for the southern bay, which was said to be packed with whales. Rubén spotted whales in the water, flew straight to them, and did steep turns around them at three hundred feet, while Roger knelt and shots pictures of each animal. On an outline of the peninsula, I penciled in ♀ + ♀ + (two females, with one calf each) at our approximate position and, a little farther along, another ♀ +. As Roger finished each roll of film, I handed him a fresh one and marked the number of the roll and the date on the used one. After an hour of steep turns, we headed back to the airstrip. Rubén rolled out a yellow drum of gas and attached a green hand pump to it that looked like a coffee grinder. Judy pumped gas from it into a hose, which Rubén fed into a can topped with chamois (to filter out contaminating water), and pumped the gas from the can into the wing. It was a lengthy process. Then Rubén and Judy climbed aboard and in a moment we were airborne again, flying over the great flat deserts. Sheep trails converged and overlapped at the far-flung water tanks. In a few minutes, Rubén landed on a dirt road, paused just long enough for me to get out, turned the plane around, and took off to spend the day photographing whales. Three kilometers from camp, at the spot where the camp road meets the main one, I began walking down roads that resembled gutted riverbeds. A herd of ten guanacos took flight when they saw me. Two mares ("rabbits with white miniskirts," Roger called them) scampered away as I passed, and lizards swaggered under bushes. In an hour, I stood on the rise overlooking camp. Two boat trails leading from the boathouse to the water told me that the chicos were already out at work. When I got to the house, I was struck by the stillness and silence. Everyone was gone. Climbing up to my hut, I took off my jacket and walked out to the cliff hut, a little less than a mile away. An icy morning had turned into a torrid noon, which would no doubt drop to near freezing by nightfall. From the cliff hut, I saw below in the water the same mother and baby I had seen earlier. She had a large, distinctive wound on one flank, and the callosities on her snout formed a sort of parenthesis. To some earlier observer, they resembled fangs, and thus she was named Fang. Her new calf nestled beside her. They had spent all morning close to camp. The sunlight made a glittering path over the water. Each time the whales surfaced, drops of water sparkled around them.

Fang and her calf were close below me, but the whole bay was a waltz of mother and baby whales. Right whales are pregnant for only about a year, which seems like a short time. After all, an elephant calf gestates for twenty-two months, and a whale is larger than an elephant. When an elephant calf is born it has to scramble up onto its legs, but a whale calf can go straight from the amniotic fluid of its mother's womb into the womb of the ocean. It doesn't have to support itself. Whales, being warm-blooded mammals, which breathe as we do, could, in principle, live on land, but if a whale were on land, its organs would be crushed under its own weight. It needs the water to support its massive size, which is one of the reasons stranded whales fare so poorly. Because a whale baby doesn't have to stand up, its bones are so flexible that you could take the rib bone of a baby whale and bend it back and forth as if it were made of hard rubber. Baby whales are virtually weightless. It's as though they were flying. Another lovely thing about whale mothers and babies is that a mother whale is herself 97 percent water. When she speaks, the sound she makes travels directly through the water, through her body and her womb, and her baby hears it. But because there is no air in the womb, the baby can't speak back. The baby must wait in the mother's womb for a year, listening, until it's born into a world where it can finally answer.

A newborn whale calf does not leave its mother's side but often swims along eye to eye with her. Sometimes the mother whale swims so that with every downstroke of her tail, she touches the calf. Sometimes the calf gets obstreperous and bangs into its mother, or even breaches onto its mother's back. Finally, she will lose her patience and punish it by rolling over quickly onto her back as the calf is ready to ram her for, say, the fifteenth time. Then she catches it by the small of its tail and holds it underwater so that it begins spluttering, wheezing, sneezing, coughing. In a little while she lets it go. After that, the calf resumes its eye-to-eye position and is careful not to act up again. Hungry calves will butt their mothers, climb all over them, and slide off them, trying to get their mothers to roll over and let them nurse. Occasionally, a mother will calm a hyperactive

calf by sliding underneath it and turning over to pick it up out of
the water and balance it on her chest, holding it between her flippers. Every now and then, with a flipper the size of a wall, a mother
reaches over and pats the calf sweetly.

For hours, I sat quietly and watched the busy nursery bay. Fang
rolled onto her weighty side, and her baby nursed. Then the baby
got rambunctious and strayed a little too far. Mother lowed to it in
a combination of foghorn and moo, calling it back within eyeshot.
From time to time, Fang submerged slowly, her tail hanging limp
and loose, trailing one tip of a fluke in the water. She made burpy
sounds, with occasional moans, and I think she may have been
napping.

When a whale sleeps, it slowly tumbles in an any-old-crazy, end-
over-end, sideways fashion, and may even bonk its head on the
bottom. Or it just lies quietly, looking like a corpse. When it rises
again to breathe in the midst of its sleep, it comes up as slow as a
dream, breaks the surface, breathes a few times and, without even
diving, falls again slowly toward the bottom. Right whales sometimes
sleep in the mornings on calm days in Argentina, and some of them
seem to be head-heavy, with light tails. The result is that they fall
forward and their tails rise out of the water. Humpbacks are rarely
visible when they're sleeping, because they're less buoyant and usually sink fast. But the behavior of right whales is easy to study,
because they're at-the-surface whales. They're so fat that they float
when relaxed, and they spend a lot of time with their backs in the
air. When they're asleep at the surface, their breathing rate drops
tremendously, they don't close their nostrils completely between
breaths, and so sometimes they snore. In fact they make marvelous,
rude, after-dinner noises as they sleep. When they wake, they stretch
their backs, open their mouths, and yawn. Sometimes they lift their
tails up and shake them, and then they go about their business.
Often, they sleep at the surface so long on calm days that their backs
get sunburned; and then they peel the same way humans do, but on
a big, whale-size scale. The loose skin from their backs falls into the
water and becomes food for birds. When they breach, they shed a

lot of loose skin as they hit the water, and seagulls, realizing this, fly out fast to a breaching whale. Not much skin sheds from the tail. The gulls know that, and when a whale is merely hitting its tail on the water, they don't bother with it.

A gull swept down, pulled a piece of skin from Fang's back, and Fang, in obvious pain, shook her head and tail simultaneously, flexed almost in half, then dove underwater. The gull flew to another pair of whales nearby, attacked them, and went off. A bizarre habit had developed among the gulls in this bay. Instead of waiting for the whales to shed skin, they landed on the backs of whales and carved the skin and blubber off. Two species of gulls—the brown-headed gulls and the kelp gulls—yanked off long strips of skin and set up feeding territories on the backs of their own particular whales. When Roger first started studying right whales at Valdés Peninsula, he noticed that only brown-headed gulls were peeling the skin off the backs of sleeping, sunburned whales. Soon, however, the kelp gulls not only learned this technique but also began carving holes in backs. The result was that whales like Fang were pitted with craters made by gulls. When a gull landed on a whale's back, the whale panicked. This year there were fewer whales in the bay, and Roger thought the kelp gulls might have been chasing them away, to bays where kelp gulls don't yet know the tricks.

Juan appeared at the edge of camp, on foot, apparently hiking in from a walk to a neighboring bay. By the time I got back to the main house, he was just arriving, wearing shorts, a T-shirt, and a knitted hat.

"Tired?" I asked with an inflection that said, *I really hope you aren't.* "Want to go find some whales?"

He grinned. "Just let me get a Coke, then *vamos.*"

I put on a leotard and tights and began crawling into a half-inch-thick wetsuit that included Farmer John overalls, a beaver-tail jacket, boots, gloves, and a hood. There was so much neoprene in the suit, trapping air, that I'd need to wear weights around my waist to keep from bobbing on the surface.

Sitting on the porch whale skull, John watched me suit up. He looked anxious. "Be careful," he said. "This morning, I was out in a boat with Tom collecting breath samples and the calf of that mother over there"—he pointed to Fang and her baby, just around the curve of the beach—"rocked the boat with its flipper and gave us a scare."

To tell the truth, if I was going swimming I'd have felt much safer with Roger on board, but I had been waiting all week for the water to calm down and all afternoon for Roger to get back from flying. It was already past four, and I very much doubted that he intended to return before sunset. So, some of my caution evaporated, and I knew it was now or never.

Juan returned from the Peludo Palace and tugged on a thin wetsuit and boots, and we went down to the beach, where Minolo joined us in the Zodiac. As we pulled out, I saw John and Tom on the porch, standing next to the sighting scopes. Heading north along the bay, we came upon two mothers and calves, but the mothers were naturally protective of their calves and hurried them away. We wanted to find a young adult. Juan had been collecting loose skin for Judy and then going into the water to photograph the heads of the whales it came from in order to identify them. I hoped to join him. We searched for an hour but found none in the mood to be approached. Finally, we headed back toward camp and, coming around a bend, discovered Fang and her calf still playing. We cut the motor about two hundred yards from the whales. Juan and I slipped over the side of the boat and began to swim toward them, approaching as quietly as possible, so that they wouldn't construe any of our movements as aggressive. In a few minutes, we were only yards from the mother's head. Looking down, I saw the three-month-old baby beside her underwater, its callosities bright in the murky green water. Slowly, Juan and I swam all the way around them, getting closer and closer. The long wound on Fang's flank looked red and angry. When her large tail lifted out of the water, its beauty stunned me for a moment, and then I yanked Juan's hand, to draw his attention, and we pulled back. At fifty feet long, weighing about fifty tons, all she would have needed to do was hit us with a flipper to crush us, or swat us with her tail to kill us instantly. But she was moving her tail gently, slowly, without malice. It would be as if a human being, walking across a meadow, had come upon a strange new animal. Our instinct wouldn't be to kill it but to get closer and have a look, perhaps touch it. Right whales are grazers, which have balleen plates, not teeth. We did not look like lunch. She swung her head around so that her mouth was within two feet of me, then turned her head on edge to reveal a large white patch and, under that, an eye shaped much like a human eye. I looked directly into her eye, and she looked directly back at me, as we hung in the water, studying each other.

I wish you well, I thought, applying all the weight of my concentration, in case it was possible for her to sense my mood. I did not imagine she could decipher the words, but many animals can sense fear in humans. Perhaps they can also sense other emotions.

Her dark, plumlike eye fixed me and we stared deeply at one another for some time. The curve of her mouth gave her a Mona Lisa smile, but that was just a felicity of her anatomy. The only emotion I sensed was her curiosity. That shone through her watchfulness, her repeated turning toward us, her extreme passivity, her caution with flippers and tail. Apparently, she was doing what we were—swimming close to a strange, fascinating life-form, taking care not to frighten or hurt it. Perhaps, seeing us slip over the side of the Zodiac, she thought it had given birth and we were its young. In that case, she might have been thinking how little we resembled our parent. Or perhaps she understood only too well that we were intelligent beasts who lived in the strange, dangerous world of the land, where whales can get stranded, lose their bearings and equilibrium, and die. Perhaps she knew somehow that we live in that desert beyond the waves from which whales rarely return, a kingdom we rule, where we thrive. A whale's glimpse of us is almost as rare as our glimpse of a whale. They have never seen us mating, they have rarely if at all seen us feeding, they have never seen us give birth, suckle our young, die of old age. They have never observed our society, our normal habits. They would not know how to tell our sex, since we hide our reproductive organs. Perhaps they know that human males tend to have more facial hair than females, just as we know that male right whales tend to have more callosities on their faces than females. But they would still find it hard to distinguish between a clothed, short-haired, clean-shaven man and a clothed, short-haired woman.

When Fang had first seen us in the Zodiac, we were wearing large smoked plastic eyes. Now we had small eyes shaped like hers—but two on the front of the head, like a flounder or a seal, not an eye on either side, like a fish or a whale. In the water, our eyes were encased in a glass jar, our mouths stretched around a rubber tube, and our feet were flippers. Instead of diving like marine mammals, we floated on the surface. To Fang, I must have looked spastic and octopuslike, with my thin limbs dangling. Human beings possess such immense powers that few animals cause us to feel truly humble. A whale does, swimming beside you, as big as a reclining building, its eye carefully observing you. It could easily devastate you with a twitch, and yet it doesn't. Still, although it lives in a gliding, quiet, investigate-it-first realm, it is not as benign as a Zen monk. Aggression plays a big role in its life, especially during courtship. Whales have weapons that are equal in their effects to our pointing a gun at somebody, squeezing a finger, and blowing him away. When they strike each other with their flukes in battles, they hit flat, but they sometimes slash the water with the edge. That fluke edge could break a person in two instantly. But such an attack has never happened in the times people have been known to swim with whales. On rare occasions, unprovoked whales have struck boats with their flukes, perhaps by accident, on at least one occasion killing a man. And there are three reported instances of a whale breaching onto a boat, again resulting in deaths. But they don't attack swimmers. In many of our science-fiction stories, aliens appear on earth and terrible fights ensue, with everyone shooting weapons that burn, sting, or blow others up. To us, what is alien is treacherous and evil. Whales do not visualize aliens in that way. So although it was frightening to float beside an animal as immense and powerful as a whale, I knew that if I showed her where I was and what I was and that I meant her no harm, she would return the courtesy.

Suddenly, Juan pulled me back a few feet and, turning, I saw the calf swimming around to our side, though staying close to its mother. Big as an elephant, it still looked like a baby. Only a few months old, it was a frisky pup and rampantly curious. It swam right up, turned one eye at us, took a good look, then wheeled its head around to look at us with the other eye. When it turned, it swung its mouth right up to my chest, and I reached out to touch it, but Juan pulled my hand back. I looked at him and nodded. A touch could have startled the baby, which might not have known its own strength yet. In a reflex, its flipper or tail could have swatted us. It might not have known that if humans are held underwater—by a playful flipper, say—they can drown. Its flippers hung in the water by its sides, and its small callosities looked like a crop of fieldstones. When it rolled, it revealed a patch of white on its belly and an anal slit. Swimming forward, it fanned its tail, and the water suddenly felt chillier as it stirred up cold from the bottom. The mother was swimming forward to keep up with it, and we followed, hanging quietly in the water, trying to breathe slowly and kick our flippers as little as possible. Curving back around, Fang turned on her side so that she could see us, and waited as we swam up close again. Below me, her flipper hovered large as a freight elevator. Tilting it very gently in place, she appeared to be sculling; her tail, too, was barely moving. Each time she and the baby blew, a fine mist sprayed into the air, accompanied by a *whumping* sound, as of a pedal organ. Both mother and calf made no sudden moves around us, no acts of aggression.

We did not have their insulation of blubber to warm us in such frigid waters and, growing cold at last after an hour of traveling slowly along the bay with them, we began to swim back toward the beach. To save energy, we rolled onto our backs and kicked with our fins. When we were a few hundred yards away from her, Fang put her head up in a spy hop. Then she dove, rolled, lifted a flipper high into the air like a black rubber sail, and waved it back and forth. The calf did the same. Juan and I laughed. They were not waving at us, only rolling and playing now that we were out of the way. But it was so human a gesture that we automatically waved our arms overhead in reply. Then we turned back onto our faces again. Spears of sunlight cut through the thick green water and disappeared into the depths, a bottom soon revealed itself as tawny brown about thirty feet below us, and then the sand grew visible, along with occasional shells, and then the riot of shells near shore, and finally the pebbles of the shallows. Taking off our fins, we stepped from one liquid realm to another, from the whale road, as the Anglo-Saxons called the ocean, back onto the land of humans.

Chapter 4

WHITE
LANTERNS

Above San Diego, a smooth blue sky
stretched to the horizon. The Pacific
Ocean kept tapping its brains on the
coast. The air felt like hot silk as you
inhaled. It was spring in Southern
California, and at Sea World the
male turtles busily courted the
females by swimming straight up to
them, staring them in the face, and
waving their feet in a come-to-me
gesture. Flamboyant, stilty flamingos
had already built volcano-shaped nests
for their young, using their beaks as
trowels. My destination was an old
prefab freezer behind the Penguin
Encounter and a heavy door that
opened like a meat locker. Just inside,
in a cramped cloakroom, green
medical clothes hung from pegs, a
row of black rubber boots stood
below them as if left by a brigade of
firefighters, and street clothes
threatened to cascade from a high
shelf. Like a decompression chamber,
an air lock, or locker room, the
cloakroom was the place where

different worlds converged and linked with visible humanity: satchels, hats, purses, nametags—*belongings*—stowed with familiar gestures of care or disregard. Adding my clothes to the blur, I suited up, dipped my booted feet in a dishpan of disinfectant, and opened the door to Penguin Quarantine.

A rush of cold air chilled my face, a smell of oiled leather dusted with salt hit my nose, and I heard a fugue of high whistles that struck the ear right on the edge of pain. In twenty white wooden cribs scattered at floor level around the cold room, big, fluffy penguin chicks stood upright and toddled, whistled to the handlers, beak-fenced with one another, or peered over their cribs. Only six weeks old, these roly-poly king-penguin babies had a thick brownish down, like a carpet of the deepest plush pile. When not waddling around the crib or roughhousing with each other, they watched the roomful of bustling humans, whom they had adopted as their parents. Never mind that we were the wrong color, wrong size, had the wrong smell and wrong sound for adult king penguins. When their natural mothers gave birth to them on the sub-Antarctic island of South Georgia, it was already late in the season—too late for most of the chicks, which hatch from pear-shaped eggs, to survive. Frank Todd, formerly corporate curator of birds at Sea World in San Diego, collected these chicks as doomed eggs and brought them back in incubators and padded sea chests, to rear safely and then to distribute among the country's four Sea Worlds.

Each crib was lined with smooth dark pebbles of the sort they would find on South Georgia, and the cribs were arranged in rows, with narrow alleyways between them. If this was a rookery, it was an odd one of wood, paint, cement, and—strangest of all—a ceiling, but the essential layout seemed right. The short, potbellied penguins, whose necks wobbled with baby fat, huddled together like Russian businessmen in fur coats. Occasionally, one batted a neighbor away with its small flipper. Raucous, shrill, they high-whistled with operatic strength and waddled around their cribs to get a better view of the human beings, crying to each passerby to stop and feed them, cuddle them, or play. Weaving their beaks back and forth, they wrenched emotion from you, and now and then squirted a stream of yellow from their rear ends.

In a side room known as the kitchen, staff biologists and some of the one hundred or so volunteers tended the incubators and hand-reared fresh hatchlings. Two young men prepared the babies' formula, which they called penguin milkshake (a gruel of krill, predigested protein, Half & Half, herring fillets, and vitamins, kept at 90° F.), in pots of hot water and tested its warmth. The littlest babies were fed five times a day, the larger ones four times. A local hospital had donated two incubators it used for preemies, and inside the incubators, kept at a constant temperature and humidity, naked hatchlings flopped all over themselves in the spastic disarray we associate with newborns. Their eyes were not yet focused and alert, and they could manage only a weak little whistle. On the table in the center of the room a shoebox held cookies someone's mom had baked: white iced Scottie dogs and green iced turtles. One volunteer separated eight colors of yarn and made up flipper bands, which had to be changed every few days because the chicks grew so rapidly. With everyone wearing green medical clothes, the kitchen looked like an intensive-care ward, and everything was scrupulously clean. Penguins are unlikely carriers of disease, but U.S. poultry farmers fear contagion, so when Sea World brings back penguin eggs, the staff must go into quarantine with them for thirty days. A large dishpan of disinfectant was at every doorway, and volunteers in rubber boots dipped their feet hundreds of times in the course of their shift.

The air was cold enough to make my breath steam, but not the breath of baby penguins. Slender black beaks turned toward me, and pairs of black eyes, soft and glossy. The curiosity of penguins in the wild is legendary. They have been known to walk right up to scientists and carefully handle and study *them*. Penguins have no land predators. So they do not instinctively fear people. Just the opposite: They're curious and alert, and the babies waddle around like human two-year-olds, eager to untie one's shoelace, slide a beak up one's sweater sleeve, or muss one's bangs.

In a back room, which was kept warmer, I found a white wooden diapering table and more cribs, this time full of chicks only fourteen to sixteen days old, which looked much more fetal and helpless than those in the cold room. A heat lamp, attached to each crib, bathed them in red light. In each crib, six chicks huddled together—gawky, rubbery, scruffy. Sections of skin looked like black oilcloth tufted with stringy would-be feathers—down that was just beginning to form. Their whistle was a faint urgent chirp, and when they tried to sit up, they rocked unsteadily and leaned all over each other. They liked to sit with their heads tucked together at the center of a circle, as if conferring in private about the decline in the quality of care, or playing one-potato-two-potato. They needed the heat lamp and their collective body heat to stay warm. In the wild, hundreds of baby penguins huddle, with those at the outer edges frantically trying to push their way into the middle. A small animal has more surface area relative to its body mass than a large animal does, so it loses heat fast and has to make up for it with a high metabolic rate. A good example of this is a shrew, a little mammal whose metabolic rate is so high it has to feed all the time.

Occasionally, a penguin chick stood up and toppled forward onto its beak in a clumsy lunge, picked itself up, and toddled around again. White terry-cloth towels laid out over the pebbles in each crib provided a surface soft and motherlike to sit on and protect their beaks when they fell over, as they inevitably did. The towels and human attentions were no replacement for the constant touching they would have had in the wild, but every touch helps. From the time it hatches, a baby king penguin stands on a parent's feet and presses into the parent's tummy, against a toasty area just for that purpose, the brood patch (or pouch). Father and mother take turns holding the chick, which wouldn't survive long on the icy ground. Nuzzling is instinctive. After all, it takes between ten and thirteen months to fledge in the wild—a long time to be exposed to the cold and wet, and to surprise attacks from hungry, dive-bombing skuas.

I like handling newborn animals. Fallen into life from an unmappable world, they are the ultimate immigrants, full of wonder and confusion. Gathering a chick up in my hands, I lifted it by the feet and rump and held it close to my body to support its neck as I carried it to the diapering table. One has to be careful of the air sacs under the wings, which can be easily damaged. While heat lamps coated it in a warm glow, it sat on a towel with its rump against my belly, nestling against its ersatz mother, and mewed gently. The baby looked like an old weathered tennis ball whose covering had frayed. First, I checked its general health and pinched a little of the skin on the back of its neck. If the skin stood up, the penguin might be dehydrated. I checked its scruffy, leprous-looking skin, which was normal for a hatchling. The baby sat quietly as I measured its beak with calipers. Kings are docile penguins, although alert, and do not seem to mind our measuring the length of their feet and flippers, or their weight. I set the chick on a digital scale and wriggled my fingers over its head like a spider to hold its attention so it wouldn't toddle away. It turned its neck around and scratched its shoulder.

"Honey, you don't got nothing to preen. What are you preening? You're still naked," Carol Strilich, a staff member, said as she jotted down the figures from the scale.

I returned the chick to the towel and rested it against my tummy. Carol and Chuck Williams, another staff member, picked up chicks of their own. Swiveling, I reached across the table to grab a small mackerel fillet, and Carol called, "Watch it!" pointing to my chick, which had quickly backed up to the edge of the table and begun to topple. My hand caught it. Even though it couldn't stand properly yet, evolution had gifted it with thigmotaxis, an overwhelming drive to press up hard against a parent. When I reached for a fish, it scooted back to find my body. If we had been mother and child, we would constantly be making "spoons." To see how thigmotaxis worked, I set the chick against my tummy and cupped my hands over its head and shoulders, making a warm living pouch for it. Quieting, it looked up at me, blinked, opened its mouth, and whistled to be fed. Normally, it would tap on its mother's beak and the mother would open her beak and pour regurgitated fish down its throat. Just the sight of a parent's open beak would be signal enough for the baby

to open *its* beak and get ready for lunch. I opened my mouth wide
and leaned over in what I imagined would be a penguin mother's
posture, but my mouth was not the right shape to trigger the baby's
beak to open. Carol laughed. This had been tried before. However,
there was one sure-fire thing to do. Making a V of my first two
fingers, I slid them over the baby's beak, which sprang open. As with
many animals, it's the right shape that matters, the right semaphore.
With my other hand, I slid a syringe full of formula down the baby's
gullet, slowly pushed in the plunger, and pulled it out when empty.
The formula must make it past the trachea or the penguin will stop
swallowing. Like human beings, they have a gag response. This I
followed with two herring fillets, the baby's first taste of whole fish.
The exact amount of food had been worked out beforehand. Carol
kept a logbook of weights and feedings, and at this stage, the chicks
were fed 10 percent of their morning weight. They should grow
about 5 percent each day.

Carol, Chuck, and the other biologists, zoologists, and volunteers
had been raising all kinds of penguin chicks, but the king babies were
unanimous favorites.

"Some of the gentoo chicks we had last time would run right off
the table," Carol said. "Emperor chicks would turn around and try
to nail you with their beaks. Chinstrap babies are cute as can be but
a real handful. They're constantly snapping at and bickering with
each other. But king babies are so affectionate. They just want to
nuzzle."

"Most penguins aren't endangered," I said, "and yet you're raising them with extraordinary care."

"But they're extremely sensitive to disturbance. And they live in
a fragile ecosystem. We're hand-rearing them now, *before* they're
endangered and . . . well, the world being what it is . . . if there's
a problem in the future, then we'll be all set to help. If only we had
done that earlier with the condor." She slid her fingers over her
chick's beak and fed it a long swill of formula followed by two small
fillets. Then she weighed it again and carefully returned it to its crib.
Because their stomachs are so full, the penguins sometimes vomit

up their food while being set back in their cribs, so handlers must be exquisitely light-handed with them after a meal. Chuck weighed his chick, then set it back on the towel in front of him and leaned over to jot down the data in his logbook, nuzzling the chick with his chin, curling it into the crook of his arm.

At day's end, I stopped at Frank Todd's office and found him in the midst of hundreds of pages of raw journal entries, which he was trying to make sense of for a book. A slender man with a dark mustache and a slightly windswept look, he sat surrounded by clouds of cigarette smoke in a cluttered office. This would be his sixteenth season in the Antarctic, and there were suitcases with RAF tags in one corner, patches from the Antarctic stations he'd worked at on a wall and, around the room, an array of artifacts, including a taxidermized penguin and a coffee mug that had printed on it: LIFE IS A BITCH. THEN YOU DIE. Each year, Todd made his way to the Antarctic, collected up eggs that would otherwise perish, and flew them back to San Diego, then began the intensive process of incubating and hatching the chicks in quarantine, finally sending them to the several Sea Worlds, as well as to other zoos, on long-term breeding loan.

"We keep the polar penguins in relative darkness all summer long," Todd explained, "to provide the exact cycle of darkness and light they would find in the Antarctic. Remember, the seasons are reversed south of the equator. And when we bring back adults, we choose mated pairs, which we can determine from bioacoustics. It's tough to move highly specialized birds. Among other things, you need a refrigerated airplane."

"I know you have a great success rate, but do any of the hatchlings die?"

"Occasionally. Hunchbacks, for instance . . ."

"Hunchback penguins?"

"Oh yes. And some penguins refuse to molt on schedule or are undersized. We keep our polar penguins indoors, so we don't have the problem with their catching avian malaria from mosquitoes. Other zoos do have that problem."

"Penguins catch malaria?"

"It can be a serious problem. In the early sixties, all the penguins at the San Diego Zoo were thought to have died of malaria."

The Southern California sun poured through the window. "Don't you find your life split up? The contrast must be unnerving."

"Everybody's life is split up. People might not want to recognize it, but it's split up between what they do in the wintertime versus what they do in the summer. Or they devote a whole year to planning the two weeks they're going to spend on vacation. So the fact is that in October the people around here begin to detect a change in my behavior, which they attribute to something they refer to as polar fever. I don't consider that necessarily disruptive. It's an aspect of my life that I consider almost normal now. In the fall, that is the *northern* fall, my eyes start to turn to the south. In fact, that's the way it is for most scientists who work with penguins. We migrate, just like the animals we study." The very idea of it made his conversation swerve into a moment of heightened emotion: "There's no place as pristinely beautiful, where the air is clearer, the grandeur more overwhelming, the animals more fascinating. If God took a vacation on this planet, he would go to the Antarctic."

I volunteered to spend the following day in the cold room, tending the toddlers, who were already boisterous and quite tall (between one and two feet), full of energy, and insistently affectionate. With their big round bodies and small heads they appeared to be miniature bears. Their eyes were as black as poppy seeds. Long flippers—wings, actually—hung almost to their feet. Their heads nested in rolls of soft down, and they had little paintbrush tails. The toddlers looked so different from the spectacularly colored adult penguins they would become that the first scientists who saw them thought they were a different species altogether and named them woolly penguins. When a few weeks old, penguin chicks develop their thick down, and, round at the bottom and narrow at the top, they become pot-bellied dolls.

Their high-pitched whistle is the only noise that can penetrate the din of a rookery in the wild, where perhaps a hundred thousand birds are busily feeding, nesting, mating, and quarreling about territories. When the baby is big enough to leave behind in a crèche of hundreds or even thousands of babies, the parents go off to fish, and return to find legions of identical-looking babies in the rookery's madding crowd. It's confusing, and in some species a number of chicks will chase after one adult, thinking it's their parent, until eventually all but the real offspring realize they've made a mistake and drop out. Unimaginable as it may seem, parent and chick recognize each other *by voice.* Every bird has its own personal voiceprint. Just as a mother bat can recognize its pup's unique scent, a baby penguin can recognize its mother's whistle. I tried to imagine a rookery in which there are a hundred thousand separate, recognizably different whistles. As small as this room was compared to a rookery, it was full of confusing sounds and penguin whistles interrupting one another, overlapping or entwining until they quickly blurred into a solid wall of noise.

In Penguin Quarantine, handlers identify penguins by their flipper bands, color-coded strands of yarn or plastic encircling a flipper. Blue-red-right in the C-1 crib was the first penguin we fed in the cold room. I took the syringe, filled it with formula, made a V with my free hand to trigger the feeding response in the chick, and carefully slid the tube down the chick's throat. The chick was to get eight silvery whole fish from a bucket. By then, all the other chicks in the crib were lunging greedily for the food, and it was hard to remember which beak to feed. When I located blue-red-right by its flipper band, I tapped the side of its beak with a fish and the beak sprang open long enough for me to slide one fish down whole, then another, then the next six. In this crib, the chicks were hefty, around fifteen pounds, and full of spunk and clangor. When we finished with the first crib, we disinfected our hands in a tub of chlorine and water and moved on to the next one. The second group got more formula but only five fish. We dipped our hands again in chlorine and water. The third crib got more formula but two and a half fish, which meant ripping smelt in half with my hands, not one of my favorite things to do, especially when blankets of roe poured out. But the wail of the hungry penguins was heartbreaking, and it was designed to be. They opened their mouths, looked up at you in anguish, and swung their beaks back and forth, while squeaking plaintively, *Feed me! And if you can't feed me, cuddle me!* I leaned over and wrapped my arms around three penguin babies at once, pressed their silky down to my face, and hugged them tight. They relaxed. Then one of them put a beak up and tapped at my face. It was lunchtime. Didn't I know anything? As we traveled down the alleyways between the cribs to feed formula and smelt, penguins behind me tried to pull the towel out of my back pocket. They shrieked to get my attention. After feeding, they quieted down and stood like sentinels.

In the last crib, F-1, six chicks wailed for food and climbed all over each other to get at the smelts. One of them, brown-white-left, was a little smaller and less forthcoming than the rest and had its own light, tinkling music-box voice. Its flipper band made it look like a veteran of war, someone who had worked out an armistice with nature. When the time came to feed it, I wrapped one arm around it, to keep the others away, and gently tapped its beak with a smelt. Nothing can tug at your parenting instincts harder than a baby penguin looking up at you, eyes moist with helplessness, crying to be fed, just to be fed. Brown-white-left held its beak open wide between fish, and I noticed that its tongue was pale and thick, like the fuzzy comb of an iris, except that it had tiny backward facing hooks, a raspy surface to hold fish and urge them down the throat.

"Mind if I stroke?" I asked brown-white-left, so that it could hear the sound of my voice. I chatted to it about summer, the Antarctic, my home in the East, as I stroked its tongue with a finger. It felt rough and slightly plastic. Then I stuck my finger down its throat and its tongue gently rasped on my finger, its neck rippling as it tried to swallow my finger. I pulled it out. "You're just a feathered dinosaur, you know," I told him in as high a voice as I could manage. For most animals, a growl, or anything resembling it—a low voice, for instance—signals danger. Around his eyes, a white ring of down had begun to shed and would soon be replaced by feathers, but for the moment it looked like a sunburn that had begun to peel. When I slid a hand under one of his boomerang-shaped wings, it felt warm. But his feet were quite cold. King penguins look as if they're wearing black surgical gloves on their feet. Thanks to an adaptation known as rete mirabile, the blood in their nasal passages and feet stays the same temperature as the cold water they swim in. Blood from the warm arteries is right next to the cold venous blood, which cools it. According to the laws of thermodynamics, heat will always travel to cold. But these animals had evolved a way for that to happen inside their bodies instead of outside, so they would not get frostbite or suffer in icy weather.

Lifting him out of his crib, I set him on my rubber boots, and he instinctively pressed up against me, threw his head back, and called for me to feed him. Since he'd been fed enough for lunch, I leaned over and wrapped my arms around him and snuggled him tight. His beak, edged in thick glossy black like a vanilla bean, searched under my shirt collar and slid up my sweater sleeve. When the chicks are older, they preen themselves and coat their feathers from oil glands so that the water will run off. But at that moment he was buttery-soft and warm, like the inside of a fur-lined glove on a cold day. In the wild, one of the most critical times for a fledgling chick is during a rainstorm. Snow doesn't bother them much. But their down is water-absorbent, so if it should grow suddenly warm and then rain, their down would get drenched, hold the water in, and the penguin could become chilled to its skin and die.

A penguin's sex organs are internal, so it's difficult to know if it's male or female until it mates. One staff woman was attempting to tell gender difference from the pattern of calls, which she confirmed by measuring hormones in the feces. Another scientist was trying to tell gender from the remains of feces in the shells. Brown-white-left gently probed into my hand, up my sleeve, into my hair, nestling, groping, as it whistle-chirped its own distinctive call. I thought brown-white-left was male, but I had no way of knowing. While I went about my chores, he followed me with his eyes, making little chirps and whistles, and I chattered back, regularly pausing to hug him. Then the obvious dawned on me. In the almost-deafening clamor of Penguin Quarantine, the only individual penguin's voice I recognized was brown-white-left's; he recognized my voice. Imprinting, they call it. The image that flashed to mind was a film I once saw of Konrad Lorenz up to his neck in a lake, with a flock of baby geese following him as he swam. I put the smelt I was holding back into the pail, wiped my hands, and returned to the F-1 crib yet again. Wrapping an arm around brown-white-left, I pulled him close, and he nuzzled deep into my collar, found my warm neck, and whistled quietly. Outside a small glass window, where Sea World's visitors stand and watch the nursery doings, rows of people sighed in unison. Although I couldn't hear them, I saw a crowd of human mouths rounding to a sound like "Awww."

Penguins are the most anthropomorphic of all animals. Everyone identifies with them. Nor had I ever been with an animal that brought out such a mothering instinct. Why do we have such strong responses to penguins? First, they stand straight and walk upright like humans, so we see them as little humanoids—a convention of headwaiters, ten thousand nuns, plump babies wearing snowsuits. On land, they have a comical waddling walk, which is similar to a human toddler's. Free of terrestrial predators, they are very curious about humans and tend to walk right up to you. When you look down, you find an affectionate creature standing tall and straight as a young child, perhaps offering you its flipper the way we shake hands. Adult penguins are easy to anthropomorphize, too, because they sometimes seem so much a caricature of human life. They like company but also bicker with their neighbors; they give their mate gifts of pretty stones but also quarrel from time to time, have affairs, and divorce and remarry; they're affectionate, attentive parents and share the child rearing; they live in colonies that function like cities; they're plagued by adolescent gangs; they're forever waddling around at high speed, as if out on important errands. They are creatures of instinct, but so are we. Our instincts dwell under layers of inhibitions, social codes, bridled emotions, feats of mental dressage, and hand-me-down wisdom, but when it comes to the basics of hunger, sex, child rearing, and other obbligatos, they are as strong as any penguin's, and that unites us with them in a small way. If someone were to design an adorable animal that acted enough like a human being to be endearing but was different enough also to be exotic, a penguin would do perfectly. When I was a girl, and home air-conditioning was rare, I used to look for a shop with a tiny penguin decal on its door, which meant that it was blissfully air-conditioned inside. Penguins adorn ice cream bars, greeting cards, calendars, wool, postage stamps, cigarettes, chocolate-covered mints, and many other attractive products. British pubs are sometimes named The Penguin, as is one of Batman's archenemies. Gary Larson uses penguins as caricature humans in his enchantingly sick "Far Side" cartoons. Berke Breathed draws cartoon penguins, too. But probably the most famous are those adorning Penguin Books. In the mid-thirties, Allen Lane wanted to launch an ambitious paperback house, but he didn't have a name for it. His secretary suggested Penguin; it captured for him just the right attitude of "dignified flippancy." Small wonder, then, that during the Falklands war, one English town I know of collected money (or "had a whip-round," as they put it) to help save the large population of penguins. The fate of the pilots, infantrymen, shepherds, and sheep, on the other hand, didn't seem to concern them as much.

Avid bird-spotters know how easy it is to confuse birds, so many of which look alike. Indeed, most birds are LBJs, as birders call them—little brown jobs. Penguins, on the other hand, are uniquely identifiable, not just among birds but among all animals on earth. Everyone knows what a penguin looks like. Yet there are shocking misconceptions about penguins. For one thing, they don't live at the South Pole. Not only is the South Pole about eight hundred miles from the closest body of water, it's at an altitude of almost ten thousand feet. Nor do they live with Eskimos and polar bears, both of which are at the other side of the world, in the Arctic.

"Penguin," you might say to a friend in a game of free association, and your friend is bound to answer "snow" or "ice" or "South Pole." But only four species of penguins live on the Antarctic continent, and only two are restricted exclusively to the Antarctic. Most live in slightly balmier climates, on sub-Antarctic islands like South Georgia or the Falklands, or along the coast of South America, South Africa, Australia, and New Zealand; and one species even lives in the Galápagos, near the equator. No penguins live north of the equator, nor have they ever. The ocean currents aren't favorable for carrying them that far north. And anyway, northern coasts wouldn't be as welcoming a locale for them. True, their cousins the ostriches survive among lions, leopards, and other land predators because of their extraordinary speed, size, and strength. But penguins, out of water, aren't such hot rods.

Penguins don't have fur, even though the babies may feel minky-soft. Mammals have fur; penguins are birds, and they have feathers. Although they're known as flightless birds—like ostriches, emus, kiwis, rheas, cassowaries, and the now-extinct moas and dodoes—they're on the same branch of evolution as hummingbirds. According to the fossil record, both flying and flightless birds evolved from the same ancestor. It's just that penguins adapted to their environment differently than did the songbirds. To escape a predator, a wren needs to fly away from a cat or a fox. But a penguin's chief enemies are skillful oceanic predators like leopard seals and killer whales, and the bird needs to be agile in the water, not on land or in the air, which is why it's so vulnerable to human hunters. The sky is almost irrelevant to its style of life. What's more, penguins haven't changed much in forty million years. Oddest of all, perhaps, penguins are dinosaurs. They're not just descended from dinosaurs, they *are* dinosaurs. Once they were larger—standing over five feet tall and weighing around three hundred pounds—and not a few scientists have observed that they would have made great football players. The biggest penguin alive today, the emperor, is about four feet tall and weighs as much as a hundred pounds. In contrast, the smallest, the fairy, weighs only two and a half pounds and stands a mere twelve inches tall. People see films of penguins waddling across the ice, hear them referred to as flightless birds, and naturally assume that penguins can't fly.

But penguins do indeed fly. They fly in water. Using flat, tapered wings that have a rounded leading edge, and flapping like any swift or lark, penguins fly through the water as they feed, or to escape predators. Although penguins may be hefty, in the ocean they're essentially weightless. Their wings are strong and paddlelike, to power them through the dense water at speeds up to fifteen miles per hour. They use their short brushlike tails and webbed feet to steer. Magnificently aquatic, penguins arc out of the water like whales—called "porpoising"—to breathe as they swim. They don't fill their lungs with air but take in just enough to keep the lungs from collapsing, and in fact breathe out rather than in before they reenter the water. When penguins dive, their pulse goes from one hundred beats a minute to twenty beats a minute, and because they take only one shallow breath, they don't get the bends. They are streamlined like torpedoes; indeed, at one point the Navy studied their shape. The simple reason why penguins can't fly in the air is that they have too much body weight for such short, narrow wings to support. At some point in their evolution, it became more important for them to have weight than wingspan, even though that meant they would lose the ability to fly. This may sound like a profound sacrifice, but in matters of natural selection it was so great an advantage that only flightless penguins have survived. After all, birds use flight to evade predators, search for their food, and migrate. But if those aren't problems, or if there are attributes for greater survival value (a big body and fast running speed for the ostrich, for instance), then the ability to fly becomes irrelevant. Most of a penguin's life is spent at sea, where it needs sea skills.

Photographs show penguins on ice floes or against a backdrop of towering Antarctic ice mountains, so people assume that penguins live on land. But some species spend as much as 75 percent of their lives in the water. Scientists only see them on land during their brief courting, mating, molting, and brooding season. The rest of the time they migrate, and may stay at sea for as long as five months at a stretch. This means that when on shore, they aren't in their pre-ferred element, the watery atmosphere they're designed for. To us, they waddle and stumble like "animated laundry bags," as penguin expert Olin Pettingill, Jr., dubbed them, and we laugh and assume that they're just naturally clumsy beasts. But underwater they're streamlined, agile, and fast. Almost everything we know about penguins comes from observing them during only one misleading phase of their life cycle—the land phase. They would find us lethargic and clumsy too, if they only saw us stumbling around in the dark. People think of penguins as slow movers. Though they can't outrun a lion, penguins can skedaddle on land if they really need to. In powdery snow, they can outrun a human being. Their best trick is to fall onto their stomachs and toboggan, picking up speed as they career down an icy hill. To leap onto huge icebergs, they need timing, balance, and coordination. They would make grand tight-rope walkers.

Penguins are birds, and birds have hollow bones, right? Other birds do have hollow bones, making them light enough to fly through the air, but penguins do not. Penguins need to be buoyant in the water, but not too buoyant, or they wouldn't be able to dive for krill and fish. It's more important that they have some sort of ballast, so penguins have solid bones, like ours. Films often show penguins standing on an ice floe eyeing the ocean until one is "pushed" in as a "sacrificial victim" to test the waters for a hungry leopard seal. This, if true, would require more malevolent presence of mind than penguins have. Instead, what usually happens is that so many penguins are crowded on an ice floe that those near the edge get nudged off. When that occurs, the others plunge right in, since they're very much creatures of the mob.

There is some confusion about how the penguin got its name. One story insists that the word comes from the Welsh *pen gwyn*, or "white head," referring to the white spot on the head of the now-extinct great auk, a black-and-white flightless northern bird originally named penguin. Another story credits the Latin word *pinguis*, meaning fat, and refers to the penguin's many layers of blubber. Yet another traces the word back to British seafaring days, when sailors supposedly called the birds *pin-wings*. The Argentinians call the penguin *pajaro niño*, "child bird."

• • •

When my quarantine period was up, I sat quietly inside Sea World's Penguin Encounter, a large, public, glassed-in environment that was as much a display as a home for the many species of penguins that lived there. Nesting, mating, swimming in a small, deep pool, they led a reasonably normal life. They did not seem to mind the sudden flashes of light that now and then glittered like distant supernovas. Although their world was brightly lit, moving walkways just beyond the glass window carried thousands of zoo visitors past in relative darkness. I could see their ghostly outlines from the corner where I was seated on shaved ice. I leaned against a rock ledge while one penguin tried to eat my shoelace and another climbed up into my lap. Closed-circuit video cameras jutted out from the ceiling to monitor the penguins' activities. An adult king penguin dove into the pool and moments later sprang out the other side. It was tempting to think of these display penguins as displaced creatures, but they knew nothing of their true homes so many latitudes away. What must their lives be like in the wild? To seek an answer to that question is to begin what Apsley Cherry-Garrard in 1922 called "the worst journey in the world." A member of Scott's final expedition, he survived to write a memoir recalling his long, courageous trek across the Antarctic in 1911. Though it was winter, Cherry-Garrard and two colleagues went by sled 130 miles across the continent on an extremely hazardous trip from Scott's base camp to Cape Crozier. The trip took five weeks in the polar night, just to obtain a few emperor-penguin eggs. They thought emperors were very primitive birds, and they needed to study some embryos. The temperature plunged to $-77°$ F., and the winds howled at well over a hundred miles an hour, yet they survived. Later, two of the men died with Scott on his tragic bid for the South Pole, and Cherry-Garrard returned to write about the Cape Crozier crossing in the sensitive classic *The Worst Journey in the World,* whose title became synonymous with trekking to Antarctica. Now, one can sleep at night on a luxury cruise ship, where a chef serves gourmet meals, and there are lecture halls and movies, but the trip is still arduous.

• • •

One cold bright Sunday in January 1989, I flew fifteen hours to Santiago, Chile, where I stayed overnight at a hotel. The next day two more flights carried me to Puerto Williams, a bleak Argentinian outpost that included barracks for the military personnel stationed there, a museum, and one out-of-place-looking bowling alley. There I boarded the *World Discoverer,* a German-owned cruise ship that travels the world with lecturers, naturalists, tourists, and a large crew, mainly Filipinos and Germans. On the previous year's trip, the weather had been so rough in Drake Passage that many passengers went to their cabins, tied themselves into their beds with belts provided for that purpose, and stayed there for two days. This year, I hoped the seas would be calmer, but I had brought seven kinds of anti-seasickness medication in case. When Shackleton, the explorer, made the trip early in the century, he used sled dogs and wooden ships. What would he have made of a cruise ship complete with a library, laundry, infirmary, sauna, gym, and Art Deco dining room? In addition to 129 tourists from all over the world, there were also, as usual, scientists hitching a ride (Frank Todd had been on the previous sailing, coming aboard from a British Navy vessel, where he had been doing research). Although this may sound like a large pilgrimage to the South Pole, it's really small. All such trips are.

You see, on any Saturday or Sunday afternoon in the fall, there are more people in a single college football stadium than have ever been to the Antarctic in all of history. It is a distant, largely unknown world, and its problems seem remote. Yet it, and its animal life, fascinates people. Sea World in San Diego sells hundreds of books about penguins every month. The Penguin Encounters at the four Sea Worlds combined draw ten million people a year. One day soon, we may need to decide the fate of the largest desert on Earth, one of the last wildernesses, even though most of us have never seen it and will never see it in our lifetime. We will be responsible for deciding the fate of its penguins, seals, birds, and other creatures. The Antarctic Treaty outlaws such acts of environmental sabotage as nuclear-bomb tests and the harboring of weapons systems and insists that the continent "shall continue forever to be used exclusively for peaceful purposes." But perhaps the most important thing it does is to protect the future of people who live as far away as Phoenix or Beijing. The Antarctic ice cap contains 68 percent of all the fresh water on earth, and we may one day need it.

As much as anything, the Antarctic's problems are political. The treaty has been in effect for almost thirty years, and twelve nations were the original signers. Since then, twenty-six countries have joined, eight as voting members. Remaining essentially intact for the entire time that it has been in effect, the treaty has to some extent protected the Antarctic from exploitation. That doesn't mean, though, that science has been compromised or that the Antarctic is a self-protected, hands-off kind of a place. But the treaty has been a good mechanism for keeping the status quo, as much as possible, within the many political climates of the world. One of the reasons the treaty was successful is because two sensitive issues weren't really dealt with: mineral exploitation (such as gold, copper, silver, beryl, iron, zinc, graphite, coal, and oil) and fishing rights on the high seas (including whales, seals, penguins, and krill). With the treaty up for review, those two issues still haven't been resolved, and may not be resolveable. Many scientists would like the treaty to be extended *because* those key issues can't be sorted out. Greenpeace would like the Antarctic declared a global park (an idea implied by the treaty itself). This is not as outlandish as it sounds. In 1990, the Planetary Society's magazine, *The Planetary Report,* solicited its readers' opinions on passing a law to protect all of Mars and any other planet we explore in the coming decades, to declare each one a planetary park, so that no nation could exploit its resources or ruin its environment. Although Antarctic scientists from different lands get on well together, visit one another's outposts, go to one another's parties, and generally wish each other well in the name of science and the mutually stranded, their countries constantly bicker. A number of countries claim the same prime pieces of the peninsula. If you look at a map of Argentina, it includes the Antarctic. A map of Chile includes the same Antarctic territory. The British claim the territory, too. The United Nations also wants control of it, on behalf of all peoples. But many scientists think that wouldn't work, either. After all, they argue, the UN has not been able to solve the problems of the rest of the world. Why give it Antarctica?

One complication is getting there in the first place. Only a handful of C-130 airplanes operate in and out of the Antarctic. If a number break down, traffic stops and everyone's marooned. Todd one time found himself in just that predicament, and he quickly discovered the frontier camaraderie among the multinational researchers. "So there we were," he had told me at Sea World, "an American team, dicking around in Chile, trying to figure out what to do. We got on board the *World Discoverer,* a German ship chartered by Americans, were taken to the Antarctic, and had our cargo offloaded by Indonesians and Filipinos into a Russian LCM steered by East Germans to a Chilean base, then we were flown by the Chileans to an Argentine *refugio* and had our communications to the States sent via the Chinese at the Chinese station, and the Brazilian Air Force brought us and our eggs out at the end of our stay. There's no place else in the world where you can do that."

But such political concerns drifted into the suburbs of our minds in Puerto Williams when we gathered in the ship's large lounge to meet the lecturers and one another and begin talking about penguins, which some of us had come from as far away as Switzerland, Germany, and South Africa to see. Two large groups, led by expert birders Brett Whitney and Bob Ridgely, had also come to pursue exotic seabirds. Some of these birders had traveled together before, on jaunts to Ecuador, the South Pacific, New Guinea, the Galápagos, and other locales. They were easy to spot in a crowd, wearing their heavy stigmata—a pair of Zeiss 10x40B birding binoculars ("armored" and with "close focus" features) draped down the chest, with the lens cap looking like a rounded black bow tie that had slipped to the back of the neck. They had two long lists of birds they hoped to spot, with boxes in which to check off each sighting, or to just write an *H* if they only heard the call of the bird. (The rules of bird-spotting are as mazey as international law.) That night, on the ledge of the journey, though all of us were excited, the birders had begun rubbing their collective mania together like high-quality flints. Before going to bed, they met with their leaders to run down their checklists and get ready for the morning's landing at Cape Horn, right at the tailbone of South America. The ocean currents and winds at Cape Horn are legendary for their ferocity. People assume the name comes from the shape of the 1,300-foot peak on the south side of the island, which in rough weather seems to impale the sky. But it was named by Dutch navigators in 1616, after the Dutch town of Hoorn, and though only five miles square, it has come to symbolize a breakaway from the known world and civilization. Like a last handhold, Cape Horn reaches into the southern ocean, and beyond it floats Antarctica.

At five o'clock on a cool, damp morning, I woke in a narrow bed to many movements at once: From the knees down, my legs felt as if they were dropping down an elevator shaft, my torso shimmied twice, and my chest rolled like a bag full of peaches. For a few moments, I drifted into sleep, then woke to someone sitting down on the bed beside me. When I opened my eyes, no one was there. When I closed them, someone sat down beside me again. Opened them, no one was there. Plunging and swaying, the ship surged through the waves, hitting them crosswise, and the motion set my stomach revolving. Like Stephano in *The Tempest,* I wanted to cry: "Prithee do not turn me about—my stomach is not constant." Finally, to keep from throwing up, I tried to picture the motion that was seizing me, a motion familiar in my joints and in my nervous system: that of cantering on a fresh, high-spirited horse with a tantrum lying just under his surface. In my mind's eye, I was cantering bareback on a black Arabian stallion on a black sand volcanic beach. The air was hot and salty and the sunstruck waves poured like liquid glass onto the beach. Meanwhile the rocking and swaying was a half ton of snort and lather flexing its muscles beneath me, full of outbreak and alarm, its graceful power held in check by my small human hands. In time, my stomach settled. The alarm clock rang, and holding on to the wall, I stood up and looked out through a porthole onto a mountainous landscape, alien, barren, and cold.

A six-bell melody sounded over the intercom, and then the voice of the expedition leader told us that it would be a "wet landing" and to wear full gear, which included waterproof pants, knee-high boots, a bright-red hooded parka, waterproof gloves, a scarf and hat, a life vest, and a rucksack to hold our cameras, binoculars, and other supplies. Breakfast was to come later, when we returned from the morning's trek. A hundred and twenty-nine people lined up on B deck to turn 129 numbered tags hanging on a board to the red side to signal to the crew that they were going on land (returning, they would flip them to the black side, so that everyone would be accounted for before the ship sailed on), and stepped one by one into the waiting Zodiacs. The tag system worked. The previous year, a traveler on shore who had stumbled, hit his head, and passed out was discovered hours later by a search party after his tag was found unturned. The Zodiacs carried us to a sheltered bay to the east side of the island, where large ocean-smoothed stones and seeweed made up the beach, and our naturalist guides waited at the bottom of a steep staircase. We gathered in groups around Peter Harrison, birder; Bernard Stonehouse, a world authority on penguins, whose wife, Sally, was with him; Commander Angus Erskine, retired British naval officer and Arctic and Antarctic explorer; Richard Rowlett, specialist in marine mammals, who had just spent six years on a Russian whaling ship; and Robert Ridgely, an ornithologist from the Academy of Natural Sciences of Philadelphia. Then we began the climb up 150 feet of steep, slippery wooden steps to the top of the hill, which opened out onto a windswept field of dense tussock grass, rocky outcroppings, a small chapel, and a Chilean weather station.

"Up the stairs and turn left," Erskine instructed us matter-of-factly. "Turn right, and you'll be in a minefield." Laughter from the climbers. "No," he insisted in a well-tempered English accent. "It is a real minefield." It was not difficult to picture Erskine in command of a 2,500-ton destroyer, as he had been in the Royal Navy for many years. Tall, sandy-haired, bearded, he was the epitome of the British officer—someone who maintains good posture even in bad terrain.

At the top of the stairs, thick tussocks of poa grass sprawled toward the distant spire of Cape Horn. Harrison was dressed in a white sweater with a pattern of black dashes stitched through it, which looked like the dappled plumage of a bird. Slender, with a blondish beard and mustache, he looked a bit avian himself as he stopped suddenly, lifted his binoculars to his eyes, and crept forward. "*Pshhh, pshhh, pshhh,*" he stage-whispered. He had heard the call of the thorn-tailed rayadito, a little white-throated, russet-eye-browed, brown-backed bird with a children's-toy squeak for a call, and he was hoping to flush it from its cover. A small flutter in the brush. "A thorn-tailed rayadito!" He extended one arm, pointed, followed the bird with his hand. Devout birders lifted their cameras and binoculars to their eyes.

"Oh, I've seen one of those," one woman said wearily, and continued climbing the winding staircase toward the summit.

"They often go around in small family parties," Harrison continued excitedly—"Not there!" He interrupted himself to warn a wayward birder, who was drifting into a field to the right. "That's a minefield!" She laughed. Erskine had told her the same thing. What a card these lecturers were. "No, that's a *real* minefield," Harrison said, letting his binoculars fall to his hand for a moment while he followed her movements. By that time Erskine had reached the top as well and, putting a hand gently on her shoulder, explained: "The Chileans always feared Argentinian invasion, so they put a machine-gun nest here, a helicopter pad"—he pointed to a ring of white stones—"and all sorts of land mines, some of which are still unexploded." Slightly addled, the woman turned crisply and hurried left, over bogs of spongy peat mixed with penguin guano, through fields of poa grass as impenetrable as muscle. An oven bird sang sweetly. On a distant promontory, a twenty-five-foot-high red-and-white lighthouse marked the tip of Cape Horn. Then a raucous braying, as from donkeys, began, and we looked toward a cliff, where two Magellanic penguins popped up beside their nest. With concentric circles of black and white on their cheeks, pink splotches around their eyes, and a smile-shaped pink stripe below their bills, they looked impish. Almost immediately they disappeared. It was our first sighting of wild penguins, and we were not expecting to find them here, such an arduous climb above the sea. To nest where the drainage is good and their eggs will be safe from flood, Magellanics may climb as much as nine hundred feet. Another pair popped up and brayed from another clump of grass, flashing pink eye masks. We did not expect them to bray like jackasses. Turning a slow circle, I scanned the poa grass. They popped up like targets in a shooting gallery, watched us for a while, then disappeared into their burrows. Far down the hill, along a crescent-shaped beach, stood hundreds more penguins, which were getting ready to swim out to sea to feed, or had just returned with full bellies. Some made long, honking mating calls, others short, rapid "rallying calls," just to let the world know they were Magellanics. The wind had risen to forty miles an hour, and the cold air started to creep into my clothes. A striated caracara, a brown-and-gold bird of prey related to the falcon, slipped sideways across the sky, its huge wings carrying it like a solar sail. Between the quicksandlike mix of mud and guano and the coarse poa grass, there was only one route to travel: along the penguin pathways, which led in a hard-to-see labyrinth across the hillside and down to the sea. At the base of many of the grass-hut-size tussocks, among clusters of veronica, were holes that the penguins had dug as nests.

"For those of you who haven't ticked off a Chilean skua yet," Bob Ridgely said, "there are two of them flying low over that ridge." The birders turned their heads in unison.

"Oh, what's this, then?" Stonehouse said. Scuttling through the brush was a baby Magellanic penguin, and in a moment he and Harrison had grabbed it, pinning its wings and holding it gently but securely. It had a black face, with tufts of brown at the neck and a pinkish splotch at each eye. "This is a juvenile penguin whose parents have deserted it," Stonehouse said, "making its way down to the ocean. When it gets there, it's going to stand on the beach for a few days and then will go to sea. If it has enough fat, it will make it. All around here you'll find burrows where the chicks were raised. Unlike the Antarctic penguins, which hatch out onto stones or onto the feet of their parents, these penguins are safe underground. Some animals become able-bodied and alert soon after they hatch, so that they can flee a predator. But these penguins don't have to hatch out feathered and alert. They hatch out blind and quite helpless and are covered in a fine layer of pale grayish down." When they put the chick back in the grass, it flopped onto its belly and tobogganed downhill toward the beach part of the rookery. The term *rookery* first referred to a group of rooks, which are also colonial birds. Then the term was carried over to crows and, finally, to other collections of breeding birds, even to some mammals, like fur seals. And penguins are supremely colonial, or social, making rookeries that can sprawl for hundreds of acres. Living together means they can unite against predators, protect their young, and migrate together.

As the others hurried across a field in pursuit of a rare plumbeous rail, Stonehouse and I moseyed among the tussocks of deep, rich, bent-over poa grass. Tall and slender, with his blue rucksack and his purple-and-pale-blue college scarf, he looked for the moment like the Cambridge don he was. And when he spoke, you could detect the Cambridge "r" that Jacob Bronowski introduced to many American viewers on PBS. In fact, Bronowski lodged in the house when Stonehouse was just a boy and was the first to encourage his smart, inquiring young mind. He smiled, pulled aside the tussock grass, and revealed a round burrow. "Smell," he said, and I knelt in the sod and inhaled the sweet oily saltiness of penguin. Suddenly, a beak jutted out of the darkness and swept swiftly back and forth. We laughed. The burrow's resident was at home and dueling with its sharp bill, at the ready for intruders.

"How on earth do they find their way from the beach to their nest through all this vegetation?" I asked. Only coal miners and spelunkers faced trickier tunnels.

"We don't know that for sure. Penguin navigation is a mysterious thing. It could be magnetic, they might be using the sun, or they could be memorizing the details of their neighborhood and finding their way back by signposts alone."

Almost everything we know about penguins is based on the slender period of time, during breeding season, that they spend on shore; and their shore life is a compromised one, since they're designed for the sea. Many questions remain. What do they do when we don't see them? What happens to them during the winter, I wondered, when they live at sea, constantly swimming and porpoising for air? Where do they feed? In the summer, the waters are murky and full of kelp and sediment, but in the winter the water grows lucid and clear. Most adult penguins die at sea, and winter must be a time of considerable hazard for them. Although they can see their food better, leopard seals can see them better. Do the various colonies stay together, or do they scatter throughout the ice packs? Penguins are like icebergs—a scintillating mystery, most of which is hidden from view.

Withdrawing carefully, and then sinking and stumbling through the compost of peat, guano, and lichen, we made our way back up the hill to a small log cabin chapel. Inside, a wooden altar sat on two tree stumps, and a vase holding a dry brown stalk of evergreen trimmed with tinsel and one pinecone reminded us that Christmas mass had been celebrated here not very long before. A print of the Virgen del Carmen, Reina de Chile, adorned the wall. She was a beautiful teenage girl holding a child whose head and arms were slightly out of proportion, like a dwarf's. In another corner, a statue of the Virgin and Child sat on another tree stump. On the altar ran the words: *"Madre de todos / Estrella del Mar, ruega por nosotros."* As blustery winds whistled through the cracks in the log chapel, it seemed a good place to send one's prayers to heaven: at the windswept edge of the known world, with penguins popping up from minefields. Outside again, we pressed our collars tight against the cold and began the slippery trek down to the beach, where the Zodiacs waited to ferry us, hungry and tired, back to the ship.

After breakfast, I crawled into bed and slept. The boat started up, and soon it began plunging again. Camera, binoculars, books, watch, papers all skidded across the desk and shelves and hit the floor one at a time. The waves began to crash against the boat with such fury that when they struck the portholes, they exploded like cannonfire. All those sea movies with their relentless creaking and swaying were right. The boat creaked like a new shoe. Lying in bed, bolstered by a pillow at each side so I didn't roll out, I looked hard at the cabin walls, trying to grip them with my eyes. Their cream-colored ersatz marbling was supposed to look randomly done with a plasterer's knife, but a horse's head, the face of a man with a mustache, and three penguins walking single file was repeated. (In his notebooks, Leonardo tells his students to stare at the cracks in a marble wall until they see a world reveal itself, and centuries later, Alain Robbe-Grillet would begin his novel *Project for a Revolution in New York* in a similar way.) When we were summoned to lifeboat drill, I staggered upstairs with the others, clinging to the handrails. Tucked between most of the railings and the wall were seasickness bags. Some people carried their own. It was the sole topic of conversation as we waited for drill. I began a bout of yawning I couldn't explain, my gorge began to rise, and I swallowed it back down. When the drill ended, everyone rushed back down to their cabins. But on the way, I staggered to the stern of the boat and there found a scene right out of storybooks, as albatrosses, sooty shearwaters, and white-chinned petrels slid across the keel of the boat, banking, wheeling, stalling, climbing, touching their wingtips to the whitecaps, rushing low through the spray, skidding, diving, and soaring.

At twelve-thirty, lunch was announced over the intercom, and also the news that the seas were too rough for the afternoon's landing; wild and rollicking, they were rearing up higher than the sides of the ship. A calm, well-tempered voice on the intercom announced that because of the "swell," the afternoon's lectures had been postponed. So, too, the captain's welcome cocktail party and dinner. A stewardess stopped by with a plateful of crackers and a cup of tea. Even she was feeling seasick. If I chewed the saltines very slowly, I discovered they would stay down. They reminded me of the biscuits the explorers in the Antarctic's "heroic age" relied on as a staple of their diet, along with pemmican, sugar, tea, and cocoa. Hardship did not stop the early explorers; indeed, it seems to have been a lure. As notorious as Drake Passage was, we were actually experiencing it in one of its calmer moods. Most people kept to their cabins and missed meals; some bundled up in parkas and blankets and sat out on the deck in chairs. Stalwart birders and those with enviable sea legs spent the crossing in the observation bridge, binoculars pressed against their eyes like the fists of sleepy children. We were an odd lot of travelers. There were doctors of every denomination, lawyers, anthropologists, professors, an assistant secretary of state (in the Carter administration), a venture capitalist, a psychologist, a painter, professional photographers, middle-income couples who had saved for years to make the trip, and wealthy tourists, one of whom, when I asked what she did in Marin County, had the candor to reply, "Oh, I don't have to do anything." The average age was between sixty and seventy, and many on board were retired.

On the observation bridge, between bird-spottings, a radiologist and a physicist discussed subatomic theory, string theory, and the Michelson-Morley experiment. "Einstein woke up the physicists from their dogmatic slumber," the radiologist said.

"Storm petrel," the physicist advised, and both followed with binoculars as it fell-swooped and then skidded out of sight. "I think Bertrand Russell said if he had to do it over again he'd be a physicist," the physicist continued. "There comes that moment of yearning to tie your tent to the pegs of existence." The other man nodded. They were far from the mirage oasis of academic life or the lucrative caravansary of medicine. But existence was pegged out plainly, in the harsh seas luxuriant with krill and the birds that had migrated as far as ten thousand miles from the Arctic to feed on such abundance.

By early morning we had reached the Antarctic Convergence, a wedding of the freezing Antarctic Sea and the warmer waters of the north, which often reveals itself as a line of foam with fog and mist and large flocks of seabirds moving in and out across its five-mile width. In our wake flew Wilson's storm petrels, which tap-danced on top of the waves, black-and-white-splotched pintados, tiny black-bellied storm petrels, Antarctic prions, sieving the surface for food, the stubby-winged diving petrels, and huge wandering albatrosses that seemed not to flap at all but to carry chunks of the sky on their wings. Minke, humpback, and southern bottle-nosed whales crossed our path from time to time, as did hourglass dolphins. We scouted the water keenly for penguins, which travel many miles to feed, but saw none. The waves continued to rear up on either side of the boat, cup us in thick green hands, and hurl us forward into another pair of waiting hands, which hurled us forward yet again. Night fell late and suddenly, without the usual pastel preamble of twilight.

At first light, on calmer seas, I opened the two porthole covers like a second pair of eyes and looked out onto Antarctica for the first time. White upon white with white borders was all I expected to see; instead, colossal icebergs of palest blue and mint-green floated across the vista. Beyond them, long chalky cliffs stretched out of view. Throwing on a parka, I raced upstairs to the deck and looked all around. As far as I could see in any direction, icebergs meandered against a backdrop of tall, crumbly Antarctic glaciers, which were still pure and unexplored. Human feet had not touched the glaciers I saw; nor had many pairs of eyes beheld them. In many ways, the Antarctic is a world of suspended animation. Suspended between outer space and the fertile continents. Suspended in time—without a local civilization to make history. Civilization has been brought to it; it has never sustained any of its own. It sits suspended in a hanging nest of world politics. When things die in the Antarctic, they decay slowly. What has been is still there and will always be, unless we interfere. *Interfere* is such a simple word for what is happening: the ozone hole, the greenhouse effect, disputes over territory, pollution, mining. Who discovered Antarctica we may never know. We re-member the Shackletons and the Scotts, but it was the whalers and sealers who opened up the Antarctic, not the explorers. Because the whalers and sealers didn't talk much about their good hunting grounds, they have sifted between the seams of history.

Soon we dropped anchor at Harmony Cove, Nelson Island, in the South Shetland Islands, whose ice cliffs are layered with volcanic ash from the Deception Island eruption of 1970. Piling into the Zodiacs, we dashed toward a cobble beach, where one of the crew, who had gone ashore early, had teased the other Zodiac drivers by spelling out LANDING in stones against the snow. A blue odalisque of ice floated offshore. Hundred-foot white glacial cliffs stood next to huge rooms of pure aquamarine ice. Ah-hah! A small welcoming party of gentoo penguins, ashore to feed their waiting chicks, waddled close to look us over. One penguin tilted its head one way, then the other, as it stared at me. This made the bird look like an art dealer, quietly thinking and appraising. Penguins don't have binocular vision as humans do, so they turn one eye to an object, then the other, to see it. Although they can see well underwater, they don't need long vision when they're on land. The last time I saw a look quite like that gentoo's was in the Penguin House at the Central Park Zoo. There, in a shower of artificial Antarctic light, in a display created by a theatrical-lighting designer, gentoos and chinstraps had eyed the crowd of people watching them—including some of the homeless of Manhattan, who used the Penguin House as a favorite warming-up spot.

According to one saying, "There are two kinds of penguins in the Antarctic, the white ones coming toward you, and the black ones going away from you." All penguins are essentially black and white on their bodies, a feature known as countershading. Their white bellies and chins blend in with the shimmery light filtering through the water, so they're less likely to be spotted from below when they're in the ocean. That makes hunting fish easier, as well as escaping leopard seals. Their black backs also make them less visible from above as they fly through the murky waters. To the krill, the white belly of the penguin looks like a pale orb, harmless as the sky. To the leopard seal, the black back of the penguin looks like a

17 DIFFERENT

shadow on the ocean bottom, unpalatable. Researchers found that if they marked penguins with aluminum bands, the tags flashed and leopard seals could spot them too easily. A lot of their study birds were killed, and they switched to black tags. Another advantage of being black and white: If they're too hot, they can turn their white parts to the sun and reflect heat; if too cold, they can turn their black parts to the sun and absorb heat. Because most of a penguin's body is below water, it's the head that has developed so many interesting designs and colors. A field guide to penguins would only need to show you the heads. Adélie penguins (named after Adélie Land, a stretch of Antarctic coast below Australia that was itself named after Adélie Dumont d'Urville, the wife of the nineteenth-century French explorer Jules-Sébastian-César Dumont d'Urville, who first sighted it; among Captain d'Urville's other accomplishments was sending the Venus de Milo to the Louvre) have black heads, with chalk-white eye rings. They are the little men in the tuxedo suits we see in cartoons. Rock-hoppers have lively red eyes, long yellow and black head feathers resembling a crewcut that's been allowed to grow out, and thick yellow satanic eyebrows that slant up and away from their eyes, giving their face an expression that says, *I dare you!* Chinstraps get their name from the helmet of black feathers that seems to be attached by a thin black "strap" across their white throats. Their amber eyes, outlined in thick black, look Egyptian, like a hieroglyph for some as-yet-undecipherable verb. Emperors have black heads, a tawny stripe on the bill, and a bib of egg-yolk yellow around their neck and cheeks. The most flamboyant of all, king penguins display a large, velvety-orange comma on each cheek, as if always in the act of being quoted about something. A throbbing orange at their neck melts into radiant yellow. And, on either side of their bills, a comet of apricot or lavender flies toward their mouth. Fairy penguins are tiny and blue-headed. Each of the seventeen different species of penguins, though essentially black-and-white, differs from all others in head pattern.

Rock Hoppers

Chinstrap

Emperors

King

On shore, of course, a mass of penguins with predominantly black-and-white bodies looks a bit like linoleum in a cheap diner.

Human beings tend to be obsessed with black-and-white animals, like killer whales, giant pandas, and penguins. "We live in a world of grays, could be's, ambiguities," Frank Todd once observed. "Maybe it's just nice to see something that's cut-and-dried. It's black-and-white. It's there, and that's the way it is."

Gentoos feed their chicks every eighteen to twenty-four hours, and the adults that had just arrived were fat-bellied, crammed with fish and krill. Native to the Antarctic and sub-Antarctic, the gentoos were white-breasted and black-backed like all penguins, but they had a white bonnet on their heads. Though quiet and friendly, they drifted just out of reach. Along with Adélies and chinstraps, the gentoos belong to the genus *Pygoscelis* ("brush-tailed"), because of their short, paintbrush-shaped tail, and they are shy penguins, whose chicks grow slowly, staying close to a parent's warm body for weeks after hatching. The gentle gentoos are docile and may not have to pair-bond as vigorously as other penguins; otherwise they would need to declare their territory and mate more stridently and become more aggressive about intruders. The name gentoo is from the deceit of a British Museum man, who received a gentoo skin from an Antarctic explorer, thought it was a new species of bird, and decided to hide the information for a while. Later, he went off to Papua New Guinea, and when he returned, he described the bird as if it were one of the local species, naming it after the Gentoo, a religious sect on Papua New Guinea.

As we straggled along the shore toward granite outcroppings where penguins nest, two large brown birds began forays, dive-bombing. This was our first close encounter with the skua, nemesis of the baby penguin, and I held an arm above my head because, like lightning, skuas strike at the highest spot. They can pick an animal's eyes out before it knows what has happened. Hawklike, cunning, and bold, they are the ace predators of sick, young, or abandoned penguins. Some claim that skuas divide up a penguin colony into thousand-pair lots and that if you want a quick population estimate of a penguin colony, count the skuas and multiply by two thousand. A skua will carefully monitor a rookery, find a deserted chick, knock the bird senseless on the back of the head to kill it, then consume almost every scrap. When it devours an adult, it eats the viscera first, turning the carcass inside out like a sleeve, leaving only the head, skin, and bones. A big skua landed in front of us, spread its wings, and noisily proclaimed its territory. Then we saw why it was so anxious: A fluffy skua chick, head tucked into its shoulders, scurried away in the other direction and crouched. Another skua arrived, and both parents tried to draw our attention away. A little farther on, we found a small rookery of chinstraps, one with its flipper out straight, as if it were signaling a left turn, all looking like a gathering of crosswalk guards. Another was lying on its stomach and turned the soles of its feet up to cool off. Moving its flippers, it revealed an underside that had gone pink in the penguin equivalent of a blush. It was a warm day for them in Antarctica. A group of gentoo penguins ambled by, going anywhere, going nowhere. Penguins are born followers. If one begins to move with purpose, the others fall in behind it.

"Those poor penguins, living in this awful cold!" one woman lamented in a Southern drawl as she pulled her red parka tight around her neck and dragged a knitted cap down almost over her eyes. In fact, penguins rarely mind the cold. Quite the opposite. More often, they overheat. Like mammals, penguins are warm-blooded, which means that they're able to make their own heat and carry it with them wherever they go, instead of taking on the temperature of their environment. This allows them to migrate and to live in otherwise inhospitable regions of the earth. Of course, keeping warm can become something of a problem in the Antarctic. Penguins have evolved thick layers of blubber, which their bodies make from krill and plantonic oils, and because blubber conducts heat poorly, a layer of it below the skin acts as an excellent insulator. It is also a place to store fuel for the long, cold breeding season. The farther south you go, the bigger the penguins get, since big animals find it easier to stay warm. About one third of the weight of the emperor penguin, which lives in the coldest regions, is blubber. In addition, as anyone who skis or spends much time outdoors in the winter knows, air makes one of the best insulators. Travelers to the Antarctic are advised to dress in many layers of clothing with plenty of air in between them. Penguins do that with tightly overlapping feathers, which don't ruffle very easily and, as a result, trap a layer of warm air against the skin. Also, each feather develops a fluffy down at the base of its shaft, and that downy layer adds even more insulation. Penguins are watertight and airtight and thought to have more feathers than any other bird. The feathers are shiny, long, and curved, arranged like carefully laid roof shingles. Dipping into the oil gland at the base of the tail, a penguin spreads a layer of oil on the feathers to keep them slick and tight. Of course, feathers do get tattered after a year or so, and then the bird must molt, to slough off the old feathers and grow new ones. If it molted gradually, it wouldn't be waterproof any longer, so it goes through all the steps of molting at the same time, a process that takes about thirty days. New feathers grow in underneath the ones that are molting and push the old ones out. It makes the penguin look scruffy and slightly crazed, as if it were ripping its feathers out in some avian delirium. What is worse, since they're not waterproof while they're molting, they can't go hunting food in the ocean. *Fasting* is what it's called by scientists, although that word suggests choice on the part of the penguin, which loses about 30 percent of its body weight and is bound to be hungry and is not exactly a volunteer.

But heat is a problem. There are few things as ridiculous as a penguin suffering the equivalent of heat stroke in the middle of the coldest place on earth. All around the rookery, overheated penguins resort to what look like vaudeville moves: Ruffling their feathers, they release some of the hot insulating air next to the skin. They hold one arm out, as if parking a 747, then they pirouette and signal a turn in the other direction. They flush pink under the wings, where capillaries swell with blood. Baby penguins like to lie down on their bellies and stick their feet up behind them, so that they can lose heat through the soles of their feet. They radiate heat through the few featherless zones on their bodies (usually around the eyes, flippers, and feet). A large adult suddenly ruffles up all over and extends its flippers at the same time, as if someone had scraped a fingernail across a blackboard.

The cold, on the other hand, isn't really a problem. If the temperature drops too low (around 15° F. with a strong wind), thousands of birds will huddle together to stay warm in what the French researchers call *tortues* (turtles). Using one another for insulation, they don't burn up their fat stores quickly. Huddling birds lose only half as much weight as birds braving the winds solo, because only a small portion of their bodies are exposed to the wind. It is akin to the protection apartment dwellers get, surrounded by apartments on either side that act as insulation.

"Come and look at this krill poop," Harrison said, bending down to consider some guano. "It's not very fresh. See those black spots in it?" He held up a handful and smudged it between his fingers. "That's the eyes of krill, which are indigestible, like tomato seeds to us. When you see the ground stained red like this, it's probably a chinstrap or an Adélie rookery rather than a gentoo, because the chinstraps eat krill and poop red. White poop comes from a diet of fish or squid. And green poop means they're not eating at all; what you're seeing is bile." Across the hillside and around the large slabs of rock, the ground was stained pink. Even if the rookery had been deserted, we could tell chinstraps or Adélies lived there. Most of the zoologists I know are, by necessity, coprophiles. A living system leaves its imprint on what passes through it. So I'm no longer surprised to find a naturalist sifting through bat, alligator, or penguin excrement. Some even study petrified dinosaur excrement, or coprolites, as they're called.

Beyond the rookery, molting elephant seals snoozed on the shore like overgrown salamis. They rolled around the sand together and against each other, to rub off the old fur, which wears out and has to be replaced each year. Pieces of molted fur and skin littered the beach. One often finds elephant seals with penguins, lying on the beach like so many old cast-off horsehair couches. It takes seven or eight years for the long nose of the bulls to develop. These pug-nosed ones were young males, which would grow larger, although they were already around twelve feet long and weighed about three thousand pounds. A gang of penguins strolled among them, seemingly without care. One in the center scratched his neck with a five-clawed flipper. Sluggish as they may look, elephant seals can dive to more than three thousand feet to feed on squid and fish.

On a rise, three fur seals sat up and stared aggressively as we passed. If they wanted to, they could gallop across the sand at great speed, tucking their pelvic girdles and undulating like fast worms. Fur seals will attack human beings. The previous year, a fur seal had grabbed a lecturer as he was getting into a Zodiac and punctured his lung. The man needed thirty-six stitches, and it took many months for the wounds to heal, since, to add to their armament, fur seals have an enzyme in their mucus that keeps their bites from healing properly. "I hate these," one of the guides said under his breath. "I have nothing whatsoever against fur-seal coats. I tell you, I'm sincere about this." As a territorial male started toward him, Stonehouse clapped his gloved hands, shouted, and kicked black volcanic sand up at its face. The seal stopped, huffed loudly, and sidled back to its original spot.

Between two rock knobs, a chinstrap-penguin colony sat on red krill-stained rocks. The gentoos choose a flat shelf area to nest and breed on; chinstraps prefer rocks, and gentoos a flatter terrain, so even though living in close quarters, they don't compete with one another for nesting sites. A baby gentoo put its head up and made a metallic gargling sound. The babies, forming little crèches with their flippers wrapped around each other, achieved a look of intense mateyness. (Other animals, like young flamingos, eider ducklings, and baby bats, form crèches, too.) While the parents are away hunting food, the babies are open to attack from skuas and other birds and are a lot safer in a nursery of chicks. Not only is there strength in numbers, but adults wandering through to feed their young can help ward off attacks by skuas. King penguins feed their chicks for nine or ten months, so their young spend a long time in crèches. Returning from the sea, adult gentoos easily recognize their babies by voice. The pattern of white dots, bar over the eyes, and other characteristics also varies slightly from one individual to another.

A chick flapped rubbery flippers. It takes time for the bones to set into the strong, hard flight-muscles of the adult. As immature birds, gentoos have a great tendency to wander and may migrate as much as two hundred miles. But in the second year they will return to the rookery, ready to breed. Because they're a mated pair, the gentoo couple doesn't have to go back to the same site each year to nest. Like all other penguins, they take two to three weeks to build a nest and copulate, but they're mobile and can change their nests. Because they don't split up when the breeding season is over, they probably remain together as mates year-round. Gentoos are the most passive penguins, and perhaps that has been their undoing. There are only about forty thousand gentoos left in the world, but at least their numbers are not declining.

In some areas, the ground was streaked with beautiful white star-bursts—squirted guano—so that it looked like a moonscape. And it was pungent! Sailors have been known to use the smell of a well-known rookery as a navigation aid, especially when fog is too thick for them to see any of the birds. A pink tinge of algae glowed from beneath the snow, which acted as a greenhouse. Frost polygons had turned the sod into a six-sided design. A chinstrap raised its bill into the air, its air sacs puffed up, and it worked the bellows of its chest. Just offshore, a row of giant petrels waited for the chicks. The range of light was so wide it was taxing for the eye to take everything in—the round, dark, wet, sullen rocks, the brilliant white snow reflecting against low clouds in a visual echo chamber of white.

On the ground were the remains of that morning's breakfast for a skua: a pair of orange penguin feet, a head, a skeleton. Stonehouse picked up the half-eaten chinstrap, showed me the flight muscles, the thick red ribbons that were the salt glands, and the concertina ribs. He handed me a small white feather, revealing the main shaft, and then, at its base, a second feather of silky down.

"Why would *this* one have died?" I said. "Why would a skua have singled it out?"

Turning the skeleton over, he discovered its eccentric bottom bill, bent at a ninety-degree angle. "You occasionally see penguins like this, with deformed bills. There's no way they can feed correctly, but even if they did manage to feed, they still wouldn't be able to preen themselves. So they would get heavily infested with lice. It's very sad, like seeing a deformed and neglected child. That's a simple, small thing to go wrong, when you think about it—just a misshapen bottom bill. But the chick would lead a difficult life for about nine months and then die of starvation. Before that happens, a skua usually identifies it as a weakling. Chicks running around without parents in this colony soon die, and they eventually form the debris on the floor of the colony that you see."

Looking more closely at the ground, I saw the long scatter of bones for the first time and was stunned. We were standing in an ancient cemetery. This penguin colony lived on top of a graveyard that may have been thousands of years old. Under the feet and nests of the birds lay all the frozen, partially mummified remains of their ancestors. The cold had preserved their carcasses for as long as three thousand years. Most adult penguins die in the ocean, but babies die right on land, and no one removes their skeletons. The bones gradually sink into the permafreeze like designs into some fantastic paperweight. The chicks are born astride a grave. A wind gust sent feathers blowing into the air as if in a pillow fight. Penguins molt each year, some even shedding parts of their bills. The ground litter included not just corpses, but also pungent guano, spilled krill, blood, feathers, molted elephant-seal skin and hair, and miscellaneous bits of animal too dismembered for an amateur to identify.

Seeing Stonehouse with the chinstrap skeleton in his hands, his wife, Sally, walked up and smiled. Her lovely English complexion had gone ruddy in the brisk Antarctic air and a few wisps of brown hair strayed from under her knitted hat. "We're so used to Daddy bringing home dead finnies," she said cheerfully. "When we were in New Zealand, if we could find a dead penguin, he was always so pleased."

Just then a lone male chinstrap tossed its helmeted head to the sky, arched its flippers back, and trumpeted an "ecstatic display" loud enough to stop a train. Its chest and throat rippled rhythmically as it called, as if with all its soul it hoped to lure a willing female by telling her that he was available and ready with a lovely little nesting site. Penguins are not profound thinkers, but their instincts guide them through all the demands of the landscape and of their hormones. An ecstatic display sounds both desperate and automatic. It may happen at any time, sometimes with good reason, sometimes by mistake, sometimes in a chorus of tens of thousands of voices screaming at the top of their lungs the equivalent of *Tell me you love me! I said, Tell me you love me!* It is a little like overhearing thousands of actors auditioning simultaneously for a Sam Shepard play. All summer, their frantic ecstasy fills the Antarctic air. Plighting their troth, an Adélie pair will do an ecstatic display, then the male will give her a precious and, to her eye, perfect stone. The actual copulation takes only seconds, and has been termed a cloacal kiss. Foreplay is everything—a complex drama of eye contact and body language. Courting males repeatedly bow to females, and the female has her own balletic gestures to use in reply.

"Well, he *is* eager, isn't he?" Sally said good-naturedly. We laughed. Life goes on, having nowhere else to go.

Among green algae-covered rocks, thick whips of red algae streamed into the water. Fur seals and Weddell seals both lazed along the shoreline, and Stonehouse strolled over to photograph them. A chinstrap swayed back onto its heels and sat with its toes off the ground. A fur seal threatened us, bluffing, and Stonehouse tossed pebbles at it until it retreated.

"Fur seals, you know, have a bearlike ancestor; whereas those Weddell seals over there are descended from an otterlike ancestor." He pointed to a pair of reclining seals with mottled, small heads and huge spaniel eyes, which were round and black as peat bogs. I suspect we are predisposed to like animals with large eyes. "They are *very* different," he continued. "We think they are so similar because they look so different from other animals, but that really says more about us and our desire to group things together than it does about them."

From iridescent-shelled limpets to wingless Antarctic flies to shrimplike krill to many species of seals to whales, porpoises, and birds, life teems around penguins. Of Antarctica's 5.5 million square miles, only about 2 percent is not covered by ice, which is where small amounts of liverworts, algae, lichens, and mosses can grow. Large animals like penguins, seals, whales, and flying birds migrate, using the lands of Antarctica, to raise their young and to breed, but feed in the waters. To see most of Antarctica's permanent land animals you would need a microscope or a magnifying glass: arthropods that live in the soil and moss; various species of mites; metezoa; tardigrades (tiny invertebrates that live in water); protozoa; worms; crustaceans; and one species of wingless fly, *Belgica antarctica*, which grows to a length of about half an inch. The wingless fly is the largest full-time resident of Antarctica. The frozen waters house a transparent, mysterious ice fish, which has no hemoglobin (red pigment) in its blood. A special blood protein acts as an antifreeze, so that ice crystals don't form even though the fish lives among ice floes. But mainly, Antarctica supports herds of migrating animals—like the penguins, which come to feed in its crystal lagoons and raise young on its ragged shores before returning to their vast home of the sea.

Earlier that day, we had heard about an Argentinian oil spill nearby. The *Bahia Paraíso*, a supply ship carrying diesel fuel, jet fuel, compressed gases, and gasoline to the Argentine base Esperanza, had run onto the rocks. The ship had also been carrying passengers, and the captain had ignored warnings from local scientists and sailed into a dangerous area, called the pinnacles, not marked on Argentinian charts but clearly shown on others. When the ship ran aground, everybody climbed into the inflatable lifeboats. Fortunately, two tourist ships—the *Society Explorer* (the *World Discoverer*'s sister ship) and the *Illiria*—were in the vicinity and changed course to rescue the stranded passengers, towing the lifeboats to Palmer Station. But an estimated three hundred thousand gallons of diesel fuel spilled into the waters; some penguins, south polar skuas, and krill were killed outright; and sealed barrels of oil were turned loose to detonate later like time bombs and contaminate unknown shores. We had heard a rumor that the United Nations was trying to raise money to remove the young penguins that hadn't gone into the water yet. But anyone who knew penguins knew that such efforts were futile. Penguins return to their home rookery to breed. If they avoided the oil now, they would find it when they returned home. The much ballyhooed oil-eating detergent we have read about wouldn't solve the problem, either; it grabs hold of the oil, in effect, and drags it to the bottom of the ocean. That may save the life-forms at the top, but not those at the bottom. At the very least, it would agitate the krill, squid, and fish on which the penguins feed. Although the sea freezes at about 29° F. and doesn't rise to beyond 32° F., it makes a thriving home for phytoplankton, the microscopic plants that are at the bottom of the food chain in the Antarctic.

The ecosystem thereabouts is simple in the sense that the food chain is very short, with only four or five steps. But contrary to what one might think, colder waters tend to be much more fertile than tropical waters. Because of the short summer season and intense sunlight, a tremendous amount of photosynthesis takes place and great seas of plantlife bloom, which means that tiny, grazing invertebrates have an unlimited supply of food, and so the population explodes. Ninety percent of an animal's time is usually spent just trying to feed itself; if it doesn't have to worry about that, it can devote itself more to breeding and the rearing of young. One result is the huge population of krill in the Antarctic, on which other creatures feed. There aren't as many types of animals as you might find in warmer waters, but their sheer numbers are vast. And it all begins with phytoplankton and krill. The krill hang on underneath the ice floes, like upside-down sheep, grazing on the plantlife. In the austral summer, huge shoals of krill become visible in the water and whales feed on them. Weddell seals and penguins that breed in this season also feed on the krill. Around the sub-Antarctic islands, offshore kelp beds grow richer and more luxuriantly than anywhere else on earth. Vast numbers of krill graze, catching onto the plants with their hairy legs. Fish feed on the krill, squid feed on the fish, penguins feed on the squid, and seals, whales, and birds feed on the penguins, and so on. As Gregory Bateson once said, the world is only a small tide pool; disturb one part and the rest is threatened.

"Suppose it turns out to be a bad year for krill," I said to Stonehouse, with a seriousness that needed no explanation.

"Penguins don't trawl for krill the way whales do," Stonehouse explained. "They catch them one at a time. Think about that. One study showed that when feeding, gentoo penguins have to catch a krill every six seconds to eat enough to survive. If it's not a good krill season and the krill are small, then a penguin may have to catch twice as many in twice as many movements. That uses up a vast amount of energy, and they don't have much to spare."

"At least the ones here will probably make it."

Stonehouse stopped, looked at me kindly, put one hand on my shoulder, and turned me to face the large, sprawling rookeries of noisy, courting, chick-rearing, squabbling, feeding penguins.

"For every hundred chicks we see there and there and there, only twenty-four will come back. They die mostly of starvation. The chicks don't always know how to fish. Or they may be abandoned too early by their parents. Or hatch too late in the season. Or be malformed. Or be underweight. Or the sheathbills we can see flying about may attack them. Sheathbills often attack penguins feeding their young, but not to grab the baby. What the sheathbill wants is the krill the parent has collected. So it flies right at the penguins," he said, using one hand to demonstrate, "startling them, and causing the parent's regurgitated krill to splatter all over the ground, where the sheathbill can get it. Or the skuas may kill a chick. Or a leopard seal. The natural wastage among penguins is very high indeed. And, of course, human beings have been the most skillful penguin predators of all."

He was correct, of course. Early visitors to penguin islands were so thrilled to have fresh food that they feasted on great herds. They boiled down penguins to make oil, and they collected their guano (an Inca word) for fertilizer. When in danger, a penguin instinctively leaps onto the land; and penguin hunters walked right up to them and clubbed them to death. Before Europeans "discovered" penguins, South American Indians used their hide for purses, slippers, and clothing, and collected their eggs. Penguin eggs have red yolks, because of the orangy krill they feed on (just as flamingos have pinkish feathers because of their diet) and translucent whites. There are records of early European ships collecting fifty barrels of penguin eggs at a time. In 1867, one trading company recorded boiling down 405,600 birds for their oil. Sir Francis Drake reported killing three thousand in one day. Probably the most famous penguin-oil distillery was on Macquarie Island (850 miles southeast of Tasmania), where visitors can still see the boilers. Although fishing for penguins is now outlawed, they are still endangered by oil spills and other forms of pollution. Beaches that are easy for penguins to land on are also easy for boats to land on, and many penguins end up having to compete with man and his pets and products. Perhaps the most ghoulish encounter between the two cultures happened when the Chilean base permitted its pet husky to roam and amuse itself. The dog, not all that far in evolution from its wolflike cousins, hunted down and ate a considerable number of penguins. I understand this also happened, but with packs of sled dogs, at Esperanza base. As if that weren't bad enough, DDT metabolites have already been found in the tissues of Adélie penguins. As birder Roger Tory Peterson has observed: "Penguins may eventually prove to be the litmus paper of the sea, an indicator of the health of our watery planet."

"What was that sound?" I said suddenly. "A gunshot?"

Stonehouse looked around carefully, searching the rookeries. "Possibly an exploding egg. Yes, I know it sounds strange, but it happens all the time. Addled or rotten eggs will begin to stink and then become explosive. Sometimes you can hear the explosion, and then you'll see a very puzzled penguin and know what happened— he was incubating a bad egg and it blew up under him."

On our way back toward the waiting Zodiacs, keeping an eye out for a puzzled penguin, we passed a wallow of elephant seals, whose belching stench hit us like a mallet. We saw leopard seals cruising offshore. Fur seals may occasionally take penguins, and even wait for them at the shoreline when they stumble through the surf, but the real killers of penguins are leopard seals. One was found to have the remains of eighteen Adélie penguins in its stomach. When a leopard seal grabs a penguin, it beats it to pieces on the surface of the water, and the smacking sound is audible for considerable distances. It leaves the skin floating in the water, sometimes with the head still attached. Roger Tory Peterson reports that penguins have a warning "babble that plainly means 'leopard seal.' " Small wonder penguins are so tentative about entering the sea. Any dark object in the surf may be a leopard seal. Or any clapping sound, as of flippers hitting the water. Such seals are beautiful, of course, as predators frequently are. They have a snakelike head, canine teeth, a slender, grayish-black back that becomes silver-gray, or even bluish, on the belly, and tawny spots on their underside. The males grow to nine feet long and weigh around seven hundred pounds, the females even larger, at ten feet long and up to a thousand pounds. Leopard-seal ultrasonic "chirps" have been recorded, noises similar to the echolocation sounds of bats, and some scientists think leopard seals must be able to echolocate when they feed under the opaque winter ice. Even if they don't echolocate, they're expert at telling the direction of an underwater sound. They are supreme predators, and as we climbed back into the rubber rafts to return to the ship, we watched them with horror and awe.

At night, we gathered in the ship's lounge to decry the oil spill, as well as the insensitivity of the French engineers who were building an airstrip right through the middle of an important Adélie penguin rookery. Stonehouse, who edits the *Polar Record* (a magazine of Antarctic research, which also monitors the latest political developments related to the region), solicited our ideas on how best to protect the fragile ecosystem of the Antarctic.

A woman across the room raised her hand, explained that she belonged to Greenpeace, and was anxious about Antarctica for many reasons. "I understand the Japanese are harvesting krill to make pet food," she said, her voice thick with emotion.

"Which nobody wants," Stonehouse said, "because it's cheaper to get pet food from other sources. But sometime in the near future they may find a way to bring krill up to human standards. At the moment, it isn't convenient to harvest. It spoils easily. You've got to put it straight into a deep freeze. Now, that means a different kind of ship and much more expensive processing. And then you've got to find a way to make it highly valuable, say, the equivalent of caviar. I don't think using it as dog food will ever be a threat. But it will be very much worth the taking when they find a high-quality market for it."

"They're trying to go after penguins, too," she said, smoothing the hem of her khaki skirt. "I understand they recently attempted to take four hundred thousand penguins, and the Argentinian government was all for it."

Stonehouse nodded. "You believe in the sanctity of wild animals."

"Yes," she said emphatically.

"Let me show you what a complicated issue this is. It wouldn't be if all of the players in the drama were at the same level or had as much to gain or lose, but that's not the way it is. Now, supposing a third world country came to us. Supposing the Indonesians said: 'We want to take twenty thousand seals a year because we've found a market for fur-seal skins in China—an unlimited market.' It could be quite a modest number in terms of the size of the population of seals. 'We'll monitor the operation scrupulously. In other words, we'll do everything properly. We're going to bring a lot of prosperity to Indonesians, many of whom are poor and hungry. It will build up a little leather and fine-fur industry and the quality of life in Indonesia will improve.' What would your answer be? Whose side are you on?"

"I would suggest that they find something else to profit from—improved crops, for instance."

"That won't satisfy people with empty stomachs."

"Ah, but what about rice? Rice can feed people."

"Don't forget, in many third world countries there's a great premium on the land. You see, this is not just an emotional problem—

it's a political problem, a social problem. If anybody is going to starve, you can bet it won't be the Americans or the British. We've gone through our industrial revolutions. We didn't get prosperity and the standard of living we're enjoying by not using our resources. Now, who are we to tell people in developing nations, 'Your right to use nature's resources is over.' It would look to them as if we wealthier nations felt that they should starve so that we could have the luxury of a zoo without walls."

"Surely you don't believe that!" she said, leaning forward and slicing an open hand through the air.

"Of course not. But I think this is how the argument is going to go. And we've got to be prepared with much better reasons than conscience—the fact that the Antarctic greatly affects the weather all over the world, for instance, just as the rain forests do; that the world's drinking water is tied up here—reasons that will make practical sense to people with other things on their mind, like getting from day to day. Remember, most people know very little about Antarctica."

Yes, I thought, they know more about the moon or the planets. I remembered going to the grocery store one summer day, when Viking II had just landed on Mars, and hearing people in line casually discussing Martian weather. They marveled at the surface winds and the sunsets. Yet did they know about Antarctica, the world of penguins? One of the Apollo astronauts, returning to Earth, said that there was a "white lantern" shining at the bottom of the world. All of us on this sailing had seen it shining, had used its light to construe some of the dark corners in our lives, and were afraid that its ice and other wonders would one day vanish.

"I just feel that Antarctica should be kept as a world park instead of exploiting it for minerals and wildlife and oil," she said.

"Yes. A lot of people, including many scientists, are extremely arrogant about their view, and want Antarctica as a continent for scientists. I think that's a mistake. I don't think it's for scientists alone at all. It's for anybody to get to know, people like you."

"Well, I mean, keep it as it is—no more population and no

more pollution. There would be an international agreement to preserve it."

"All right," Stonehouse said. "I might begin to go along with this,
it sounds like a good idea. But who is going to rule the damn place?
Who knows enough about it to be able to manage it except the
people who are already involved with it?"

"Well, it wouldn't be one person or another, it would be a group
of countries."

"Are we going to turn the United Nations loose on it? They can't
even run their own building."

"Whoever has claims there right now and research stations right
now. Maybe those people combined with . . ."

"But they have conflicting claims."

". . . combined with scientists, environmentalists . . ."

"Okay. Who's going to police it? You see, there isn't an Antarctic
Treaty authority."

"How does it work now?"

"If you're working in the Antarctic, you're working under the
control of your own country, not under the control of Antarctica.
You are controlled by your own government, your own law. An
American couldn't arrest me for doing something wrong. All he
could do is report me to the British government. In the same way,
I can't stop a Chilean or an Argentinian from doing something I
don't like. I can only point out that I intend to report him to his
government. Which he might find laughable."

"Suppose," I offered, "you had a group of multinational guides,
who served a tour of duty in the Antarctic. It could be like joining
the Peace Corps. The lecturers wouldn't arrive on the boats, they
would be waiting for the boats. These people could also act as
wardens of the park. And they could rotate, so that they wouldn't
be serving one country's ships or one company often enough to
perhaps become compromised."

"I like that idea. Now, whom do they report to?"

I laughed, dispirited. "We're back to a world court."

"Exactly. One with the power to embarrass or fine or punish

wrongdoers. Don't misunderstand me. I believe this is a solvable problem, but it's a difficult one. It has to be solved in a clearheaded way, with good, practical solutions. How we decide the fate of the Antarctic is extremely important, because we're going to face this problem over and over again as other crucial ecosystems become endangered."

With more questions raised than answered, we finally retreated to our cabins for the night. Some stayed up late, roaming the open decks, in long johns and parkas, to savor the eerie sparkle of moonlight on the wild ice.

Somewhere along the way, we had lost the nighttime. Where did we lose it? In the deserted whaling station, in whose smoky hall we ate a barbecue of reindeer meat and danced to Glenn Miller? At the Polish station, whose greenhouses grew snapdragons and tomatoes? In the volcanic ring of Deception Island? Watching rippling terraces of Adélie penguins go about their lapidary business, obsessed with nesting stones? At the small British base, Signey, whose young men had not seen strangers, or women, for nearly two years? (Visiting with us in the lounge, some of them were trembling; and we sent them away with handshakes, good wishes, and sacks of potatoes, onions, and other fresh food.) At the Valentine's Day dance, on seas so rough that dancers held on to the ceiling? On Elephant Island, a forbidding snag of mountain but a thriving chinstrap rookery, where Shackleton and his men landed after their trials on the pack ice? At the eerie, deserted penguin rookery, where watching a lone penguin chick face the death machine of a rampaging skua, which played out its instincts blow by blow, tortured our hearts? Among the guano-thick beaches, where waves of hungry penguins bobbed in the sea and babies clamored to be fed? Listening to the assistant cruise director, a fine pianist, give recitals of Debussy, Haydn, Bach, and Beethoven against a backdrop of sunstruck glaciers?

Now we lived only in a late summer twilight. Icebergs clustered around us like statuary as the ship sailed through the Gerlache Strait, which separates the Antarctic Peninsula from Brabant and Anvers islands. Each narrow waterway seemed to lead into another one, until finally we sailed through the Lemaire Channel, which narrows to a mere sixteen hundred feet wide at its southern end. This too was the penguins' world. On either side of the ship, glaciers spilled into the sea, jagged mountain peaks rose into the clouds, and icebergs roamed freely. In the channel, the water was like lucid tar, with icebergs of all sizes drifting through it, their white tops a thin reflection of mortality—their blue bases pale and inscrutable. The blazing white of an iceberg lay on a thick wide base of blue ancient as the earth, older than all of the people who had ever seen it or who had ever visited the Antarctic combined. The icebergs took all sorts of shapes, and some had fissures through which a searing blue light shone. In the wake of an iceberg the water looked like oiled silk because the surface of the water had been smoothed by the ice's palm. On both sides of the boat, black, jagged, ice-drizzled mountains reflected in the mirror surface. On a small berg, five gentoo penguins sat, their white bonnets sparkling in the sun. On another small berg sat their death—a leopard seal, sprawling on one side, idly scratching its flank with a five-fingered paw.

"*Seehund,*" a woman from Frankfurt said solemnly. We were all on the side of the penguins, though nature should have no partisans, no sides, no center, except the center that is forever shifting, as Emerson said, a center that moves within circles and circles that move.

Great tongues of ice stretch out from the continent and speak in a language like music, with no words but with undeniable meaning. And like music, the vista is a language we don't have to learn to be profoundly moved—we who do not just use our environment but also appreciate, admire, even worship it. True, we kill other life-forms to survive, but we feel a kinship to them, we apologize for stealing their life from them. We are the most vital creatures ever to inhabit the earth, and the one truth we live by is that life loves life. Still, nature proceeds "red in tooth and claw," as Tennyson said. This becomes simpler to see in a simpler environment. When you walk through a penguin rookery, where the underweight chicks stand doomed and the skuas maneuver like custodians of death, pages of Darwin's *Origin of Species* spring to life in front of you. All the cozy denials we use as shields fall aside.

The sky that day was clear, and the air as astringent as ammonia vapor. The sun poured down but had no heat, and the ice mountains occasionally revealed weavings of blue and green. After the darkness of winter, the five months of summer sun did not warm things up much. Because the sun rode so low on the horizon, it seemed to have little warmth. The ice reflected the heat back into the sky. Most people on board had greatly dilated pupils by then, a side effect of the scopolamine patch they wore behind one ear to ward off seasickness. It made them look a little like zombies, but it also allowed their eyes to take in big gulps of light. In Zodiacs, we drifted along the peninsula, through an ice-sculpture garden. Heraclitus said you never step in the same stream twice. The Antarctic version of that is that you never see the same iceberg twice. Because each iceberg is always changing, one sees a personal and unique iceberg that no one else has ever seen or will ever see. They are not always smooth. Many had textures, waffle patterns, pockmarks, and some looked pounded by Persian metalsmiths. A newly calved iceberg lay like a chunk of glass honeycomb, spongy from being underwater. (At some point it was other-side-up.) Another had beautiful blue ridges like muscles running along one side. So many icelets thickened the water, each one quivering with sparkle, that the sea looked like aluminum foil shaken in the sun. There were baths of ice with blue lotion, ice grottos, ice curved round the fleecy pelt of a lamb, razor-backed ice, sixteen ice swans on an ice merry-go-round, ice pedestals, ice combs, ice dragons with wings spread, an ice garden where icebergs grew and died, ice tongs with blue ice between their claws, an ice egret stretching its wings and a long rippling neck out of the water. Apricot light spilled over the distant snow-tipped mountains. Chunky wedges of peppermint-blue ice drifted past us. Behind us, the Zodiac left a frothy white petticoat. And farther beyond, shapes arched out of the water—penguins feeding, oblivious to what we call beauty.

We paused at Paradise Bay, where blue-eyed shags nested along the cliffs, a whale maneuvered at a distance, penguins porpoised to feed, and crabeater seals lazed on small icebergs, red krill juice dripping down their chins. Through pale green water, clear and calm, a gray rocky bottom was shining, along with red and brown seaweeds and patches of yellow-blooming phytoplankton. A loud explosion startled us and, turning, we saw ice breaking off a glacier to become an iceberg, which would float for four years or so before it succumbed to the sea. I looked down through the fathoms of crystal water to the smooth rocks on the bottom. Suddenly an eight-foot leopard seal swiveled below the boat, surfaced to breathe, cut a fast turn, and began circling the Zodiac, around and around, underneath it and alongside. Each time it spun underwater, large blue air bubbles rose to the surface like jellyfish. Mouth open, baring its sharp yellow teeth, it lunged up through the water and bit a pontoon on the Zodiac. "Back away from the edge!" David Kaplan, our driver, said with contained urgency, and the twelve passengers leaned inward, away from the attacking seal, which could leap out of the water and seize an arm, pulling a person under. Circling, fast, handsome, wild, ferocious, it spun below again, dove, and leapt to the surface. It was attacking us as it would penguins on an ice floe. We who live at the top of our food chain rarely get the chance to feel like prey, to watch a predator maneuver around us with a deftness that's instinctive, cunning, and persistent—and live to tell about it.

"Just an average day in Paradise," Kaplan said, brightening the motor and heading for shore. We climbed out at an abandoned Argentinian base. As the clouds drifted behind the peninsula, the continent itself appeared to be moving, as of course it was. On a rock ledge, an Antarctic tern—a small white bird with black cap and startling red beak and matching red feet—thrilled the sky with song. A teal vein of copper ore cascaded down the rocks among patches of fiery orange lichen and green moss. As the rest of our party climbed up a steep slope of glacier to the top of a mountain where a wooden cross had been planted, I stood like a sentinel, still as a

in, watching my kind struggle up the hill from the sea. Across
y, the snow mountains were glazed in a dusky pink light
and the water was cerulean blue. Gray clouds hung in front of and
below the powdered tops of the mountains. The air was so pure that
the clouds looked cut-out and solid, suspended by a sleight of hand,
a magician's trick. Mirrors lay scattered on the surface of the water,
where there was no ice to disrupt the flowing light. A blue iceberg
shaped like open jaws a hundred feet high floated near shore. Corrugated-metal buildings shot off hot orange. A long hem of brash ice
undulated across the south end of the bay. Somewhere the leopard
seal sat looking for less elusive quarry, and would find it.

The birders were up early as we approached Coronation Island, in
the South Orkneys; they were desperate to spot an Antarctic petrel,
a bird that resembles but is slightly larger than the many pintados,
or painted petrels, swirling in small tornadoes behind the boat. Most
Antarctic petrels are in their rookeries as much as a hundred miles
inland from the ice shelf. When one finally winged across the water,
the birders went berserk.

"Oh! There it is! Beautiful!" a woman cried.

"Wow! The nape is almost buff!" said an enraptured man.

All the Antarctic petrels we saw that day were pale. They were
in molt, a wonderful coffee-tan color, and flapped stiffly because
their new feathers weren't in yet. To see one or two at this time of
year so far out was a bonus. However, many of us were not looking
for petrels but for a rarer sight: the emperor penguin. Largest of all
penguins, emperors can dive to nearly nine hundred feet to feed on
squid and stay submerged for nearly twenty minutes or more. When
they stand in the snow like vigilant UFO watchers, they have the
usual black-and-white coloring, but also a spill of honey at their
throats and cheeks. Emperor penguins are such altruistic parents—
or fanatical, depending on your point of view—that they will even
pick up a frozen or ruined egg and try to incubate it, or try to
incubate stones or an old dead chick. An abandoned or wayward
chick will immediately be adopted. Sometimes adults even squabble

so much over a chick that the chick gets hurt or killed in the process. Emperors rarely, if ever, touch bare ground. They live out their whole lives standing sentry on shelf ice or swimming in the ocean. Unfortunately, their rookeries were too far south for us to see them.

A small flock of Antarctic prions hydroplaned over the water, plowing a furrow through it, using their tongues to sift krill into a feeding pouch under the jaw, feeding the way baleen whales do.

"Bird alert! Bird alert!" sounded over the intercom, waking passengers from their slumber and early diners from drowsy breakfasts. "EP alert! EP alert! A juvenile emperor penguin has been spotted off the stern of the boat!" I ran to the stern, colliding with people frantically running up the stairs from the cabins below. HOLD THESE RAILS it said on brass plates at each stairway on every deck, as if in rebuke to excited birders who had been turning the ship into an aviary. The stampede ended with a clash of bodies on the stern deck. And there it was: porpoising out of the water, looking like part of an inner tube with a flash of yellow showing every now and again. Then it vanished, and we were left standing quietly with our amazement. To glimpse an emperor penguin in the wild, feeding this far from its home, was a benediction.

Stowing my binoculars, I went downstairs to breakfast, which I barely touched. Despite the elaborate meals, I'd been losing weight at a reckless pace. It was as if I was being nourished so thoroughly through my senses that I felt too full to eat. Before coming to the Antarctic, I had thought that penguins lived in a world of extreme sensory deprivation. But I had found just the opposite—a landscape of the greatest sensuality. For one thing, there was so much life, great herds of animal life to rival those in East Africa. Many people have compared Antarctica to a wasteland; instead, it is robust with life. For another, the range of colors was breathtaking; though subtle, it had changing depths and illuminations, like flesh tones. The many colors were in the ever-bluing sky, in the cloud formations, the muted light, the midnight sun, the auroras dancing over still waters with icebergs and crash ice, and in areas that dazzled like small hand mirrors, through which black-and-white penguins dove. Who would

gined the depth of blue in the icebergs, appearing as sugar-
~~kes~~ with muted sunlight bursting off them?

~~...~~ scale, the massiveness—sitting alongside an iceberg, you
couldn't see around it in either direction. One day the water was so
smooth that you could use it as a mirror, and four hours later the
wind was howling at ninety knots. And was as beautiful at ninety
knots as when crystal-calm. Huge ice caverns formed arches of pastel
ice. *Glare* had so many moods that it seemed another pure color.
The mountains, glaciers, and fjords bulged and rolled through endless displays of inter-flowing shapes. The continent kept turning its
shimmery hips, and jutting up hard pinnacles of ice, in a sensuality
of rolling, sifting, cascading landscapes. There was such a liquefac-
tion to its limbs. And yet it could also be blindingly abstract, harrow-
ing and remote, the closest thing to being on another planet, so far
from human life that its desolation and iciness made you want to do
impetuous, life-affirming things: commit acts of love, skip Zodiacs
at reckless speeds over the bays, touch voices with a loved one by
way of satellite, work out in the gym on thrones of steel until your
muscles quit, drink all night, be passionate and daring, renew the
outlines of your humanity.

Nowhere, yet, had we seen king penguins, the species I helped raise
at Sea World, the most gaudily colored of all. To find them, we had
to sail again across galloping seas, and when at last we dropped
anchor at Cooper Island, at the tip of South Georgia, and climbed
into our Zodiacs, we realized that we had arrived at one of the most
astonishing places on earth.

Our first sight of land was from the rafts, on seas that smacked
them hard against each swell. The mountains of Cooper Island
stretch high and green to ice-capped peaks. When American ornithologist Robert Cushman Murphy visited it in 1912, he called it
"a stretch of the Alps in mid-ocean." Macaroni penguins, named
after the Yankee Doodle dandies because they have orange spaghetti
bangs hanging from their heads, clotted the hillsides, and their
collective clamor—part bray, part clack—resounded louder than the

surf. Albatrosses, terns, petrels, and other birds swirled in relentless squadrons overhead, planed low over the water, squealing and chirping, or clustered on the hillside. Schools of macaroni penguins porpoised through the water all around our Zodiacs, which quickly seemed to be boiling in a cauldron of penguins. Fur seals clambered onto the many rock outcroppings near shore, and gave gargling barks. The whole scene shimmered, fluorescent with life. So many animals moved in the foreground, and in the background, that your eyes strained to focus on both at once. It was like traveling through the middle of a pop-up storybook. Magic realism had sprung to life. In each cove, penguins leapt out of the water like solid balls of rubber to land safely on the rocks, as we staggered toward one shore after another, looking for a safe place to land. Finally, we headed for a small, wave-tossed beach, hit hard, climbed out fast, and let the Zodiac return to deeper waters. Fur seals basked on the shore, some hidden behind large boulders, some sitting on top of the thronelike tussocks. Those steeply tussocked cliffs gave way to a high field above us, and beyond that stood a scree-torn mountain capped with snow.

Brittmarie, a Swedish-born climber from California, whose candor and zest I liked, looked at me, then at the craggy bluffs overhead.

"Let's do it," I said, and we exchanged grins.

Sneaking away far left, around the sleeping fur seals, we started to climb up a steep, rocky creekbed.

"Three points!" she yelled down to me as I scrambled up behind on the slippery rocks. "Always be secure at three points!"

"Words to live by!" I called back. Soon we found ourselves walled in by thick cliffs with dense tussocks hanging from them.

"It's straight up," Brittmarie said, smiling. "What do you think?"

There is an art to climbing tussock-grass mountains, I'm sure. An amateur like me could only improvise. Because the grass clumped tightly at the base, I held on securely there as I pulled myself up, stepping in the mud between the tussock clumps. Petrels had made burrows among the tussocks, which I used as footholds whenever possible. If you have the upper-body strength, you can hold on with both hands, as if climbing a rope ladder, and find safe footing.

Halfway up the hill, panting hard, we paused to rest. If anything, the hill above looked even steeper, the tussocks bulging overhead. Suppose the edge tussocks weren't firmly rooted and broke off? We decided to angle up, and finally we reached the top, where a field of tussocks led across promontories to a distant group of nesting albatrosses with their chicks. Half an hour later, we managed to steal up on them in the grass. Fluffy gray chicks swiveled around to face us, each with a black bridle-shaped stripe across its mouth. One or two began clacking to warn us away. Their parents flew overhead or at eye level or soared along the cliffs below us. Perched on that height, in the windy mist, while albatrosses maneuvered, we saw the ship rolling on the freshening sea, where Captain Lampe, whose skills we had learned to respect in the iceberg-clotted channels, was holding steady against wind and current. We saw Zodiacs plunging through the water to unload. We saw lens-shaped clouds prowling the mountains, and knew they signaled stronger winds. But our goal was higher still. Hand over hand, leaping small pits and bogs, we climbed toward an unmistakable sound—a chattery braying. There, hundreds of feet above the sea, sprawled a rookery of macaroni penguins. Plump, slightly farouche-looking, with orange hair parted in the middle, they ran around like miniature Zero Mostels. How on earth they managed the climb we did not know. But climb it they often did, with their stomachs full of food, to feed their waiting young. We knew that it would be almost impossible for a creature that can't fly to get up the mountain. Fortunately, the penguins didn't know it, and here they were.

"Think of the energy it must take for a little, short-legged bird to walk up over all those sharp, rocky slopes to get to the top to breed," Brittmarie said, pulling a camera from her blue knapsack. "It's beyond comprehension."

"Tenacity," I said, thinking out loud—and not meaning the macaroni penguin's tenacity, exactly, but life's. Life hangs on in such out-of-the-way places, pushes on with such ingenuity and bravado. Turning over a mother-of-pearl-lined limpet shell on Elephant Island a few days earlier, I had seen a hundred squirming wingless flies.

Life just seemed to keep reinventing itself—inside a limpet shell, or hundreds of feet up a rocky cliff above a roaring ocean.

When the seas started to grow dangerously rough, we were summoned back to the boat, and set sail at long last for the king penguin rookeries at Gold Harbor and Salisbury Plain, on the island of South Georgia. At Salisbury Plain, our Zodiacs cut through thick curling waves onto a steep beach. For some reason there was the sound of harmonicas and, occasionally, distant oncoming trains. Turning, I saw a nearby hill seemingly squirming in the sunlight and automatically walked toward it. All at once it reeled into focus as a bustling, fidgeting, buzzing, clamorous, colossal king-penguin metropolis that sprawled for miles, pouring along the scimitar-shaped beach, through interfolding valleys, spilling down the hillsides. It was penguin heaven. The adults stood tall, with those splendid pairs of orange commas on their cheeks, a radiant sun-yellow blooming at their throats, and an apricot or lavender comet along each side of their bills. Stately, curious, they allowed me to sit down right among them. One slightly potbellied king, carrying an egg on its feet, "head-flagged" with its mate, bobbing and sweeping heads like signalmen with flags, or shadow boxers. Then the female touched her bill to her brood patch—a vertical opening where she held the egg—tossed her head up, and rubbed her bill back and forth across her mate's neck, as if to sharpen it on the whetstone of his desire. A neighbor bashed them both with its flippers and they screeched a rude reply.

Kings don't like being crowded. Thousands of birds stood close together in the rookery. Like soldiers in line, replying to the command of "Dress left!" or "Dress right!" they occasionally put out a flipper to keep their neighbor at a comfortable distance. Any attacking skua would face an impenetrable sea of sharp upturned bills. It would be like flying into a bed of nails. King penguins know exactly how much space they need to feel secure but not hemmed in, and they are rarely more than a flipper smack or a bill lunge away from one another. Four bachelors strutted by smartly in a line, looking gallant and available. One paused in front of a female, pointed its apricot-striped bill skyward, thrust out its chest, cranked its flippers back, and flapped rhythmically as if he were trying to lift off. A hoarse drumbeat throbbed in his throat, then changed to a climactic braying of two tones at once—the harmonica I had heard. His ecstatic display was all aces, and the female responded. They head-flagged together for a while, then, for a long time, stared at each other and chattered. The male suddenly threw his shoulders back and strolled forward, in what scientists call the advertisement walk. Looking as swell as possible in penguin terms, he turned his head from side to side so that she could see what beautiful orange ear-patches he had. If she followed him, it was a marriage. Then, several other bachelors waddled up and tried to muscle in, gently chasing the female toward the shore. Demure, she held her flippers to her side while the bachelors crowed and raved. Ultimately, her original swain won out, and bumped her repeatedly, though gently, with his chest, herding her to the outskirts of the rookery, where they had a little more room. In time, he would stand right on top of her back, mate in as little as forty seconds with a cloacal kiss, and then climb down, leaving his muddy footprints behind.

To pledge their devotion, a nearby couple plunged into a suite of "mutual displays," which looked like ecstatic displays except that both male and female took part. Facing each other, they were soon weaving their heads from side to side and crying out in joy, finally pointing their bills up to the sky. Doing this every few minutes keeps their bond strong. Most penguins return to the same nest the follow-ing year, and the same mate, whose voice they recognize. Birds whose mates have died, or with whom they weren't able to nest successfully the previous year, must find new mates. If the rookery is disturbed for any reason, couples often engage in mutual displays, which they also do when an egg is laid or when they change shifts in incubating an egg—in fact, whenever it seems wise to restate their vows. Insinuating themselves through the rookery, at speed, two penguins did the "slender walk." All they wanted was to get from their nests to the sea without stopping to fight or give anybody grief, so they held their flippers tightly against their sides, slicked down their feathers, and slid through as inoffensively as possible. In a major rookery, everything is happening at once and you can see just about all the phases of the king's life cycle going on simultaneously. A fluffy baby peered out from under a parent's soft white belly. A larger baby turned to hide by sticking its head under a parent's belly, leaving its oversized rump outside. A small gaggle of "mohawks," molting babies that have a stripe of down on top of their heads, chased an adult and screamed to be fed. In their fury, they raced right over the remains of disemboweled chicks.

A king stood on his heels and dusted the snow behind him with his tail. By then, I had removed my parka to reveal a bright-yellow sweatsuit. Although I'm shaped wrong and don't have cheek commas, my black hair and screaming-yellow body were the right colors to interest a king penguin, which shuffled up close, cocked a head to one side, then to the other, and carefully checked me over. There is, ordinarily, a no-man's-land between us and wild animals. They fear us and shy away. But penguins are among the very few animals on earth that cross that divide. They seem to regard us as penguins, too, perhaps of a freakish species. After all, we stand upright, travel in groups, talk all the time, sort of waddle. Still, though I was black and yellow and in a submissive posture, I was not the penguin he hankered for, he decided at long last, not one of *his* kind, and he shuffled away slowly, keeping an eye on me until he disappeared into the gyrating sea of black and white.

A low, smothery cloud bank drifted overhead. It was going to be a rainy night in South Georgia. Surrounded by penguin society, which began to close its ranks behind me, I thought of brown-white-left, the fluffy chick I helped raise at Sea World in San Diego. Moved to Orlando, his final home, he would already be fledging. Even if he could understand me, how could I begin to describe his homeland and the rigors of penguin life in the Antarctic? How poor his odds would be of survival? I was probably with his parents, perhaps his brothers and sisters, certainly cousins, right here in this rookery. When I thought of the horror of a penguin being flayed alive by a leopard seal, my skin crawled. Nature neither gives nor expects mercy. I gently touched the sleek oiled back of a lovely nesting penguin, with a fine set of commas, whose feathers were tipped in a bluish gleam. For brown-white-left, life would be more artificial, of course, but also much safer, and it was good to know that he was alive a world away. Safe from hunger, leopard seal, and skua, he was probably sitting like a pensioner on a park bench as he watched the silent pageant passing on the moving sidewalk beyond the glass, where ghostly humans floated in a darkness deep as the Antarctic night.

INDEX

ABOUT THE AUTHOR

Diane Ackerman was born in Waukegan, Illinois. She received her B.A. in English from Pennsylvania State University and an M.F.A. and Ph.D. from Cornell University. She is the author of five volumes of poetry: *The Planets: A Cosmic Pastoral* (1976), *Wife Light* (1978), *Lady Faustus* (1983), *Reverse Thunder: A Dramatic Poem* (1988), and most recently *Jaguar of Sweet Laughter: New and Selected Poems* (1991).

Her books of nonfiction include *Twilight of the Tenderfoot* (1980), *On Extended Wings* (1985), and the best-selling *A Natural History of the Senses* (1990). She has received the Academy of American Poets' Peter I. B. Lavan Award and grants from the National Endowment for the Arts and the Rockefeller Foundation, among other prizes and awards. Ms. Ackerman has taught at Washington University, New York University, Columbia University, and Cornell University, among others. She is currently a staff writer at *The New Yorker* and is working on several books, including *The Rarest of the Rare*, about endangered animals. She lives in New York State.